S0-BIF-436

Spirituality and the Ethics of Torture

Spirituality and the Ethics of Torture

Derek S. Jeffreys

SPIRITUALITY AND THE ETHICS OF TORTURE
Copyright © Derek S. Jeffreys, 2009.

All rights reserved.

First published in 2009 by
PALGRAVE MACMILLAN®
in the United States—a division of St. Martin's Press LLC,
175 Fifth Avenue, New York, NY 10010.

Where this book is distributed in the UK, Europe and the rest of the world,
this is by Palgrave Macmillan, a division of Macmillan Publishers Limited,
registered in England, company number 785998, of Houndmills,
Basingstoke, Hampshire RG21 6XS.

Palgrave Macmillan is the global academic imprint of the above companies
and has companies and representatives throughout the world.

Palgrave® and Macmillan® are registered trademarks in the United States,
the United Kingdom, Europe and other countries.

ISBN: 978–0–230–61731–5

Library of Congress Cataloging-in-Publication Data

Jeffreys, Derek S., 1964–
　　　Spirituality and the ethics of torture / Derek S. Jeffreys.
　　　　　p. cm.
　　　Includes bibliographical references and index.
　　　ISBN 0–230–61731–X
　　　1. Torture—Moral and ethical aspects. 2. Torture—Religious aspects.
　　I. Title.

HV8593.J44 2009
172'.2—dc22   2008054869

A catalogue record of the book is available from the British Library.

Design by Newgen Imaging Systems (P) Ltd., Chennai, India.

First edition: July 2009

10 9 8 7 6 5 4 3 2 1

Printed in the United States of America.

To W. Norris Clarke, S.J.

CONTENTS

ACKNOWLEDGMENTS

This has been a difficult book to write because I had to read through accounts of many horrible acts of inhumanity. I first want to thank my dear wife, Celestine, for her patience and understanding as I often responded with anger and sadness at what I read. My sons, Zachariah and Caleb, are fortunately still too young to understand the horrors of torture, but supported their father wonderfully. I also thank Paul J. Griffiths, whose guidance I deeply value and whose friendship has sustained my entire family. Thanks also to David Burrell, who supported me in writing this book. I thank the Philosophy Department at Fordham University, where I presented a portion of the manuscript. I am grateful to the American Civil Liberties Union and Human Rights Watch for the work they have done in making public key documents about torture. For helpful conversation or assistance, I thank Sid Bremer, John F. Crosby, John Deely, Dan Fromkin, Karen Greenberg, Stanley Hauerwas, Harvey Kaye, Fred Kersten, Gyula Klima, Joseph Koterski, S.J., Patrick Lee, Lisa Magarrell, Joseph Margulies, Alfred McCoy, Gilbert T. Null, Mark Osiel, Jerrold Rodesch, and Anthony Simon. At Palgrave Macmillan, I thank Christopher Chappell, Samantha Hasey, and Matt Robinson for all of their hard work and support. I also thank the wonderful copyeditors Maran Elancheran and Anula Lydia, who did a fabulous job editing the manuscript.

Finally, I dedicate this book to W. Norris Clarke, S.J. (1915–2008). Mentor and friend Father Clarke inspired me with his enthusiastic spirit and deep knowledge of Thomism. This book reflects many of our wonderful conversations.

Introduction

But I refused to have him tortured. I trembled the whole afternoon. Finally, the bomb did not go off. Thank God I was right. Because if you once get into the torture business, you're lost... Understand this, fear was the basis of it all. All our so-called civilization is covered with a varnish. Scratch it, and underneath you find *fear*. The French, even the Germans, are not torturers by nature. But when you see the throats of your *copains* split, then the varnish disappears.

Paul Teitgen[1]

In late 2007, Americans got a rare glimpse of torture in the "War on Terror."[2] A former Central Intelligence Agency (CIA) official, John Kiriakou publically admitted that the CIA tortured a suspected al-Qaeda operative. He detailed how the CIA captured Abu Zubaydah in a March 2002 raid. Zubaydah was almost killed, but the CIA flew in skilled doctors to nurse him back to health. Once he recovered from his wounds, CIA officials begin interrogating him. According to Kiriakou (who chose not to participate in the interrogation), Zubaydah initially resisted nonviolent interrogation. Believing another al-Qaeda attack was imminent, the CIA subjected him to "enhanced interrogation techniques," one of which was waterboarding. During waterboarding, interrogators place a detainee on a flat board, perhaps with his feet elevated. They cover his face with cloth and then pour water into his nostrils and mouth. The water immediately produces a powerful sensation of suffocation that few can withstand. Kiriakou reports that Zubaydah resisted for thirty-five seconds, but then immediately began cooperating. When questioned about this episode, Kiriakou acknowledged that waterboarding amounts to torture, but defended it by noting its beneficial effects. He claimed it produced valuable intelligence that saved

American lives and maintained that the CIA had no time to employ nonviolent interrogation.[3]

The Zubaydah revelations illustrated diverse elements of the debate about torture and the War on Terror. Like many, Kiriakou justified torture by claiming it saves lives in extreme circumstances. His view also reflect that of the Bush administration, which fought unsuccessfully against restrictions on interrogations. Some public commentators even denied that waterboarding is torture whereas others insisted that it is self-evidently torture. They condemned Zubaydah's treatment, maintaining that torture is never morally justified. They also mounted a campaign against violent coercion that successfully found its way into U.S. Army field manuals, Congressional legislation, and Supreme Court decisions. Finally, debates about the Zubaydah case focused on sensational instances of torture and other cases. They ignored hundreds of other incidents that did not seem like torture. Waterboarding "looks" like torture, whereas sensory deprivation appears less threatening. In reality, however, sensory deprivation, sleep deprivation, isolation, and stress positions can destroy one's personality. The attention to the Zubaydah case, thus, illustrated the sad truth that "we are less likely to complain about violence committed by stealth."[4] For many, torture that leaves no discernible marks is not leaving torture at all.

The Zubaydah case also reflected a new post–September 11 willingness to openly discuss torture. For example, noted legal scholar Alan Dershowitz infamously proposed that the United States issue "torture warrants" specifying precisely when torture is permitted. Maintaining that governments invariably engage in torture, he argued that we should legally control them. Columnist Charles Krauthammer went further, insisting that we are obligated to torture terrorists with information about violent acts. Krauthammer, Dershowitz, and others provoked a storm of controversy. Organizations such as Amnesty International and Human Rights Watch insisted on an absolute ban on torture. In contrast, political philosopher Jean Bethke Elshtain adopted a "dirty hands" approach arguing that interrogators may be tragically forced to abuse and torture.[5]

The debate about torture shows no sign of abating and will likely persist for many years. Unfortunately, ethically, it has ignored important issues, more often focusing on imaginary or sensational cases. It has also uncritically embraced contemporary ethical ideas thereby ignoring religious and philosophical traditions that help us understand torture.

Finally, although religious leaders and scholars have issued statements on torture, discussions on this issue remain largely secular.[6]

This book corrects these lacunae in the public debate by considering spirituality and torture. To introduce the book, I first discuss the deficiencies of ticking bomb scenarios, arguing that they do little to illuminate the ethics of torture. They make artificial assumptions, rely on uninformed intuitions, and encourage us to calculate consequences. Second, I describe how current debates about torture ignore spirituality. By focusing entirely on human rights, autonomy, or other topics, they fail to consider how torture assaults our spiritual nature. Third, I introduce Thomistic personalism, noting in particular its conception of spirituality. Fourth, I consider the difficulties in writing about torture, acknowledging the need to listen to torture victims. I also discuss how Nazi and Communist examples detrimentally affect discussions of torture. Fifth, I describe how I use the sources in this book, expressing modesty about classified information. Finally, I outline the book's structure discussing in turn the contents of each chapter.

Torture and Ticking Bombs

Many contemporary debates about torture feature a ticking bomb scenario. In this scenario, a public official captures a terrorist who knows the location of a bomb that is about to kill numerous people. To prevent carnage, should he or she torture the terrorist? Or, should the public official retain an absolute ban on torture, thus allowing innocents to die? In the aftermath of the September 11 attacks, many believed we ought to torture in ticking time bomb situations. Those disagreeing accepted the terms of the debate, but insisted that they would refrain from torturing even in extreme circumstances. In this way, reflecting on ticking bomb scenarios became a cottage industry in political ethics.

Unfortunately, the ticking bomb scenario presupposes artificial circumstances with little relevance for real interrogations. It assumes that interrogators possess great certainty that a terror suspect knows the bomb's location. However, this is rarely the case, and the ticking time bomb scenario never indicates an appropriate level of certainty. At what point should an interrogator conclude that he knows enough to torture? Moreover, the ticking bomb scenario mistakenly presupposes that torture reliably produces true statements rather than lies. Undoubtedly, it yields useful intelligence at times, but how do we know that torture as a *practice* produces reliable intelligence? As I discuss in chapter two, its advocates offer no scientific studies supporting its general reliability. In fact, we "really have no idea how reliable torture is as a way of obtaining information," and we learn little from occasional instances when it produces good intelligence.[7] Perhaps torturing someone will yield false and damaging information. For example, suppose we torture a suspected terrorist who then falsely claims he received support from a nation-state. We then use this information to launch a preemptive strike, initiating a destructive war. The moral of such a tale is that once we fabricate hypothetical scenarios, many possibilities emerge. In the absence of detailed empirical or historical studies, we have little reason to know which outcome will prevail. Finally, the ticking bomb scenario overlooks important institutional realities. Interrogators operate within rules and bureaucracies and are rarely as unencumbered as they appear in the philosopher's hypothetical cases. They require special training that few people can undergo. Training and institutional culture shapes character, and individual acts have long-term consequences for institutions.[8]

The ticking bomb scenario also trades on uninformed moral intuitions. One person refuses to torture despite the threat of thousands of deaths whereas another agrees to torture, arguing that her act produces positive consequences. How can we respond to such profound disagreements? What usually transpires is charge and countercharge or anecdote against anecdote. Those supporting torture accuse its opponents of moral self-indulgence or political irresponsibility. Torture opponents respond by accusing them of moral callousness or they raise the specter of Nazism or other forms of totalitarianism. These exchanges do little to further our understanding of ethics and torture.

By engaging in this fruitless discussion, we also learn little about why torture is wrong. What makes it so uniquely horrible? Why should we refrain from it and risk the lives of numerous people? Some people believe torture is self-evidently wrong and simply refuse to discuss the topic. However, such a stance cuts off conversation, ignoring people of good will who think torture is sometimes morally legitimate. Other thinkers condemn torture because it destroys autonomy, violates rights, or represents the ultimate form of tyranny.[9] Undoubtedly accurate, these analyses fail to capture our deepest feelings about torture. Is the specter of tyranny the main reason we recoil when looking at the

Abu Ghraib photographs? Or, is there something deeper here about how torture affronts human dignity? Without addressing this issue, we are left wondering why torture is so morally objectionable. Torture proponents quickly capitalize on this confusion, arguing that torture is no different than self-defense or other such acts.

Torture and Spirituality

We cannot adequately comprehend the immorality of torture without considering our inner life. Approaches to torture emphasizing human rights, autonomy, or utilitarianism rarely penetrate a person's inner core. For example, human rights thinkers infrequently discuss the nature of a torture victim's suffering. In fact, they often assume a shallow conception of the human person, identifiable only with autonomy or external actions. Similarly, utilitarians presuppose moral agents maximizing pleasures, interests, or utility functions without acknowledging the person's deeper dimensions. Yet, we cannot understand torture's horror simply by identifying it with physical pain because the "vastness and the many forms of moral suffering are certainly no less in number than the forms of physical suffering."[10] Some thinkers like Elaine Scarry and David Sussman recognize these dimensions of torture.[11] However, they focus almost entirely on the body and agency, ignoring the spiritual dimensions of torture. We suffer in ways that are irreducible to our being's physical dimensions. A person's suffering "manifests in its own way that depth which is proper to man, and in its own way surpasses it. Suffering seems to belong to man's transcendence."[12] Torturers subtly exploit and undermine these inner dimensions of our being. Contemporary thinkers often cannot understand such evil because they lack a rich conception of the human person.

The superficiality of contemporary debates is particularly disturbing because of events in the War on Terror. We have reputable accounts of U.S. personnel who deliberately attacked the religious beliefs of suspected terrorists. We have also seen, as I demonstrate in this book, the revival of psychological methods of torture harkening back to the 1950s. They subtly assault the human psyche often without ever touching the person. Finally, religious movements are proliferating globally, affecting the lives of millions of people. However, few scholarly treatments of torture draw on religious traditions. All these developments should lead us to think more carefully about spirituality and torture.

The Human Person as an Embodied Spirit

To respond to these shortcomings in contemporary analyses, this book draws on a conception of spirituality grounded in Thomistic personalism. Personalism, a twentieth-century philosophical and theological development, makes a person the center of ethical and political analysis. Thomistic personalism grounds its understanding of the person in Thomas Aquinas's thought, at the same time retrieving insights from phenomenology, a philosophical movement analyzing consciousness and experience.[13] It focuses particularly on the fundamental difference between persons and things. For example, if I kick a chair, my friends might suggest that I take anger management courses, but will hardly accuse me of cruelty. In contrast, if I kick a random stranger, they will be naturally horrified. Unlike things, persons are living, rational beings with inner lives revolving around truth and goodness. They possess self-awareness and the capacity to respond to others. They also exercise freedom and self-determination, actively cultivating relationships of giving and receiving. These capacities reveal each person's unique existence and value.

Thomistic thought offers a rich conception of spirituality. Many contemporary philosophers misunderstand spirituality. They are unaware that it has a long history marked by philosophical and theological sophistication. For centuries, thinkers insisted that our spiritual nature differentiates us from things and nonhuman animals. They conceived of the human as a "frontier" or "horizon" being situated in both the material and the spiritual worlds. For example, Aquinas maintains that we are embodied spirits with spirit and body linked intimately. The intellectual soul, he says, "is said to be on the *horizon* and *confines,* of things corporeal and incorporeal."[14] For Aquinas, the human person is an immaterial and material being who rises above the body and the world of things and other animals.

We express spirituality through knowledge, self-possession, and communication without loss—capacities I discuss in this book. Through knowledge, we transcend our biological, historical, and cultural circumstances. We relate to objects and gradually learn about their essences.[15] We pass from object to object, unify them into wholes, and locate them into hierarchies.[16] We pursue ideals or values opening us up to beings beyond our immediate environment. Knowing also empowers the person to develop a remarkable inner unity called self-possession. As a knowing being, I am no slave to my surroundings but respond to them through a center of activity. I act internally learning to be a source of action.[17] I appear as someone who "possesses myself and who is simultaneously possessed by myself."[18] I can thus take responsibility for my character and actions.

This capacity for self-possession enables us to communicate with others in amazing ways. One such mode is what philosopher Kenneth Schmitz calls "communication without loss," an "enjoyment of free activity" not "governed intrinsically by the laws that govern physical motion."[19] Human beings often interact in a zero-sum way with distinct winners and losers. Persons, in contrast, can give to one another without loss and actively accept the gifts of others. This extraordinary capacity reveals our nature as embodied spirits able to transcend narrow self-interest.

Considering these spiritual capacities helps us define torture. The War on Terror has seen deeply troubling definitions of it, particularly those in the 2002 Office of Legal Counsel's "torture memos." Secretly written by a small group of lawyers, they justified inflicting terrible pain on suspected terrorists. Scholars have also defended lesser forms of abuse they call "torture lite." Many carelessly analyze torture treating it simply as a physical matter. In contrast, in this book, I carefully define the elements of torture. I characterize it as voluntarily and intentionally inflicting severe mental or physical suffering on a helpless victim for the purpose of breaking the will.

We see torture's spiritual horror clearly if we think about sensory deprivation and self-inflicted pain. These techniques have a long history, particularly in European colonies and Asian countries. However, as Alfred McCoy and Michael Otterman have demonstrated, they emerged as CIA interrogation techniques in the 1950s and the 1960s, aided by social-scientific research promising to unlock the mind's secrets.[20] The Bush administration revived them, subjecting detainees to extreme sensory deprivation and stress positions. As I discuss in this book, sensory deprivation powerfully assaults spiritual transcendence, cutting us off from essential sources of knowledge. It disorients the person internally, creating powerful hallucinations. Similarly, stress positions create deep internal conflicts in the person. Both these practices illustrate torture's true character as an assault on the human spirit.

Should We Ever Torture?

Despite this horror, many people believe that torture is morally legitimate. They often justify it by appealing to consequentialism, the idea that consequences should determine an act's moral character. In current debates, torture proponents allege that torture sometimes produces vital information that saves lives. If we rationally calculate consequences, they maintain, we should sometimes be willing to torture.

Some critics respond to consequentialism by denying that torture ever "works," but they fail to refute consequentialism. They point to how torture often produces false confessions. This is a strong argument that I evaluate in this book, but I maintain that it misses the larger ethical point. Those defending torture's reliability presuppose we can accurately predict its consequences. I reject this idea, drawing particularly on twentieth-century critics of utilitarianism like the famed economist Friedrich Hayek. I argue that with large institutions, we cannot often accurately predict an act's consequences. I add to this uncertainty by considering how spiritual goods are immaterial and thus difficult to measure. Consequently, although torture sometimes yields accurate information, we cannot establish its reliability as a social practice.

Some contemporary thinkers recognize consequentialism's limitations but argue that torture is still tragically necessary. Their position, known as the "dirty hands" approach, has been championed by Michael Walzer and Jean Bethke Elshtain and appeals to many people today. For them, we should not hubristically demand precision in political life. Political actors operate in a foggy world of imperfect information and demands for immediate action. Unlike academic theorists, they make no pretence to possessing complete information and know they cannot calculate all the consequences of their action. International politics is marked by violence and pursuit of power and interest, and all politicians in such an arena roughly estimate consequences, hoping to protect spiritual and material goods. Often, they confront intense clashes of goods or obligations admitting of no easy resolution.

Although the dirty hands position is very attractive, I argue that it suffers from philosophical liabilities. Like consequentialism, it cannot coherently measure consequences and ends up appealing to intuitions or emotions. In the dirty hands account, the politician mysteriously decides when to disregard moral norms. More significantly, the dirty hands position underestimates torture's horrible consequences because it ignores our spirituality. Torture shatters personalities leaving a perverted moral residue in persons and institutions. Once we recognize the damage it causes, the dirty hands position loses much of its attraction.

Rejecting both dirty hands arguments and consequentialism, I defend an absolute ban on torture insisting that it is always wrong. I recognize that a ban may yield tragic consequences and acknowledge that leaders may ignore it. However, I distinguish between objective wrongness and subjective culpability. Torture is objectively wrong, but human beings in terrible circumstances may torture with varying degrees of culpability. We must insist they act immorally but be sensitive to their mitigated responsibility.

Nazis and Communists

American discussions of torture refer misleadingly to Nazis, Communists, or other mass murderers, comparing the United States to their crimes. We are not like them, we are told, and we should avoid exaggerating our crimes. For example, when the Abu Ghraib scandal broke, some Americans claimed that unlike terrorists, the United States does not behead people. Or, they maintained that Saddam Hussein committed far greater crimes than any American ever did. Such a response, however, is a misleading distraction, an attempt to change the subject. To forestall it, I declare unequivocally that I see no moral equivalence between the Nazis or Communists and the United States. Totalitarian regimes committed enormous crimes that we should remember as unprecedented, but we cannot use this memory to ignore lesser crimes. Many nations torture in horrible ways that nevertheless fall short of the evils of totalitarian regimes. We should be able to analyze their crimes without constantly discussing Nazism. I draw on many examples in this book most of which will come from the United States. With this focus, I in no way endorse the thesis that the United States produces all evil in the world. Nor do I suggest that all American soldiers or interrogators are war criminals, a false and pernicious thesis. However, I do not seek a contrived and self-serving balance by constantly comparing us to the world's worst offenders. We cannot absolve ourselves of wrongdoing by claiming we are not totalitarians. On the contrary, by identifying our crimes, we hope to avoid descending to the level of Nazis and Communists.[21]

Torture and Ineffability

Writing about torture presents particular challenges that I keep in mind throughout this book. First, we cannot fully capture torture's horror in writing. Words fail to capture many experiences, but torture differs from others because of how it assaults the person. It undermines the victim's capacity to speak, often reducing him or her to an organism in pain. Like other kinds of profound suffering, torture creates a subjective world that seems "almost inexpressible and not transferable."[22] Journalist Jean Améry captures this insight in his famous account of his torture in Belgium and Auschwitz. He notes that "if from the experience of torture any knowledge at all remains that goes beyond the plain nightmarish, it is that of a great amazement and a foreignness in the world that cannot be compensated by any sort of subsequent human communication."[23] To apprehend torture, visual or cinematic representations may be preferable to written accounts. Recognizing this reality, I quote as much as possible from the writings of torture victims. Second, defining torture presents dangers because lawyers and politicians manipulate definitions to excuse crimes. Some commentators, in fact, reject any attempt to define torture because they think definitions encourage evil. Mindful of this danger, I nevertheless think it important to subject torture to analysis. Without defining it, we allow governments to abuse language and obfuscate their crimes with propaganda. Moreover, we weaken our opposition to torture by adopting confusions. Facing terrorism, we might revert to intuitions about torture and embrace its use. To counteract these dangers, we need intellectual clarity. Finally, discussing torture can corrupt us because other people's horrible experiences become vehicles for self-aggrandizement. Those disfigured by torture recede into the background, eclipsed by people capitalizing on their lives for political or academic gain. Throughout this book, I am attentive to this danger.

A Word about Sources

Before outlining the structure of the book, I want to say a few words about sources. Choosing sources for a book on torture and the War on Terror presents difficulties. New revelations about the early years of the War on Terror constantly emerge. With Internet technology, new documents also become available. Others remain classified, rendering it difficult to make judgments about policy. Finally, scholars sometimes uncritically use documents to support a case. In this book, I draw extensively from documents available on the Internet. The American Civil Liberties Union has made thousands of them available, and I work through some in the book. Whenever possible, I use multiple sources to substantiate controversial claims. As more participant accounts of the Bush administration emerge, we will piece together a fuller account of its interrogation policies. In the meantime, our picture remains necessarily incomplete, and those without access to classified information must modestly work with public sources.

Torture presents the additional problem of possible deception and political manipulation. As I argue in this book, we have ample evidence that torture occurred in the War on Terror, and cannot dismiss it as mere al-Qaeda manipulation. Nevertheless, in individual cases, we may encounter manipulation and mendacity. Therefore, we cannot incredulously accept all accounts of torture. To address this problem, I pay particular attention to cases for which we have strong documentation. Sadly, they abound, and we need no longer entertain the idea that all allegations of torture originate in al-Qaeda's deceit.

The Book's Structure

In chapter one, I discuss a Thomistic conception of spirituality and describe why we should refrain from using persons as mere means. Drawing on the work of philosopher W. Norris Clarke, S.J., I consider the human person as a "frontier being" occupying both spiritual and material realms. I also emphasize the spiritual capacities of transcendence through knowledge, self-possession, and communication without loss. This chapter includes some philosophical heavy lifting, but I ask the reader to bear with me as I work through complex concepts. For those interested mainly in the discussion of torture, I recommend reading this chapter's conclusion to get a sense of what I mean by spirituality. In chapter two, I define torture, emphasizing how it seeks to break the will using spiritual and material means. I focus on torture's purpose responding to possible criticisms of my definition of torture. In chapter three, I consider why torture is morally repellent. I argue that it uses persons merely as a means and seeks to destroy their spiritual natures. Here, I use recent work on sensory deprivation and self-inflicted pain (Alfred McCoy, Michael Otterman). I argue that such torture undermines our spiritual transcendence and capacity to know. In chapter four, I discuss consequentialist defenses of torture. Using Friedrich Hayek's and Russell Hardin's work on utilitarianism, I argue that we often cannot accurately predict torture's spiritual and political consequences. In chapter five, I turn to dirty hands justifications of torture, a position I once found deeply attractive. I reveal its dangers, maintaining that torture is always morally wrong. In the book's conclusion, I discuss memory and reconciliation. Drawing on the writings of the German philosopher Max Scheler on repentance, I urge Americans to recall and discuss what has occurred in the War on Terror.

CHAPTER ONE

"The Soul Is Somehow All that Exists": Spirituality and Human Dignity

> The two aspects, combined—dwelling most intensively within itself and being *capex universi*, able to grasp the universe—together constitute the essence of spirit.
>
> Josef Pieper[1]

When the Abu Ghraib scandal broke, many people reacted with disgust at the sight of naked prisoners standing in pyramids and sexually compromising positions. They were appalled to see military policemen treat Iraqi prisoners like playthings. Sadly, this revulsion soon gave way to excuses, rationalizations, and defense mechanisms designed to shield people from horror. Nevertheless, the initial reaction to Abu Ghraib bears close scrutiny because it reveals something important about our experience of persons. If soldiers abused dolls, we might worry about their mental health, but we would not morally condemn them. However, we are troubled when they target prisoners for abuse. Why do we react this way? What precisely distinguishes things from persons?

In this chapter, I explore the person–thing distinction, maintaining that the human person is valuable because he or she occupies both spiritual and material realities. First, I discuss how we experience the difference between persons and things. Second, examining this experience, I retrieve a classical view of the human person as a frontier being living on the edge of the material and immaterial worlds. This majestic vision explains why persons are valuable, but many contemporary thinkers find it strange or unappealing. Third, to defend it, I sketch three elements of spirituality: transcendence through knowledge, self-possession, and communication without loss. Finally, returning to ethics, I maintain that our frontier status bars us from treating persons merely as means to an end.

Things and Persons

When witnessing the horrors of Abu Ghraib, we experience the "great gulf that separates the world of persons from the world of things."[2] Encountering a thing, we regard it as "an entity which is devoid not only of intelligence, but also of life; a *thing* is an inanimate object."[3] In contrast, we experience a person as a "somebody," set apart from all other entities we encounter.[4] He or she appears as a being with a "specific inner self, an inner life."[5] We apprehend this inner life when people act on us or when we witness horrific acts against them. For example, at Abu Ghraib, Army Private Lynndie English was photographed holding a strap around a prisoner's neck. When this picture became public, people immediately realized that something was wrong, displaying their recognition of the person's value.

We undoubtedly experience this difference between persons and things, but what precisely distinguishes us from inanimate objects? For centuries, thinkers insisted that our spiritual nature differentiates us from things and nonhuman animals. They conceived of the human as a "frontier" or "horizon" being situated in two worlds. For example, in the *Timaeus*, Plato describes how the Demiurge made a "mixture of *the Same*, and then one of *the Different*, in between their indivisible and their corporeal, divisible counterparts. And he took the three mixtures and mixed them together to make a uniform mixture, forcing the Different, which was hard to mix, into conformity with the Same."[6] Philosopher Plotinus says the soul is "of the boundary order, situated between two regions and has tendency to both."[7] Christian theologian Nemesius of Emesa marvels at how "man's being is on the boundary between the intelligible and the phenomenal order."[8] In the Italian Renaissance, Pico della Mirandola has God say to Adam,

I have placed you at the very center of the world, so that from that vantage point you may with greater ease glance round about you on all that the world contains. We have made you a creature neither of heaven nor of earth, neither mortal nor immortal, in order that you may, as the free and proud shaper of your own being, fashion yourself in the form you may prefer. It will be in your power to descend to the lower, brutish forms of life; you will be able, through your own decision, to rise again to the superior orders whose life is divine.[9]

These and many other thinkers locate the human being on the edge of the material and immaterial worlds. They identify this status as that which differentiates humans from things and nonhuman animals.

Some thinkers decry this intermediate status and urge humanity to exit it. For example, Plotinus describes a tragic double existence in which the human soul "is a deserter from the totality; its differentiation has severed it; its vision is no longer set in the Intellectual; it is a partial thing, isolated, weakened, full of care, intent upon the fragment, severed from the whole, it nestles in one form of being; for this it abandons all else, entering into and caring only for the one, for a thing buffeted about by a world full of things."[10] He adopts this negative assessment of humanity because for him only the soul, not the entire person, lives on the frontier. This leads him to occasionally denigrate the body.[11] For Plotinus, our frontier status appears alien thereby preventing us from reaching our true destiny.

Thomas Aquinas differs from such thinkers by attributing frontier status to our embodied substance. We are embodied spirits, with spirit and body linked intimately. By the body, the human person "sinks his roots deep into the material cosmos, which provides the initial input for his thought and action and the theater (in this life) for his journey toward self-realization."[12] However, as spirit, the person rises above the body and the world of things and other animals. He is thus an "amphibian" existing in two worlds.[13] Consequently, the intellectual soul "is said to be on the *horizon* and *confines* of things corporeal and incorporeal."[14] Aquinas also says that "there is yet another reason why the human soul abounds in a variety of powers—because it is on the confines of spiritual and corporeal creatures; and therefore the powers of both meet together in the soul."[15] He uses the term *confinium* to describe the frontier, emphasizing that the human being unites two realities.[16] This status signifies "not so much a separation, but rather a bond; it does signify a 'difference' but also a unification."[17] Some ancient thinkers held that the material and immaterial differ so much that a supernatural being must compel their unity. For example, Plato maintains that the Demiurge "needs a great deal of strength" to bring together the spiritual and material because "the components concerned are incompatible."[18] In contrast,

Aquinas maintains that this unity is natural requiring no force or violence to actualize it.

Nevertheless, despite its natural character, the spirit/matter connection should amaze us. Through the human person, we are "able to contemplate the marvelous connection of things" through which exists "something supreme in the genus of bodies, namely, the human body harmoniously tempered, which is in contact with the lowest of the higher genus, namely, the human soul."[19] The body links the person to other animals, whereas the soul connects him to higher forms of intelligence. The wonder of man is that he "combines both spiritual and material components in his one person so that he really assumes an intermediate position."[20] Purely spiritual beings (if they exist) occupy only one world requiring no contact with the material realm. In contrast, the human person is a "citizen of two worlds" who integrates two realms, albeit slowly and often tragically.[21]

Contemporary thinkers may see this majestic vision of the person as a premodern relic long rendered obsolete by modernity. Politically, the past century's deliberate and systematic violations of persons mocked attempts to esteem the human race. Conceptually, many contemporary intellectuals explicitly repudiate the person's unique status. For example, some writings in environmental ethics harshly criticize anthropocentric ethical theories rejecting the idea that humans exceed other living entities in value. Animal rights activists oppose the notion that the human species has exceptional value, labeling it "specieist," an irrational attitude akin to racism or sexism. Following Ludwig Wittgenstein and others, some philosophers object to language about the person's spiritual life, replacing it with a concern for language or behavior. Finally, materialists (those who think that the material is all that exists) attack the person's moral distinctiveness. They maintain that genetics, cognitive science, and neurology all reveal that humans differ only in degree, not kind, from other animals. These and other developments challenge the idea that human persons occupy a special place in the cosmos.

For many contemporary philosophers, language about spirituality is also deeply puzzling. For example, Ghanaian philosopher Kwasi Wiredu believes that one "searches in vain for a useful definition of the spiritual."[22] Is it simply the nonmaterial? Such a definition serves only as a "definition by pure negation."[23] Similarly, Wiredu suggests, identifying the spiritual with the unseen admits too many entities into the spiritual realm. Many scientific entities are unseen, yet we hesitate to call them spiritual. Like Wiredu, linguist Steven Pinker can make no sense of spirituality. Reviving the famous phrase of philosopher Gilbert Ryle, he calls the spiritual soul a "Ghost in the Machine." According to Pinker, the spiritual is indefinable and unreal. Science, he maintains, shows definitively that what we used to call the spiritual soul consists instead of "the information-processing activity of the brain, an organ governed by the laws of biology."[24] Pinker and other contemporary thinkers associate spirituality with primitive ideas about human nature. For them, talk of our frontier status makes little sense in a modern scientific world.

Spirituality and Knowledge

Contemporary thinkers correctly note how religious people use vague conceptions of spirituality. Despite a worldwide explosion of religious consciousness and practice, many people know little about the history of theology and philosophy. Today's bookstores are filled with books about spirituality or metaphysics that employ ill-defined concepts. Moreover, people often contrast the terms spirituality and "religion," without understanding either of them. Finally, those interested in religion and science mix spirituality and brain physiology, irritating both theologians and neuroscientists. Given this frequent but confused appearance of the term "spirituality," it is no wonder that some intellectuals jettison it altogether.

Despite these confusions, the concept of spirituality has a long history marked by philosophical and theological sophistication. I focus on Aquinas's account of spirituality, which he links to a complex understanding of knowledge emphasizing the intellect and senses. For him, we must know by using our senses because we possess few innate ideas. Our initial contact with the world, thus, is receptive. Through a process involving complex acts, the intellect gradually transforms what the senses apprehend into immaterial objects. Knowing moves from the material to immaterial and from the concrete to the abstract. The intellect also divides and composes what it apprehends and makes judgments about extramental realities. Aquinas's account of knowledge thus defies easy classification. We might call it empiricist because it relies heavily on the senses. However, it also grants the intellect habits and capacities foreign to modern empiricism.[25]

The Spirituality of the Person

Aquinas uses his conception of knowledge to define spirituality. The "meanings he associates" with the term differ "strongly from contemporary meanings."[26] Sometimes, he contrasts spiritual with material change. For example, material change occurs in the digestive tract, where food undergoes radical transformation once we eat it. Spiritual change, however, involves no such mutation. Knowing is spiritual because it interacts with other entities without deforming them, distinguishing it from processes such as digestion.[27]

Through knowledge, a spiritual creature gains access to a universe. In Josef Pieper's words, she places herself "into relation with the sum-total of existing things."[28] She transcends her immediate surroundings and biological limitations by relating to a world. In this sense, the intellectual soul

> has a power extending to the infinite; therefore it cannot be limited by nature to certain fixed natural notions, or even to certain fixed means whether of defence or of clothing, as is the case with other animals, the souls of which are endowed with knowledge and power in regard to fixed particular things. Instead of all these, man has by nature his reason and his hands, which are "the organs of organs" (De Anima iii), since by their means man can make for himself instruments of an infinite variety, and for any number of purposes.[29]

Naturally, human finitude limits what we know, but we can progressively increase our knowledge. In fact, for us, "existing things, inasmuch as they have being and through their being, are positioned within the knowing soul's field of reference."[30] We not only relate to them, but also gradually learn about their essences.[31] We not only move from object to object, but also unify objects into wholes. This movement unifies objects into hierarchies.[32] We organize them around ideals and values moving beyond our immediate environment.[33]

Spirituality's transcendent dimension may worry those allergic to dualism, but Aquinas emphasizes the embodied character of human knowing. For some philosophers and theologians, dualism (the idea that we are sprit/body or soul/body) is a dirty word, supposedly responsible for many of today's ills.[34] Whatever we might say of these worries about dualism have little bearing on Aquinas's ideas. He devotes considerable effort to rejecting disembodied conceptions of the human soul.[35] He repeatedly insists that human cognition requires a composite substance living in two worlds.[36] Animals, he maintains, know through their senses only without the functioning of the intellect. More cognitively advanced creatures might cognize through the intellect alone, requiring no incoming sense information.[37] In contrast, as horizon beings, humans know through both the senses and the intellect. For this reason they need a body.

The embodied character of our spirituality becomes clearer if we think about time. Our knowing is intimately linked to time (a point I return to when discussing how torturers deliberately disrupt our sense of time). Our mental acts are temporally indexed because they relate to the senses and motion. We measure motion in a variety of ways, and we usually know successively and discursively.[38] One event follows another, and we measure this succession with devices such as clocks. Consequently, how we know often involves a temporal dimension.

Nevertheless, human minds can also know the essences of things and, therefore, can cognize atemporal entities. For example, we learn mathematics at a particular time, but the objects we know are atemporal.[39] It would be absurd to say that the number 2 exists at 2:00 p.m. on June 14, 2007, in Green Bay, Wisconsin. Otherwise, no one at that time and date outside of Wisconsin could think about the number 2![40] Contemplating mathematics, therefore, includes temporal activities cognizing atemporal objects. We can identify many situations where a mind situated in time accesses atemporal objects. Our contact with them means that although "temporality undoubtedly denotes a fundamental aspect of consciousness, that aspect is not the only one."[41] The mix of temporality and atemporality characterizes our experience as knowing beings.

Spirituality and Self-Possession

Knowing empowers a person to develop a remarkable inner unity called self-possession. Oneness characterizes all beings, but spiritual beings can achieve a "more intense inner unity...a heightened and self-contained 'oneness.'"[42] An intrinsic existence is "the dynamic core of an entity from which all active manifestations originate and toward which all endurance and receptivity are focused and directed."[43] It appears only in some beings and not in others (we do not talk about the intrinsic existence of a chair). Plants and nonhuman animals possess intrinsic existence enabling them to relate actively to their environment.[44] However, spiritual beings develop a particularly strong inner unity, self-possession through knowledge. As a knowing being, I am no slave to my surroundings, but have a center of activity through which I respond to them. In fact, to be able "to say 'I' is the unique prerogative of a personal being."[45] I appear as someone who "possesses myself and who is simultaneously possessed by myself."[46] Self-possession reveals itself vividly when the "intellect knows itself, and knows that it knows," a capacity that chairs and buildings lack.[47]

The person develops self-possession by shaping her character through intransitive and transitive actions. Transitive action produces effects outside the agent, tending beyond her toward "the external world."[48] For example, when I build a house, I end up with a product that is external to my body. In contrast, *intransitive* action remains within the subject, determining the quality or value of the person. Its distinctive feature is "never to consist in the production of anything, never to be a way leading to a term distinct from itself."[49] Through intransitive action, we shape our character positively as well as negatively. We act internally, learning to be a source of action, and aware of how we affect others. As I soon demonstrate, torturers deliberately pervert and destroy self-possession, mocking our attempts to retain psychic and physical unity.

Spirituality and Communication without Loss

Self-possession opens up remarkable modes of communication available only to spiritual creatures. One such mode is what Kenneth Schmitz calls "communication without loss," an "enjoyment of free activity" not "governed intrinsically by the laws that govern physical motion."[50] It is accompanied by physical changes, but includes properties that we cannot entirely reduce to them.[51] Much human interaction yields immediate gains and losses, and items in our immediate environment cannot coexist without them.[52] For example, the computer on my desk takes up space, preventing me from stacking books on it. Given this experience of material objects, we may falsely conclude that "every movement entails an exchange that must be understood as a material transfer or a mutual give and take of some form of mass or energy such that the contributors suffer a loss."[53] However, the knowing relation takes nothing from the known object, but only alters the knower's being. Thus, when I look at my computer screen, I have interacted with it without altering its material constitution.

Schmitz uses teaching to illustrate the significance of this communication without loss.[54] A teacher communicates information, but loses none of her knowledge. Likewise, a student receives information without losing something. In this encounter, we can measure energy lost or gained, but such quantification captures only part of what occurs in the teaching encounter. It differs from many human interactions involving calculations. For example, economic transactions require quantification. If "I have four things and give away two, it is obvious that I only have two left, and that I am correspondingly *impoverished*."[55] In contrast, communication without loss enhances the giver, who "far from being destroyed or impaired as a result is enlarged and enriched."[56] At their best, teachers and students move beyond immediate interest to participate in common enterprises.

To develop this communication, persons must be willing to receive what others offer. They must cultivate "a certain readiness or pre-ordination," an active openness to another.[57] When a student receives instruction from a teacher, she is no mere passive receptacle, akin to wax receiving an imprint.[58] Instead, she actively responds to teaching. Far from being static, active receptivity represents "the most intense of living actuality, realized variously in the effort to understand, in the bliss of friendship, in the energy of artistic creation, and the acknowledgment of the divine."[59] Such experiences can only occur with some stable self-possession and minimal openness to others.

French philosopher and dramatist Gabriel Marcel illustrates active receptivity well by considering hospitality.[60] Normally, we do not say that a host "undergoes" hospitality or "endures" his guests (unless he truly dislikes them!). Instead, we say he prepares his house and accepts visitors in his domain. The host must be at "at home," possessing not only the house, but also a welcoming personality.[61] Likewise, he must in some minimal sense be "at home" with himself to be truly welcoming. Without a self to communicate, he cannot enter into positive communication. A profoundly disordered person, for example, experiences difficulty giving without expecting something in return. To return to the hospitality example, a person with a disordered home and an empty refrigerator has little to offer his guests. To actively receive means we "introduce the other person, the stranger, into a region" of intimacy and openness.[62] We welcome each other's presence, celebrating a common existence. As I discuss in chapter three, torture often deliberately mocks active receptivity by creating "guest houses" or "inns" that house detainees. Torturers show a keen sense of awareness of our capacity to freely give to others.

Active receptivity lacks the possessiveness present in other relationships. When I have something, it is external to me. I attach myself to it, but it always remains outside of me. I can also quantify it in some way.

For example, if I say "I have a computer," the computer remains external to my body, even though I spend hours before it. I can also measure and define its dimensions. Having also includes an instrumental moment where I use something for specific ends. I manipulate it with techniques that others imitate. In contrast, I can relate to the world in a way lacking possessiveness and externality. They are present to me in a noninstrumental way. For example, I say "I am sad," rather than "I have sadness" to describe an emotion. We cannot easily understand the presence of this emotion because "it is almost impossible for us to avoid a picture of activity which would be in some sense be physical. We can hardly help seeing it as the starting-up of a machine, a machine of which our bodies are the spring and perhaps also the mold."[63] To understand spiritual activity, we need to move away from strictly physical images.

Rejecting pure possessiveness, however, is crucial in social and political life. Possessive persons limit their availability toward others. People become potential objects of desire–satisfaction or means to an end. Or, they become organizational units that we manage. In contrast, spiritual beings welcome others, abstain from seeking immediate advantage, and develop intimacy. Intimacy is thus a spiritual gift that "is offered by a person in the trust that the offer will be received by another with respect, and on the basis of a certain mutual integrity and openness."[64] Rather than fixating on a person's identifiable characteristics, it acknowledges the uniqueness of the inner person.

Horizon beings exhibit active receptivity imperfectly. In fact, we must not "look to the human person for an exhibition of pure spirit, for the obvious reason that, although the human person is spiritual, integral to human person are the material and immaterial modalities of physical being."[65] If they exist, other cognitively advanced beings might communicate without loss generously and effectively. For example, we can imagine an alien who could process information without the senses and share information generously. In contrast, we must work at knowing, combating numerous internal and external obstacles. Even with the help of the senses, our intellect struggles to recognize spiritual qualities in ourselves and others.

To summarize what I have said about spirituality, it is no vague capacity or entity we posit to make sense of our lives. Nor is it simply the opposite of the material (however we define it). Instead, spirituality is intimately linked to cognitive powers. It includes the capacity to transcend ourselves through knowledge, self-possession, and communication without loss.

The Fragility of a Frontier Being

Although the human person is naturally a frontier being, his status is fragile and requires continual cultivation. Commenting on puzzles of cognition, philosopher Yves Simon quotes the famous passage from French philosopher Blaise Pascal:

> Man is but a reed, the most feeble thing in nature; but he is a thinking reed. The entire universe need not arm itself to crush him. A vapour, a drop of water suffices to kill him. But if the universe were to crush him, man would still be more noble than that which killed him because he knows that he dies and the advantage which the universe has over him; the universe knows nothing of this.[66]

Pascal perfectly expresses the nobility and fragility of our frontier existence. The person is "more than" the material universe because he integrates the material with the immaterial. He is beset by threats, but his awareness of them gives him us a dignity that things lack. Pascal is attuned to how easily our frontier status disintegrates. Like ancient and medieval thinkers, he emphasizes our physical frame's fragility. Despite modernity's advances in health and technology, we continue to confront powerful physical threats to our personhood. We are constantly subjected to attacks on our bodily integrity from other persons and the environment. Recent research in the neurosciences demonstrates just how much chemistry influences our brains. HIV-AIDS and other diseases ravage the globe. Environmental degradation and threats of nuclear and biological terrorism threaten to kill hundreds of thousands of people. Contemporary scientific advances, thus, add to our knowledge of the precariousness of our frontier status. We cannot easily separate physical debility from spirituality because the "spiritual factor both penetrates and is penetrated through and through by the bodily conditions of our existence as persons."[67] Threats to the body may also affect the spirit.

We also encounter spiritual difficulties occupying a frontier status. The person always remains a person, but he must develop his personality; he can also degrade it in many ways. As French philosopher Jacques Maritain put it, personality is "metaphysically inalienable," but "suffers many a check in the psychological and moral register."[68] We struggle to know through the senses and discursive reasoning and make many mistaken judgments. To return to our advanced alien, he might be "a person transparent to himself, who grasps himself completely in one word" and "knows all things in the depth of his self-knowledge."[69] However, such immediate self-knowledge is unavailable to us. Given constant temptations to embrace perversions, the person must win his "personality as he wins his liberty; he pays dearly for it."[70] As we will soon see, torturers take full advantage of such spiritual weaknesses, presenting their victims with temptations to betray themselves or others.

A Frontier Being and the Personalistic Norm

By contemplating our frontier status, we are in a better position to understand the fundamental moral difference between persons and things. Unlike persons, things are material entities incapable of transcending their environment and unable to unify the material and the immaterial. They are unaware of time and cannot self-consciously contemplate eternal objects. Finally, they lack the capacities of self-possession and communication without loss. These differences explain why we should refrain from treating persons as mere things. To capture this insight, the late John Paul II articulated what he called the personalistic norm, which states that "whenever a person is the object of your activity, remember that you may not treat that person as only the means to an end."[71] It is "born from" the "awakening to the inwardness of personal subjectivity."[72] The personalistic norm also acknowledges that "the person is the kind of good which does not admit of use, and cannot be treated as an object of use and as such the means to an end."[73] We use persons constantly, but we must avoid using them *merely* as means to an end. The personalistic norm, thus, rules out forms of utilitarianism that employs persons merely as instruments for promoting the well-being of others. For example, we cannot justify slavery or genocide by pointing to their beneficial consequences. Such practices use persons merely as instruments, disregarding their value a spiritual creatures. The personalistic norm has profound consequences for political life. Economic and political institutions often abuse persons and cultivate a common urge to use others instrumentally. Twentieth-century personalists wrote extensively about reforming institutions so they would respect the person. They frequently defended the person's dignity against the many forces arrayed against it.

Concluding Reflections: Hierarchies and Contemporary Thought

Linking the personalistic norm to our frontier status entails risks because some contemporary audiences find hierarchies ethically problematic. For example, writing shortly after the Abu Ghraib scandal erupted, Peter Singer and Karen Dawn linked it to animal torture. They revealed that prior to her deployment to Iraq, Lynndie English worked in a poultry factory. They reported stories of employees "ripping birds' beaks off, spray-painting their faces, twisting their heads off, spitting tobacco into their mouths and eyes and breaking them in half—all while the birds are still alive."[74] Because English worked in such an environment, Singer and Dawn suggest that we can understand her descent into cruelty in Iraq. In fact, they conclude that "in both Baghdad and Moorefield, W.Va., a simple cruel dynamic was at work. When humans have unchecked power over those they see as inferior, they may abuse it." They conclude that "we know that some humans will seek superiority over others by dominating and humiliating them. That should warn us that abuse is possible whenever power is unchecked, especially in a system constructed to inflict violence on beings seen as inferior." Singer and Dawn thus trace Abu Ghraib's horrors to hierarchical thinking and practices.

Like others who object to morally distinguishing between humans and other animals, Singer and Dawn suggest that hierarchies produce abuses. Critics of Aquinas often make this point maintaining that his hierarchy perpetuates unjust social relations. They argue that he is insufficiently critical of slavery, seems unconcerned about gender inequalities, and repeatedly affirms that humans can use other animals. On this reading, ancient and medieval metaphysical hierarchies are politically regressive, producing sexism, oligarchy, and numerous other ills.

Hierarchies can be dangerous, and contemporary thought draws attention to how they may promote injustice. However, there is no *necessary* relationship between hierarchy and cruelty, and we have no justification for jettisoning hierarchy altogether. Cruelty to animals may inure us to cruelty to humans, and perhaps such a dynamic played a role (a minor role, I would add) in the Abu Ghraib disaster. Moreover, hierarchies may lead some people to brutalize nonhuman animals. Ancient thinkers make disturbing arguments justifying natural hierarchies that denigrate slaves and women. However, others celebrate the natural order, arguing that diversity in the universe is a wonderful phenomenon.[75] Some medieval thinkers also emphasize the intrinsic equality of all humanity. For example, when discussing our final destiny, Aquinas insists that all created intellects can "attain to the vision of the divine substance."[76] Finally, modern thinkers have used hierarchies to celebrate diversity, democracy, and nonhuman animals. In contrast, twentieth-century thinkers celebrating egalitarianism committed horrific crimes. These developments demonstrate that hierarchy and exploitation are contingently related. In all cases, we must vigilantly guard against cruelty and injustice.

In defending the idea of a frontier being, however, ancient and medieval thinkers also use complex language that some contemporary thinkers find confusing. For example, philosopher Eleonore Stump suggests that Aquinas's understanding of the person in the cosmos is "unlikely to be persuasive to contemporary readers."[77] I think she is simply mistaken in this assessment. Contemporary thinkers can perfectly understand the human person as a frontier being. They can experience the fundamental distinction between persons and things. Reflecting on it, they can consider how knowing enables us to transcend our immediate circumstances, cultivate self-possession, and communicate without loss. Rather than worrying about strange vocabulary, we should invite contemporary thinkers to reflect more carefully on spirituality.

Ethically, contemporary readers urgently need to understand spirituality. Because many intellectuals downgrade the person's place in the cosmos, we lose sight of her value. The personalistic norm is no arbitrary invention of ecclesial or political authorities, but reflects instead the person's value. By integrating the material and the immaterial, the human person reveals her true dignity. We can thus see why it is true that "anyone who treats a person as the means to an end does violence to the very essence of the other."[78] This idea has far-reaching consequences for public life, as we will soon see when turning to the horrible topic of torture.

CHAPTER TWO

Breaking the Will: Spirituality and the Definition of Torture

The word "torture" lacks a stable definition.

Richard Posner[1]

A small mistake in the beginning is a big one in the end.

Thomas Aquinas[2]

Few people openly advocate torturing terrorists. Instead, they take refuge in convoluted or vague definitions of torture allowing them to support it. For example, U.S. President Bush declared that "torture anywhere is an affront to human dignity everywhere."[3] However, in the year before he made this statement, his administration radically redefined torture in its now infamous "torture memos." What exactly did the president mean when using the word torture? Similarly, when the Abu Ghraib scandal broke, Defense Secretary Donald Rumsfeld insisted that "what has been charged so far is abuse, which I believe technically is different from torture. I'm not going to address the 'torture' word."[4] Using obscure distinctions known only to him, Rumsfeld was able to deny that U.S. soldiers tortured. Other thinkers condemn torture but simultaneously legitimize it by embracing the troubling phrase, "torture lite." Publicized by journalist Mark Bowden and later adopted by Jean Bethke Elshtain, torture lite includes "sleep deprivation, exposure to heat or cold, the use of drugs to cause confusion, rough treatment (slapping, shoving, or shaking), forcing a prisoner to stand for days at a time or to sit in uncomfortable positions, and playing on his fears for himself and his family."[5] With a small semantic alternation, Elshtain and Bowden legitimize brutality, at the same time denying they advocate torture.

These responses to torture weaken our moral sensibilities allowing us to ignore its horrific character. They also leave the dangerous impression that moral acts are merely social constructs we manipulate at will. In this chapter, I oppose such moral obfuscation by carefully defining torture. First, I analyze the now infamous U.S. torture memos, uncovering their inadequate and dangerous definition of torture. Second, I discuss why some definitions of torture falter because they ignore our spiritual nature. Third, I briefly outline the moral act's structure, discussing intention, circumstances, and object. Fourth, I define torture by analyzing its elements and focusing on how it seeks to break a victim's will. I also describe how torture dethrones the human from her status as a frontier being. Finally, I consider challenges to defining torture, rejecting particularly the notion that torture seeks to promote the common good.

The Origins of Torture after September 11

In the immediate aftermath of the September 11 attacks, the U.S. government came under enormous pressure to gather intelligence. The CIA, the Pentagon, and State Department lacked sufficient information about al-Qaeda and scrambled to understand the enemy that attacked the United States.[6] As Jane Mayer notes, in the early months after the September 11 attacks, it is "nearly impossible to exaggerate the sense of moral and existential danger that dominated the thinking of the upper rungs of the Bush Administration."[7] Under such desperate circumstances, U.S. officials were willing to use morally questionable means of obtaining information. After a short but contentious debate, the United States decided that the Geneva Conventions had no application to al-Qaeda. In a memorandum dated February 7, 2002, President Bush declared that the War on Terror represents a "new paradigm" in which "none of the provisions of Geneva apply to our conflict with al-Qaeda in Afghanistan or elsewhere throughout the world."[8] The president maintained that he had legal authority to suspend the Geneva Conventions between the United States and Afghanistan but would continue to apply them to the Taliban. However, he went on to say that Common Article Three of the Geneva Conventions, which establishes a minimum of humane treatment for captives, "does not apply to either al-Qaeda or Taliban detainees."[9] Finally, President Bush emphasized that despite his conclusions about the Geneva Conventions, the United States would treat all captives humanely "to the extent appropriate and consistent with military necessity."[10] However, he never defined military necessity, permitting intelligence and military authorities to adopt an elastic understanding of it.

As the War on Terror continued, President Bush sought additional legal advice concerning detainee treatment. Unknown to the American people (and many in the government as well), the Justice Department's Office of Legal Council issued a memorandum on torture in August 2002.[11] This now infamous memo, together with a Pentagon Working Group Report document and a later memorandum by John Yoo, shaped American detainee policy for several years. In 1987, the United Nations ratified the Convention against Torture and Other Cruel, Inhuman or Degrading Treatment or Punishment (CAT). It defines torture and requires nations to actively oppose it. The United States ratified CAT in 1994 attaching legal reservations to its ratification. The authors of the memo, Jay Bybee and John Yoo, offered an interpretation of this treaty (as implemented by the U.S. Code 18 U.S.C. 2340–2340A) that radically redefined torture.[12] For Bybee and Yoo, torture occurs only under certain carefully defined conditions.[13] They intended their definition to guide and legally protect interrogators in the field.

Bybee and Yoo analyze the elements of torture. They first focus on *specific intent*, insisting that a general intent to severely harm does not constitute torture. Instead, a person must "expressly intend to achieve the forbidden act."[14] At first glance, Bybee and Yoo make an unexceptional point about intent; they simply distinguish between degrees of knowledge in intent. This distinction has a long, albeit controversial pedigree in American law, philosophy, and theology. In the Bybee–Yoo memo, however, the specific intent requirement becomes deeply problematic when the authors define "severe pain or suffering." Using dictionary definitions, statutory language, and select medical studies, they insist that severe physical pain or suffering must rise to the level of "serious physical condition or injury such as death, organ failure, or serious impairment of body functions—in order to constitute torture."[15] Turning to mental harm, Bybee–Yoo add a temporal dimension to torture. Mental harm may be severe, but does not amount to torture unless it is prolonged (such as posttraumatic stress disorder).[16]

Thus, to be guilty of torture, an interrogator must specifically intend to inflict long-term, severe mental or physical pain or suffering of a particular kind. If she intends only to cause short-term pain or suffering, she does not torture. Bybee–Yoo view their definition as a reasonable interpretation of the term "torture" in American law. Offering a complete definition, they say that it is "not the mere infliction of pain or suffering on another, but is instead a step well removed. The victim must experience intense pain or suffering of the kind that is equivalent to the pain that would be associated with serious physical injury so severe that death, organ failure, or permanent damage resulting in a loss of significant body function will likely result. If that pain or suffering is psychological, that suffering must result from one of the acts set forth in the statute. In addition, these acts must cause long-term mental harm."[17]

The Bybee–Yoo memo significantly influenced U.S. policy toward detainees in the War on Terror.[18] Defense Secretary Rumsfeld relied on it when devising interrogation techniques for Guantánamo Bay and elsewhere. In early 2003, the U.S. Defense Department assembled a working group to develop interrogation guidelines. It issued a March 2003 memo that repeated almost verbatim the Bybee–Yoo definition of torture. These two documents provided the Bush administration with a definition of torture it used for several years. They shaped the interrogation policies of the Defense Department and the CIA in Guantánamo Bay, Iraq, and secret CIA prisons. The administration revisited the memos only after they were publicly leaked. In 2004, Jack Goldsmith, the head of the Office of Legal Counsel, rescinded the memos arguing that they no longer represented a legitimate legal position. Later that year, Acting Assistant Attorney General Daniel Levin issued a new memo that removed some of the earlier memo's controversial features, but denied that the Justice Department had condoned torture.[19] The Supreme Court intervened several times insisting against the Bush administration that Common Article Three of the Geneva Conventions applies to all detainees, regardless of their combatant status. Congress also opposed aspects of the Bush administration policy, passing the Detainee Treatment Act of 2005 (also known as the McCain Amendment after its sponsor Senator John McCain of Arizona) and the 2006 Military Commissions Act (MCA). Such legislation prohibited the military from torturing detainees, but placed no restrictions on the CIA. Moreover, President Bush issued "signing statements," documents indicating how he understood Congressional legislation. In them, he continued to assert that he had the right to interrogate as he saw fit.[20] The administration also exempted the CIA from restrictions on torture and sought to include secret detention techniques in the *Army Field Manual*. Nevertheless, the military produced a new manual that repudiated much of the administration's position on torture. Finally, in 2007, the administration issued an executive order on torture prohibiting certain interrogation techniques but allowing the CIA wide latitude in devising interrogation policy. In sum, despite considerable opposition, the Bush administration did little to clarify its definition of torture.[21]

A Flawed Definition

The Bush administration's definition of torture had every sign of being a hastily constructed rationale for brutality. As soon as the torture memos became public, many voices raised concerns about them. They focused particularly on what they permit. As long as an interrogator avoids specifically intending the pain specified, she is not guilty of torture. This elastic standard allows for many horrific acts. The back teeth are not generally considered a "significant bodily function," so an interrogator could remove them without anesthesia. Significant sleep deprivation threatens neither death nor organ failure, so an interrogator could deprive a suspect of sleep for days. Finally, an interrogator could simulate drowning by covering a detainee's face and pouring water down his nose. In sum, the memos created incredible latitude for interrogators to justify terrible acts.

Individuating Moral Acts

People familiar with the memos recognized their moral elasticity but often overlooked how they take advantage of confusion about moral acts. Written by lawyers, they define acts by surveying existing law (in a very selective fashion) and emphasizing the agent's intention. This reasoning may have legal merit but is ethically confused, failing to define intention adequately. If someone specifies an act solely by her intention, she can easily deny responsibility for it. Suppose a torturer rips someone's fingernails off, but denies she specifically intends to cause him severe pain or long-term damage. She claims instead that she intends only to fight terrorism. By defining acts solely on intention, we would have to conclude that she is no torturer. However, this flies in the face of what we know about torture. We could justify any act by claiming we intended only a positive outcome. Intentions by themselves, then, are notoriously unreliable as a guide for moral action.[22]

Perhaps we should say that circumstances determine whether someone is guilty or not guilty of torture. Some people, for example, attributed the Abu Ghraib horrors to an "animal house" mentality among soldiers at the prison. For them, the photographs shocking the world revealed the work of a few sadists rather than interrogators. Given the links between official policy and what happened at Abu Ghraib, these contentions hardly stand up to critical scrutiny (see Human Rights Watch, "Getting Away with Torture"). Nevertheless, suppose circumstances do define torture, and if they changed and Abu Ghraib soldiers produced vital intelligence, we might describe them as doing their duty. Their horrific acts would be justified by changed circumstances. Obviously, something is amiss in such an analysis. The guards at Abu Ghraib placed naked detainees in human pyramids and forced them to masturbate. They humiliated and degraded them and stuck objects up their rectums. To deny that these acts constitute torture seems fundamentally wrong. Yet, if circumstances alone define the moral act, we might be forced to draw this conclusion.

As circumstances and intention alone cannot define moral acts, we need a more sophisticated theory of action. To this end, I adopt the framework of object, intention, and circumstances.[23] When discussing action, Aquinas emphasizes that every act has some goodness because it has being. For him, being and goodness are convertible, and therefore what exists must possess some minimal goodness. Ontologically, goodness means the fullness of being. A good dog, for example, does well what dogs normally do (bark, run, etc.). This technical metaphysical point has deep ethical significance because it means we cannot eliminate all goodness from action. Even the worst terrorists retain some goodness in them because they exist and seek some good. Additionally, this idea "serves as a valuable reminder that human action is intelligible as such, and therefore subject to moral evaluation, precisely insofar as it is a definite something, an event stemming from the causal powers of some creature."[24] Moral acts are never purely physical happenings but proceed from agents trying to actualize some good.

To ascertain the act's specific goodness, we must consider intention, object, and circumstances. The act's circumstances are "those elements of an action that 'surround' it, and that answer such questions as 'how, where, when, why, etc.'"[25] The object (sometimes called purpose in contemporary thought) defines the species or kind of act we are encountering. Finally, intention is the end for which the agent acts and which helps us evaluate his character. Take an act of torture at Abu Ghraib. Its circumstances might be the Abu Ghraib prison at 100 plus degrees, its object would be torture, and the intention might be to do one's duty as a soldier.[26]

The object defines the act's moral quality. It classifies the act (one of theft, murder, charity, etc.) as well as tells us whether it is good or bad. Circumstances can in some cases alter an act's moral character, but alone they cannot define it. For example, military reports about Abu Ghraib emphasize the prison's terrible conditions. Chains of command were confused, thousands of prisoners lived in awful conditions, soldiers were constantly assaulted and mortared, training was poor, and the military hierarchy exerted intense pressure on soldiers to "soften up" prisoners. In such circumstances, soldiers ended up committing terrible acts. Nevertheless, these circumstances cannot make torture into an act of mercy. Similarly, the agent's intention affects how we assess an act's moral character. If the torturer intends to torture because she is sadistic, her intention devalues the act. However, if she believes she is doing her duty, we think differently about the act. Despite these different intentions, her act remains one of torture. Finally, an intention negatively or positively determines moral responsibility for the action. A person intending to torture with considerable knowledge holds greater moral responsibility than someone knowing little about her act. Nevertheless, even though such intentions affect the value of an act, the object ultimately defines its nature and value.

Defining Torture

This structure of acts raises many complex questions, some of which I consider shortly. Turning to the definition of torture, I want to first say a word about the different kinds of torture. Some writers limit the concept of torture to state agents, emphasizing that it is something only political communities do. For example, the United Nations Convention against Torture and Other Cruel, Inhuman, or Degrading Treatment or Punishment restricts torture to action instigated "by or with the consent or acquiescence of a public official or other person acting in an official capacity."[27] This restriction is counterintuitive and arbitrary. We often talk about criminals torturing their victims, domestic abusers torturing their spouses, and abusive parents torturing children. In these cases, we have a similar act playing itself out in different circumstances. We can, however, classify torture into different kinds. For example, we have *sadistic torture* that torturers administer simply for pleasure. We have *terroristic torture* that torturers use to terrorize individuals or populations into submission. We also have *punishing torture* where the agent punishes a person for an infraction. Finally, we have *interrogational torture* in which the person tortures to obtain information.[28] I focus on interrogational torture, but my definition applies to all forms of torture. I also assume that both state and nonstate actors can torture.

Turning to the definition of torture, as I understand it, it is voluntarily and intentionally inflicting severe mental or physical suffering on a helpless victim for the purpose of breaking his will. I assume that torture must be voluntary. I act voluntarily when I act with knowledge and consent.[29] I may unknowingly inflict severe suffering on another but cannot be accused of torturing him. Here, we should distinguish between human acts and acts of the human. Human acts tend toward some good that an agent seeks, whereas acts of the human lack these characteristics. For example, a seizure is an act of the human because it does not originate in an intrinsic principle aiming at a good whereas teaching a philosophy class seeks a good.[30] I may be responsible for my acts of the human. For example, a military officer may be held responsible for failing to do her duty. Commanding General Janice Karpinski was correctly held accountable for allowing the intolerable conditions at Abu Ghraib to exist. Apparently, she knew little about torture but was still responsible for what happened under her command.[31]

The concept of intention is quite complex, and all I assume here is that it involves some aim or plan of the agent. As philosopher Elizabeth Anscombe famously argues, intentional actions are "the actions to which a certain sense of the question 'Why?' is given application."[32] Acts may have more than one intention even though they include only one object.[33] For example, an interrogator may intend to enhance his career and help his country while torturing.

By including the idea of severity in the definition of torture, I may create numerous problems. "Severe" seems hopelessly subjective—what is severe to you may not be severe to me. One person faints at the sight of blood, whereas another merely blinks. Commenting on attempts to define the term severe, legal scholar Marcy Strauss notes that "torture cannot be defined as that amount of physical abuse that causes 'significant' pain; pain cannot be measured objectively, and such a standard would provide little guidance for interrogators."[34] Physiologically, individuals differ on pain tolerance and such differences seem to doom efforts to define the term severe.

I am sympathetic with these difficulties, but think we should retain the concept of severity when defining torture. Undoubtedly, pain tolerance differs giving torture a subjective element. However, we can identify acts that generally produce severe suffering on normal human beings. Mutilations, exposure to extreme temperatures, sleep deprivation, and other such acts usually cause severe suffering. They serve as paradigm cases of severe suffering, and the word severe distinguishes them from minor acts of violence. Beyond identifying such paradigm cases, I prefer to leave the concept of severe vague. Given recent attempts to restrict the concept's extension, my approach harbors some danger. However, greater definitional precision also invites lawyers and bureaucrats to "press up against clear bright-line rules" to circumvent them.[35] By demanding precision about severity, we portray torture as "something like a speed limit which we are entitled to push up against as closely as we can and in regard to which there might even be a margin of toleration which a good-hearted enforcement officer, familiar with our situation and its exigencies, might be willing to recognize."[36] Commenting on this phenomenon with reference to the torture memos, Philip Zelikow, a former counselor to Secretary of State Condoleezza Rice, noted that "[b]rilliant lawyers worked hard on how they could then construe the limits of vague, untested laws. They were operating so close to the frontiers of our law that, within only a couple of years, the Department of Justice eventually felt obliged to offer a second legal opinion, rewriting their original views of the subject. The policy results are imaginable and will someday become more fully known."[37] We may treat some acts like speeding, but others reflect such immorality that we discourage people from pushing boundaries. For example, we dissuade citizens from thinking about how they can almost rape each other. In sum, I want to retain paradigm cases of severe pain without carefully defining severity.

Sadly, events in the War on Terror illustrate how bureaucracies push the boundaries of concepts such as "severe" suffering. In the past, torturers crudely experimented on people to discover what constitutes severe suffering. They might have broken fingers, noting who could withstand this pain and who would pass out. Today, we have scientific experts tailoring interrogations to individuals. For example, at Guantánamo Bay, Major General Geoffrey Miller created Behavioral Science Consultation Teams (BSCTs).[38] Composed of psychologists and psychiatrists, they were tasked with identifying emotional and physical weaknesses of detainees. They examined medical records, recommended interrogation techniques, and monitored interrogations. Some Teams diagnosed detainees' phobias that interrogators then exploited during interrogation. In 2002–2003, officials at Guantánamo held numerous meetings to discuss interrogation techniques. At these meetings, psychologists on the BSCTs offered detailed advice about how to break the will of detainees.[39] Apparently deemed helpful at Guantánamo, the BSCTs also operated at Abu Ghraib with disastrous effects. They illustrate that although the severity of pain differs from person to person, modern interrogators can discover individual pain threshold. They use this knowledge to push definitional boundaries with all means at their disposal.

Some analysts arbitrarily restrict torture to physical suffering. For example, Michael Davis maintains that all instances of mental torture are "either physical or something other than torture."[40] For him, sleep deprivation seems like mental suffering, but is in fact a physiological matter. Philosopher Seumus Miller discusses using phobias to extract information, but seems reluctant to include mental suffering in his definition of torture.[41] Darius Rejali defines torture as the "systematic infliction of physical torment on detained individuals by state officials for police purposes, for confession, information or intimidation."[42] Finally, Uwe Jacobs carefully demonstrates that sensory deprivation and attacks on the person can unleash terrible neurological damage on her. However, he goes beyond neurology when arbitrarily asserting that "biology gives rise to all mental processes."[43] Like many other contemporary thinkers, these scholars never consider that torture could be more than just physical.

This disregard of spirituality implies a shallow commitment to philosophical materialism or physicalism. Philosophical materialism posits that the physical is all that exists in the universe. It has appeared in philosophical and religious thought for millennia in both Western and Eastern philosophy, with champions such as the great Roman poet Lucretius and Indian skeptics. Recently, however, it has taken on a new guise with the concept of physicalism. It maintains that only the sciences provide knowledge and insists we can use them to fully explain consciousness. Philosophers of mind have vigorously debated physicalism's merits, but few writing about torture show any awareness of this debate.[44] Instead, they either assume that all torture is physical or reduce the psychological to what neuroscience reveals.[45] Neuroscience helps us understand torture but we should not arbitrarily assume that it fully explains it. If we are embodied spirits, we should expect torture to involve spiritual deformations. They may include physical suffering, but they cannot be entirely physical. Often, we cannot easily disengage the physical and spiritual but this provides no excuse for simply disregarding spirituality. By restricting torture to the physical, scholars make their task conceptually easy, but at the price of simplifying our experience.

Events in the War on Terror illustrate how torture goes beyond the physical. Periodically, controversies erupted over how U.S. interrogators treated the Muslim Holy Book, the Qur'an. In 2005, *Newsweek* magazine created an international furor by reporting that American interrogators flushed it down a toilet. After its report, riots erupted in Pakistan, and several people died. Because of insufficient evidence, *Newsweek* retracted its story, but other stories of Qur'an abuse later emerged. Intransigent detainees or boastful interrogators may have fabricated some of them. However, we cannot dismiss them all because numerous people report observing Qur'an abuse. For example, FBI documents confirm "abuses related" to "detainees' religious beliefs."[46] One FBI agent reported seeing a captain squatting over a Qur'an to offend a detainee. Another heard an interrogator bragging about forcing a detainee to listen to satanic music for hours. An interrogator reported seeing another interrogator throw the Qur'an on the ground causing a riot in a camp in Afghanistan. Finally, David Becker who supervised the interrogation of Mohammed al-Qahtani, the "twentieth hijacker" (whose case I discuss shortly), seemed to deliberately target Qahtani's prayer life by having female interrogators touch him. Becker had heard that "devout Muslims can't pray if they feel 'unclean.' Therefore, if the detainee was made to feel 'unclean' he would have to stop praying. One way to make a Muslim male 'unclean' is to be touched by a female."[47] Qahtani's interrogators also constructed a "shrine to bin Laden" and told him that he could pray only to bin Laden, and commandeered the Muslim call to prayer as a "call to interrogation."[48] From public documents, it seems that some soldiers and interrogators used disrespecting religious beliefs and practices as interrogation methods.[49]

These acts show why it is completely arbitrary to restrict torture to physical suffering. We can torture someone by threatening his most fundamental convictions, seeking to separate him from them to obtain information. For example, in a sworn statement in the Taguba Report, an Abu Ghraib detainee reported that interrogators "ordered me to curse Islam and because they started to hit my broken leg, I cursed my religion. They ordered me to thank Jesus that I'm alive. And I did what they ordered me. This is against my belief."[50] We can only say that such mental suffering is entirely physical if we presuppose a person is merely her body. However, we have no reason to adopt such an a priori stance toward spirituality. Surprisingly, however, many recent discussions of torture never consider spiritual suffering. In a world where religion matters so much to so many people, a purely physical approach to torture seems grossly inadequate.

The victim's helplessness is particularly important for defining torture. With torture, there exists a "vast inequality between tortured and torturer."[51] Améry makes this point well, noting that torturers remove "the expectation of help" that is "one of the fundamental experiences of human beings."[52] The victim cannot stop the torturer from hurting her, and the torturer decides at will when to torture. In this relationship, we see "a profoundly asymmetric relation of dependence and vulnerability between parties."[53] The inequality in knowledge is vast because the victim has no idea what will happen to her. For example, at Guantánamo Bay, the Military Commissions system created enormous confusion for detainees. Disorganized interrogations, Supreme Court rulings, Congressional legislation, and other developments made the detainees' future uncertain. Without access to intelligence data or legal representation, detainees were completely at their interrogators' mercy. In such circumstances, the torture victim sees herself as "unable to put up any real moral or legal resistance to her tormentor."[54]

Some critics maintain, however, that torture victims are not helpless because they can comply with their torturers. On this view, the victim need only provide his captor what he wants, and the torture ceases. By refusing to accede to this demand, he continues his fight, and we should treat him like a combatant. By resisting, he maintains "a second line of defense."[55] Apologists for torture and Bush administration officials made such an argument when discussing al-Qaeda prisoners. These prisoners, they maintained, "received resistance training, which taught that Americans were strictly limited in how they could question prisoners."[56] They engaged in acts of resistance, including well-publicized hunger strikes at Guantánamo Bay. We cannot, the argument goes, legitimately see such people as helpless victims.

This argument seems initially plausible because some al-Qaeda members resisted American action. However, it breaks down under careful scrutiny. First, many detainees were not al-Qaeda members and never received resistance training. Public information on this training indicates that it was based on the Manchester document (so-called because it was confiscated by the British police in Manchester in 2000), an al-Qaeda training manual with instructions on how to resist interrogations. U.S. officials have frequently cited it as evidence that detainees are lying about torture. Some detainees may have read the manual, but many others never saw it.[57] Therefore, we have little reason to think that most detainees received resistance training.

Second, complying with torture may not actually stop it. A woman suffering from domestic violence may comply with her husband's wishes, but the attacks may not cease. Third, as Shue argues, we cannot meaningfully say that detainees can comply with their captors. Lacking knowledge and power, a victim often cannot know what her captor seeks. At Guantánamo Bay, for example, detainees lacked legal representation and access to evidence and could be tried and retried at will. Joseph Margulies describes how U.S. interrogators adopted a "mosaic" approach to interrogation, which seeks to link disparate pieces of information from different sources at different times. Under this theory, "while it may seem to the uninitiated that the prisoner knows only 'innocuous' facts, the true import of his information may become known only once the military has the opportunity to reinterrogate him based on information learned from other prisoners, *including prisoners who have not yet been captured*."[58] Thus, a prisoner could comply with interrogators by confessing, but this would not necessarily stop the interrogation. Additionally, victims may yield truthful information, which torturers fail to recognize it because they seek something else. Or, they enter the interrogation with presuppositions preventing them from seeing the truth. For example, Rejali details how in the 1970s, Chilean intelligence interrogated Sheila Cassidy, an English citizen. Under torture, she revealed the names of nuns and priests who helped her, but her torturers refused to believe clergy were involved. The notion that someone can stop torture simply by complying, then, presupposes that a torturer "has gathered circumstantial information that allows" him to recognize the truth.[59] However, torturers often lack just this information.

Shue also describes the moral ambiguity in forcing torture victims to comply with torture. Some victims may hold strong convictions, and compliance means, "in a word, betrayal; betrayal of one's ideals and one's comrades."[60] Compelling a person to betray his most basic convictions "cannot be counted as an escape."[61] Naturally, we want committed al-Qaeda members to surrender their resolve to murder innocent people. However, torture uses force to alter the conscience. Al-Qaeda members have distorted ideas, but we cannot conclude that forcibly changing them constitutes legitimate compliance. Instead, it constitutes a Faustian bargain of the worst kind, a morally disordered "denial of oneself."[62] In sum, the mere possibility of compliance provides a torture victim with no real power.

Breaking the victim's will constitutes the most important element of torture. The torturer uses severe suffering to destroy someone's will to resist. A doctor may cause severe pain to helpless patients.[63] Nevertheless, she does not aim to break her patients' wills. By itself, then, inflicting severe suffering is a necessary, but insufficient, condition for torture. It also must seek to break the will. Miller helpfully distinguishes between minimal and maximal senses of breaking the will. In a minimal sense, we break someone's will when we "cause that person to abandon autonomous decision-making in relation to some narrowly circumscribed area of life and for a limited time."[64] We break it in a maximal sense when a "victim's will is subsumed by the will of the torturer."[65] The victim identifies completely with the torturer, seeing his good as hers, and identifying solely with what he wants. Breaking the will in this case radically targets autonomy. A slave, for example, might retain limited capacity to resist or shape other people's actions. We cannot say the same of the broken torture victim. He can no longer resist and is forced to do whatever the torturer desires.

A torturer may also break a person's will by undermining his or her internal harmony. Philosopher Patrick Lee has drawn attention to how torture produces disharmony between "the body and psyche, cognition and volition, bodily self from physical locale (or sense of locale), self from community, the present self from his long-term commitments and hopes."[66] Breaking the will, as Lee points out, ruptures a person's personality and distinguishes torture from imprisonment. A society may deprive a serial killer of liberty for life, but he retains a psychobodily unity in prison. If we dunk his head in water daily, this unity will disintegrate quickly.

We can understand this disintegration better by recalling our embodied nature. Unless it kills, torture cannot separate the soul from the body (which is impossible in this life). However, it can undermine a person's unity by treating him as a nonhuman animal. For example, in late 2002, the United States began using "enhanced interrogation" techniques on prisoners at Guantánamo Bay. One prisoner who was particularly targeted was Mohammed al-Qahtani. He came to the United States intent upon participating in the September 11 attacks, but immigration officials stopped him. He was released, but later captured while fighting in Afghanistan, and was sent to Guantánamo Bay. *Time* magazine obtained a log of his interrogation, which describes how the

> [d]etainee was reminded that no one loved, cared or remembered him. He was reminded that he was less than human and that animals had more freedom and love than he does. He was taken outside to see a family of banana rats. The banana rats were moving

freely, playing, eating, showing concern for one another. Detainee was compared to the family of banana rats and reinforced that they had more love, freedom, and concern than he had. Detainee began to cry during the comparison.[67]

In another log entry, the interrogator "told detainee that a dog is held in higher esteem because dogs know right from wrong and know to protect innocent people from bad people. Began teaching detainee lessons such as stay, come, and bark to elevate his status up to that of a dog. Detainee became very agitated."[68] Interrogators aimed at breaking al-Qahtani's will by degrading him to a subhuman status. They subjected him to more than forty-eight days of enhanced interrogation techniques aimed at rupturing his will. For interrogators, he was no longer an embodied spirit differing from other beings in the universe. Instead, he was an animal unworthy of moral respect.

This case illustrates a radical form of breaking the will that few contemporary writers discuss. Responding to the Abu Ghraib scandal, some people said we treated detainees like animals. Or, they commented that we "wouldn't even treat animals this way." They also described the torturers as animals. These reactions suggest we are aware that torture threatens our status as frontier beings. In the maximal sense of breaking the will, a person retains a will even if he subsumes it into another's will. In the radical case I am describing, breaking the will deliberately seeks to disintegrate the personality and dethrone the person from her remarkable status in the universe. For example, people were deeply disturbed when they saw the photo of Private Lindsay holding the strap around the neck of an Iraqi at Abu Ghraib. She went beyond minimal and maximal senses of breaking the will to embrace a profound spiritual destruction. In the next chapter, I say more about it, but for defining torture, it suffices to emphasize that breaking the will can have minimal, maximal, and more radical senses.

Does Torture Really Exist?

With these senses of breaking the will clear, I now consider challenges to the definition of torture I defend. A critic might grant the definition but may apply it to cases we would not normally call torture. For example, people sometimes claim that the military inflicts severe suffering on helpless victims with the goal of breaking the will. Yet, we would hardly be willing to accuse it of torture. Yoo makes this point stating that "[m]arine instructors don't commit torture in boot camp."[69] Others use Special Forces training to counter definitions of torture. When crafting interrogation policy, the Pentagon drew on the Survival, Evasion, Resistance, and Escape (SERE) program. This program (replicated in several services, including the Air Force and Army) exposes American military personnel to coercion, including waterboarding and sleep deprivation. In the SERE program, does the military torture its own people? For many Americans, this suggestion is patently absurd.

These appeals to military policy are unconvincing. First, we should be open to the possibility that programs such as SERE do torture Americans. We might justify such torture as preparation for combat, but it might be torture nevertheless. Similarly, drill instructors may exceed their authority, illegally approaching torture at times. Again, we may see their action as necessary preparation for war. Second, however, the military/torture analogy is flawed. Most training programs in the Special Forces and elsewhere allow participants an exit. For example, the Navy Seals permit trainees to ring a bell indicating they can no longer participate in training. In other words, unlike torture victims, trainees are not entirely helpless. Militaries may also break a trainee's will in minimal senses, but avoid breaking it in maximal or radical senses. Totalitarian regimes may demand that soldiers surrender all independence, but American and European militaries allow them to retain elements of their identities. Otherwise, they would prohibit soldiers from disobeying unlawful orders. This option, recognized by the Nuremburg Tribunals, presupposes that they retain some independent capacity for judgment. Militaries in democratic nations also permit soldiers to retain religious convictions. Chaplin services reflect a commitment to religious liberty. Finally, military training often degrades soldiers by making them behave like nonhuman animals. However, military codes of conduct like the U.S. Uniform Code of Military Justice presuppose that soldiers are rational animals. In sum, analogies between military training and torture are flawed, a product of careless thinking.

Perhaps, however, I have mistakenly identified torture by its object. Must we have all torture's elements in order to identify it? Suppose we use severe pain to break a person's will, but he is not helpless. Or, suppose we inflict severe mental or physical suffering on someone without aiming to break his will. Finally, suppose we seek to break someone's will through hypnosis or powerful leadership. In confronting these possibilities, how can we maintain that torture has a distinct moral object?

These questions correctly indicate that without all its elements, a brutal act does not constitute torture. We may try to break a victim's will, which is surely wrong in many cases, but unless he is helpless, we do not torture him. Likewise, we might inflict severe suffering on him without seeking to break his will. Our purpose in doing so determines the act's moral legitimacy. Similarly, we might have a boxing or martial arts match where combatants seek to use severe physical suffering to break the will of the opponent, but they are not helpless. Finally, we might induce a person to completely surrender his will, which is morally wrong because it destroys his freedom. However, without inflicting severe suffering, we do not torture him. To identify torture, we therefore must have all its elements.

We should not, however, think that all acts falling just short of torture are morally acceptable. Interrogations may involve many morally illegitimate abuses. In fact, international agreements such as the CAT and the Geneva Conventions distinguish between abusive treatment and torture. Striking a detainee or making him wear female underwear may fall short of torture but is nevertheless abusive. Unfortunately, contemporary debates about torture often fail to morally evaluate abuse. Some U.S. conduct in the War on Terror fell short of torture, but was profoundly abusive. Yet, citizens, politicians, and commentators were willing to countenance it as long it as it did not seem like torture.

Another challenge to defining torture concerns intent and the common good. An interrogator might inflict severe suffering on a helpless victim, but claim he intends only to promote the common good. For example, in their memo, Bybee and Yoo offer the president of the United States ways by which he could defend himself if charged with torture. Self-defense, they maintain, "can be an appropriate defense to an allegation of torture."[70] Noting standard legal requirements for self-defense, they argue that a threat must be imminent, the agent must believe force is reasonable, and he must use force proportional to the threat. Applying these criteria to torture, they argue that even if the president tortures, he can plead self-defense.

This example illustrates a difficulty in identifying an act's object. Is it entirely a subjective matter based on an agent's purposes or interests? Some philosophers maintain that we can characterize action in multiple ways. For example, we might describe torture as self-defense, promoting the common good, protecting the innocent, initiating violence, stopping terrorism, fulfilling sadistic urges, and doing one's military duty. With these available descriptions, why privilege one of them? Philosopher Martin Rhonheimer describes this problem when discussing shooting a person in the heart, asking if "it is not simply up to me to decide whether my shooting at a person's heart is or is not an action of punishment?"[71] On this understanding of human acts, we need not adopt any particular act-description. We describe an act's physical characteristics and then choose the description that best suits our needs and preferences.

We encounter further difficulties with an act's object when considering circumstances. Some critics charge that dividing an act between object and circumstances is too neat and fails to correspond with real action. Circumstances and the act's object seem so tightly linked that we cannot separate them. Is it, theologian Lisa Cahill asks, "really so easy" to speak of "acts in themselves" without identifying the "nexus of practical, physical, causal and moral relationships" surrounding an act?[72] For example, perhaps torture is an abstraction requiring us to fill it in with details about circumstances. Before declaring the Abu Ghraib acts morally wrong, we need to describe all circumstances. Without considering them, how can any of us condemn the Abu Ghraib soldiers? Circumstances would include the soldiers' biographies, their extreme living conditions, and the threats they faced. Until we provide such analysis, we cannot say they tortured.

These problems in the philosophy of action may seem arcane, but they are particularly important when discussing torture. The CIA, military, and executive branch bureaucracies all have good reasons to deny they are torturing. In this context, fuzziness about moral definitions is advantageous. Agents seeking to evade moral responsibility may heartily embrace the idea that act-descriptions depend entirely on our wills. A report on interrogation techniques illustrates the dangers of moral redefinition. In 2007, the National Defense Intelligence College presented a report called "Educing Information." Alarmed by the amateur nature of interrogations in the War on Terror, it evaluated the effectiveness of forms of interrogation. Drafted by professors and behavioral scientists, it sought to help the U.S. government conduct more professional interrogations. Whatever its scientific merits, the report replaced the word "interrogation" with "educing information." In its foreword, Robert A. Destro objected to this semantic sleight-of-hand, maintaining correctly that it undermines moral clarity.[73] Debates about defining acts, then, are no ivory tower exercises, but have great import for public policy.

The Objectivity of Action

To respond to challenges to the objectivity of action, I first note how counterintuitive they are. They suggest that we can redefine our actions as we please, depending on needs and interests. Our descriptions bear no necessary relationship to what we have done or to other people's needs. Suppose I rape someone while a college student and get away with this crime. Years later, my victim locates me and accuses me of rape. I have caused her profound suffering, and she wants to hold me responsibility for my actions. However, instead of admitting to rape, I claim it was merely a "youthful indiscretion" meriting no judicial punishment. Such a response would be morally outrageous, a deliberate evasion of responsibility. I have caused great harm, and I cannot simply redescribe my action in any way I please.

Unfortunately, appeals to moral sensibilities convince few philosophers, and we must respond more carefully to those denying the objectivity of action. I begin by conceding that we can describe action in diverse ways. An act-description "may vary with the specialized interest of the inquirer or narrator."[74] A doctor examining a torture victim might adopt clinical language to understand what happened to him. A physiologist exploring a torturer's brain might employ neurological language. Thus, pluralism in act-descriptions is appropriate in many circumstances, and those interested in moral issues should not arbitrarily dismiss it.

Nevertheless, third person descriptions bear little on action's moral dimensions because they abstract from the acting person's perspective. Human acts proceed from an agent seeking to actualize some good. They reflect a being's inner nature, and spiritual beings act with knowledge and take responsibility for their acts.[75] Once we recognize that human acts proceed from such a being, third-perspective act-descriptions loss their moral relevance. By considering the acting person, we thus delimit the act-descriptions bearing on moral matters.[76]

A critic might concede this point, but maintain that third person act-descriptions receive moral significance only when we add intention. Suppose we take the description, "causing severe physical suffering." It seems morally neutral. As a doctor, I may cause severe physical suffering to heal a patient. Naturally, my action would be praiseworthy. However, if I sadistically inflict severe suffering on my child, then I am a child abuser. In either case, what matters is the intention we add to a neutral act-description. We have "an action analysis in which acts are simply physical events" that we then humanize with intentions.[77]

This approach to action theory is deeply flawed, however, because in it, the "acting person disappears as a subject that *chooses*, and thus willingly performs concrete acts, acts that are not simply events causing consequences, but proximate ends of a choosing will."[78] "Causing severe physical suffering" is not a human act because no agent chooses it. Instead, it abstractly describes a behavioral pattern while leaving the agent out of the picture. A machine might inflict severe suffering without reason, but humans seek to actualize goods. As philosopher Robert Sokolowski notes, act descriptions like "causing pain" already presupposes some kind of human agency. Viewed from outside the agent, we would more properly describe them in terms of subatomic particles. Once we use agential language, we must then ask why an agent acts. Additionally, separating a physical description and intention artificially ruptures a complex whole. The spiritual being intending and initiating action disappears, replaced by abstract accounts of behavior or environment.[79] Why did the person inflict extreme physical suffering? Once we ask this question, we discover that acts have a basic intentional structure linked to the person. A personalist analysis of action, then, refuses to focus on events, but instead considers why a person acts. It considers action from the "perspective of the acting person" rather than from a mere description of events.[80] The spiritual person wills an act with a given structure. She also finds herself before persons who have value prior to her choice. They are no mere physical organisms, but beings demanding moral respect. In this encounter, we cannot merely describe our action clinically at the same time leaving out all elements of the person.[81]

Instead of morally neutral act-description, we confront elements of acts essential to an act's sense. Some descriptions "constitute an instance of some kind of act whose description, special contexts apart, cannot be absorbed into some other."[82] Modern thinkers call these instances "essences," whereas medieval philosophers term them "species." Both concepts express the idea that acts have a unity without which they would not be what they are. For example, among other things, theft involves taking something that does not belong to you.[83] Remove this element, and we no longer have theft. Similarly, torture involves seeking to break another's will. Remove this feature, and we no longer have torture. Act-unities, then, present themselves to us, and we cannot alter them willy-nilly.[84] We understand these act-unities vividly when considering a person's action. It embodies an act-unity, through which the agent changes the world through speech or bodily movement. We recognize a close connection between this change and the person's character, realizing that she has ownership of the change. The person, in other words, *embodies* a particular act. A torturer thus cannot merely claim that she causes severe pain. Instead, she creates pain for some purpose linked to who she is and what she wants to accomplish in the world.[85]

Critics of this act theory correctly link the act's essence and circumstance, but fail to distinguish the kinds of circumstances. In identifying an object's act, we do not, as Cahill maintains, "define acts in the abstract," without considering circumstances.[86] Instead, we distinguish circumstances relevant to the act-description. *Specifying circumstances* are those defining the essence of an act. They are "considerations that cause one kind of action no longer to be that kind of action but to become another kind."[87] For example, philosopher Janet Smith notes that if consensual sex becomes unwilling, it changes its species to become rape. The specifying circumstances of willing or unwilling enter into the act's object. In contrast, accidental circumstances do not alter the act's species. Whether a person has sex on a bed or on the floor has no bearing on the act's species. The idea of consenting to rape makes no sense because rape implies a lack of consent.[88] By distinguishing the kinds of circumstances, we counter the facile claim that circumstances always shape the act's object. Undoubtedly true, it does nothing to prevent us from identifying an act's object even without knowledge of all its circumstances. Once we have specifying circumstances, we know the act's moral character. For example, if I intentionally have sexual relations with an unwilling victim, I rape her. I am guilty of rape, and we need no further information about my psyche or the victim to understand that my act is wrong.

Although an act's object defines its character, we should not disengage it from intentions. Aiming at an object, moral agents may also have many short- and long-term intentions. The president of the United States intended to protect the nation when he authorized harsh interrogation methods in September 2001. A CIA interrogator may have intended to advance his career through torture. Some torturers at Abu Ghraib "seemed to think that they, too, were doing the right thing under the circumstances in order to protect the safety of U.S. troops."[89] An agent can have such intentions, yet still torture, or convince himself that he had good intentions. For example, after torturing detainees, a conscience-stricken interrogator might convince himself that he was only following orders. However, he cannot deny the direction of his will, which aimed at inflicting severe mental or physical suffering on a helpless victim to break his will. His intention, noble or ignoble, adds or subtracts from the act's moral value and helps us assess his moral responsibility. Nevertheless, it cannot change the moral quality of the act.[90]

Let me illustrate the relationship between object and intention. After the September 11 attacks, CIA Director George Tenet was deeply concerned that al-Qaeda might launch another attack. He seemed to have the noble and praiseworthy intention to protect the nation. However, along with it, he authorized torture. Within two years after the September 11 attacks, the CIA captured three top-level al-Qaeda operatives: Abu Zubaydah, Ramzi bin al-Shibh, and Khalid Sheikh Mohammed.[91] They were subjected to interrogation techniques such as waterboarding. As I have already noted, waterboarding involves simulated or real drowning. Interrogators place the detainee on a long board, cover his mouth, and slowly pour water into his nose and mouth. The detainee experiences panic and intense fear of drowning. In the next two chapters, I consider whether such interrogation is morally justifiable. We cannot doubt, however, that it amounts to torture. CIA officers may have acted with great concern for their country. However, they cannot deny that they aimed at breaking detainees' wills by inflicting severe mental and physical suffering on them when they were in a helpless state.

"Torture Lite?"

Once we understand how to define moral acts, we see why the recently invented term torture-lite is so morally problematic. Publicized by Mark Bowden and defended by Jean Bethke Elshtain, torture lite is allegedly an alternative to torture. As I mentioned earlier, its methods include "sleep deprivation, exposure to heat and cold, the use of drugs to cause confusion, rough treatment (slapping, shoving, or shaking), forcing a prisoner to stand for days at a time or to sit in uncomfortable positions, and playing on his fears for his family and friends."[92] Bowden rejects torture but argues that interrogators may legitimately employ torture lite. Elshtain concurs, criticizing human rights organizations for taking a moralistic stance against torture. By refusing to distinguish torture from torture lite, she maintains, these organizations "do a disservice to the complexity of the matter; they fail to discriminate between cases;

they embrace a moralistic 'code fetishism' that flies in the face of the harsh and dangerous realities of the world in which we find ourselves; and, ironically, by failing to distinguish between sleep deprivation and amputation or burning or some other horror, they elevate the former and diminish the latter."[93] For Elshtain and Bowden, torture lite offers a tragic, but morally legitimate, means of interrogation.

By employing the term torture lite, Elshtain and Bowden do a disservice to moral clarity. The term itself is jarring and inappropriate. We talk about "lite" beer and soda, but we should hesitate to use such language to analyze immoral acts. Many people believe we should never torture.[94] In lists of evil acts, torture appears along with rape and genocide. Surely, we would not talk about "rape-lite" or "genocide-lite" because we recognize the horrors of these acts. Attaching "lite" to "torture" seems equally problematic.

More importantly, neither Elshtain nor Bowden offer criteria for distinguishing torture lite from torture. Instead, they appeal to our intuitions, suggesting we can easily distinguish between torture and something like sleep deprivation. However, intuitions in this matter are notoriously unreliable. A human rights activist may see sleep deprivation as torture, whereas Bowden/Elshtain do not. In fact, the practices Bowden lists as torture lite may in fact be torture depending on the moral object of interrogation. For example, I find Bowden's mention of sleep deprivation deeply troubling. For much of the twentieth century, Soviet and Chinese interrogators used it to break the will of their detainees. During the Korean War, they employed it to devastating effect against American prisoners of war.[95] Sleep deprivation has debilitating effects on cognition, decision making, and the emotions.[96] Pentagon documents recognized these effects because when recommending disturbing sleep, they hastily denied that they advocate sleep deprivation.[97] Yet, FBI agents reported many instances of "sleep adjustment," where interrogators disrupted detainees' sleep patterns.[98] Often, detainees were allowed only four hours of sleep in a twenty-four period, not necessarily in succession. Moreover, officials at Guantánamo employed sleep deprivation, but sought to hide their behavior from the Red Cross.[99] Such disruption can produces terrible suffering. For example, in a well-known statement, former Israeli prime minister Menacham Begin described his experience as a prisoner in the Soviet Union saying that a sleep-deprived prisoner is "wearied to death, his legs are unsteady, and he has one sole desire to sleep, to sleep just a little, not to get up, to lie, to rest, to forget... Anyone who has experienced this desire knows that not even hunger or thirst are comparable to it."[100] For those with a historical memory, there is nothing "lite" about sleep deprivation. Similarly, we can torture someone by playing on his fears for his family. Reportedly, after capturing Khalid Sheikh Mohammed, interrogators threatened to kill his family. Ron Suskind reports that "according to some former CIA officials, interrogators told KSM [Khalid Sheikh Mohammed] his children would be hurt if he didn't cooperate."[101] Apparently, this tactic was entirely ineffective, but nevertheless, there is nothing lite about it. If the United States used it to break Khalid Sheikh Mohammed's will, it tortured him.

Appeals to intuition are particularly unreliable when thinking about psychological torture. Too often people discount it as a torture technique. Take stress positions and sensory deprivation, two techniques I discuss at length in the next chapter. Stress positions include standing or squatting for hours or maintaining physically painful positions. In 1976, the European Commission on Human Rights reflected on stress positions and found the British guilty of torture in Northern Ireland. In 1978, the European Court of Human Rights instead ruled that British authorities were guilty only of inhuman and degrading treatment.[102] However, as I have defined it, stress positions can be torture. They use severe physical and mental pain on a helpless victim in order to break his will. They do not seem as extreme as removing fingernails, but they are torture nevertheless. Similarly, sensory deprivation can psychologically devastate a human being. For decades, psychologists and psychiatrists have demonstrated that depriving a person of sensory input produces short- and long-term psychological damage. Because such deprivation seems different than sodomizing a person with a broom, we may not consider it torture. We could offer a similar analysis of shaking, which torturers have used to devastating effect. When used repeatedly, it damages the brain.[103] The few empirical studies we have on psychological torture suggest that it damages the victim as much or if not more than physical torture. Victims report negative effects for years after their torture.[104] In sum, we should avoid relying on our vague sense of what constitutes torture. Unlike those endorsing torture lite, we should carefully consider the moral act's structure to ascertain whether an act is torture.

Conclusion

We may concede that torture uses severe pain or suffering to break the will of a helpless victim, but wonder why it is morally objectionable.

I have already suggested that torture violates the personalistic principle, which prohibits us from using a person merely as a means to an end. It is a paradigmatic case of using another merely as a means. It offers no benefit to its victim, serving simply to yield information to interrogators. I have also maintained that the personalistic principle is no arbitrary rule, but is grounded in the person's unique value. Persons differ in value from things, and we should never erase this distinction. Torture directly assaults our unique status as frontier beings. Nevertheless, many social practices treat persons merely as a means to an end. Rape, slavery, and abusive labor practices all violate human dignity in this way. Why do we find torture particularly repulsive? In the next chapter, I consider why we react this way.

CHAPTER THREE

Assaulting the Spirit: Why Torture Is Wrong

Perhaps the greatest failing of those of us who have been arguing against all torture and "cruel, inhuman, and degrading" treatment of detainees is that we have assumed the reasons why torture is always a moral evil, rather than explicating them.

Andrew Sullivan[1]

The lack of physical signs can make psychological torture seem less significant than physical torture, but the consensus among those who study torture and rehabilitate its victims is that psychological torture can be more painful and cause more severe and long-lasting damage even than the pain inflicted during physical torture.

Physicians for Human Rights[2]

Scholars and public officials offer many reasons why torture is wrong. Some maintain that it violates human rights to life and physical integrity. Human rights language is a powerful moral idiom in international law and politics, and organizations such as Human Rights Watch and Amnesty International employ it frequently. Others argue that torture destroys autonomy. For example, Seumus Miller condemns torture because it "consists in part in the intentional, substantial curtailment of individual autonomy. Given the moral importance of autonomy, torture is an evil thing—even considered independently of the physical suffering it involves."[3] David Luban offers a liberal argument against torture that "puts cruelty first." Liberals, he argues, should oppose torture because it "is a microcosm, raised to the highest level of intensity, of the tyrannical political relationships that liberalism hates the most."[4] Henry Shue rejects torture because it assaults someone who has "exhausted all means of defense."[5] For him, the person's helplessness makes torture particularly abhorrent. Some evangelical theologians reject torture because it denigrates the image of God. When states torture, one evangelical statement says, "that act communicates to the world and to one's own people that human lives are not sacred, that they are not reflections of the Creator, that they are expendable, exploitable, and disposable, and that their intrinsic value can be overridden by utilitarian arguments that trump that value."[6] Finally, some thinkers reject torture because they think it produces inaccurate intelligence and damages individuals and institutions.

These ideas partially explain why we find torture repulsive but remain narrow because they ignore spirituality and the phenomenology of torture. When scholars mention spirituality, they appeal vaguely to the idea that torture harms the torturer as much as the tortured. Similarly, with few exceptions (Elaine Scarry, David Sussman), contemporary thinkers rarely consider torture as a personal relation with a distinct structure. Without exploring this relation, the full horror of torture rarely emerges, and we have difficulty resisting strong pressures to use it.

In this chapter, I consider torture as a spiritual assault on the person. First, I emphasize how it undermines our transcendence through knowledge. Focusing on sensory deprivation, I show how it targets our embodied spirituality. Second, I consider how torture destroys self-possession, creating intense conflicts within the human person. To illustrate this horror, I discuss stress positions producing self-inflicted pain. Third, I turn to torture and communication without loss, depicting the zero-sum struggle between torturers and victims. To illustrate this perverse world, I consider forced nudity, a common tactic in the War on Terror. Discussing the dynamics of shame, I show how forced nudity tortures the person by shaming her. I conclude by responding to those who reject torture as a spiritual assault, arguing that they disregard important elements of human nature.

Torture and Transcendence

In her well-known book on torture, Elaine Scarry describes how it is "world destroying" because it can reduce someone to pain and a torturer's desires.[7] Torture dissolves the unities of our world, mocking attempts to remain psychically and physically whole. It particularly targets our spiritual transcendence. The person is open to a universe and transcends his biological and cultural limitations. He also relates to ideals and unifies his experience in remarkable ways. Torture directly undermines these capacities. Rather than receiving diverse information, the tortured person is driven to focus only on pain and the information that the torturer seeks. Isolated, his range of knowing quickly becomes constricted. In his famous book, *Prisoner without a Name, Cell without a Number*, Argentinean journalist Jacobo Timerman powerfully captures the spiritual constriction of torture. Tortured under the Argentinean junta in the 1970s, he adopted what he called a "vegetable attitude," an absolute passivity of "casting aside all logical emotions and sensations—fear, hatred, vengeance—for any emotion or sensation meant wasting useless energy."[8] Timerman advises those undergoing torture to adopt this vegetable attitude because any attempt to relate to reality is useless and dangerous. Hopes, ideas, and thoughts all disintegrate in the torture chamber.

Sensory deprivation constitutes one such assault on spiritual transcendence. Many Americans do not view it as torture, but know little about modern interrogations. Torturers have long hooded prisoners, denying them access to sights and sounds. Among other places, hooding has appeared in South Africa, Brazil, Algeria, and Great Britain.[9] Although it is not considered full sensory deprivation, hooding powerfully disrupts our normal way of knowing. Torturers also place victims in solitary confinement, denying them access to outside stimuli. They recognize how isolation can shatter one's personality, leaving people broken and willing to share information.

As historian Alfred McCoy details, sensory deprivation took sinister turns as a CIA interrogation technique in the 1950s and the 1960s. Responding to Soviet and Communist Chinese interrogation methods during the Korean War, the CIA spent millions of dollars on psychological research. Convinced that the North Koreans had brainwashed American prisoners of war (POWs) it set out to discover the secrets of mind control. American, Canadian, and British psychologists at major research universities received funding to conduct sensory deprivation experiments. After several name changes, the CIA settled on MKULTRA, a program that supported research for more than two decades. Some researchers conducted profoundly unethical experiments on children, the mentally challenged, prisoners, and other vulnerable persons.[10] For example, Canadian psychologist Donald O. Hebb shared with the CIA his research on sensory deprivation at McGill University.[11] Devising a "black box" for isolating people, he discovered that sensory deprivation has devastating psychological consequences. After hours of perceptual isolation, subjects began disintegrating psychologically. They hallucinated, had difficulties solving problems, and failed to connect thoughts. Other researchers conducted similar experiments with identical results. For example, at the National Institutes of Health, Maitland Baldwin used Hebb's methods on Army volunteers. In one shocking episode, he kept a soldier in a sensory deprivation box for forty hours reducing him to cries and tears. The man eventually kicked his way out of the box.[12] CIA medical personnel terminated Baldwin's funding after discovering his immoral experiment. However, the CIA closely monitored sensory deprivation research to see whether it could serve as a tool for breaking the will.[13]

The most infamous CIA experiments with sensory deprivation occurred in Montreal in the 1950s and early 1960s. Ewen Cameron, a famous psychiatrist working at the Allan Memorial Institute, subjected perhaps a hundred patients to sensory deprivation, electroshock treatment, and lysergic acid diethylamide (LSD) injections. Funded by the CIA for many years, Cameron promised to reproduce and explain Soviet and Chinese brainwashing. Some CIA officials believed his work was too abstract and would be of little use in the field. Others, however, remained deeply interested in Cameron's research.[14] He discontinued his experiments in 1963 after the CIA withdrew his funding. However, he ruined the lives of many vulnerable people who came to him in desperate straits. His full involvement with the CIA became public knowledge only in the 1970s and the 1980s when CIA files became public. His victims eventually received monetary compensation from the U.S. government after a protracted legal fight.

Interest in sensory deprivation also appeared in the 1960s CIA interrogation manuals. For example, the famous 1963 CIA interrogation handbook, the KUBARK Manual, draws on psychological research on sensory deprivation. It expressed doubt about whether psychological experimented can assist interrogations, but recommended sensory deprivation as one interrogation tool. Along with other techniques, it can make detainees regress in personality "to whatever earlier and weaker level is required for the dissolution of resistance and the inculcation of dependence."[15] The CIA reproduced these conclusions in the manuals it wrote for Latin and Central American countries in the 1980s. For example, McCoy shows how an infamous 1983 Honduran interrogation manual repeats almost verbatim the KUBARK manual's "language for both conceptual design and technical details" of psychological torture.[16] It recommends extended sensory deprivation citing psychological research to show how it breaks a detainee's will.

We now have overwhelming evidence that some U.S. interrogators and soldiers used sensory deprivation in the War on Terror. They employed it at Guantánamo Bay and in Afghanistan and Iraq.[17] At Guantánamo, interrogators used extreme sensory deprivation methods. In 2002, interrogators received authorization to deprive detainees of light and auditory stimulation.[18] Evidence exists that in 2003 detainees "were isolated in single cells and allowed out of the cells only twice a week for fifteen minute periods in order to shower and exercise. No physical contact between detainees was permitted."[19] FBI documents repeatedly describe how isolation drove detainees to emotional and physical extremes.[20] Released prisoners also narrate horror stories of extensive isolation. For example, two British citizens, Moazzam Begg and Feroz Abbasi, were "put in isolation in 2003 and remained there for 18 months. They say that they were kept in solitary confinement in Camp Echo, a high security facility within Camp Delta. The cells in which they were confined had no natural light and the detainees were cut off from all communication with others; they did not have the right to recreation, group prayers or association with other detainees."[21] Falsely accused of crimes, Begg and Abbasi were eventually released. They returned to England where they continued to experience the devastating effects of sensory deprivation and isolation. Many other prisoners as Guantánamo were also subjected to extreme sensory deprivation, many of whom were entirely innocent of the charges against them.[22]

The CIA also used sensory deprivation in secret prisons in Europe and Asia, where it transferred at least one hundred detainees. It hid these so-called high-value targets from the International Committee of the Red Cross (ICRC), and we know they existed only because of media exposure and European investigations. Many detainees were forcibly kidnapped by the CIA. During transport to prison, they were blindfolded or hooded, and in detention they "went through months of solitary confinement and extreme sensory deprivation in cramped cells, shackled and handcuffed at all times."[23] For example, Khaled El-Masri, a German citizen, was mistakenly kidnapped by the CIA in 2004. (The mistake was due to a similarity to El-Masri's name with that of suspected al-Qaeda terrorist al-Masri.) Transported from Macedonia to Afghanistan, he was imprisoned in a secret CIA prison but was later ordered to be released by the then National Security

Advisor Condoleezza Rice. Here is how he describes his treatment

> I was dressed in a diaper, over which they fitted a dark blue sports
> suit with short sleeves and legs. I was once again blindfolded, my
> ears were plugged with cotton, and headphones were placed over
> my ears. A bag was placed over my head and a belt around my waist.
> My hands were chained to the belt. They put something hard over
> my nose. Because of the bag, breathing was getting harder and
> harder for me. I struggled for breath and began to panic.[24]

After his capture, El-Masri remained imprisoned for 149 days even
though he was completely innocent. Sadly, he was only one of many
prisoners the CIA treated this way, some of whom were simply in the
wrong place at the wrong time.

Sensory deprivation profoundly damages the person. In the 1950s
and the 1960s, researchers discovered that short-term isolation produced an inability to

> think or concentrate, anxiety, somatic complaints, temporal and
> spatial disorientation, deficiencies in task performance, hallucina-
> tions, and loss of motor coordination...Effects include depression,
> anxiety, and difficulty with concentration and memory, hyper-
> sensitivity to external stimuli, hallucinations and perceptual dis-
> tortions, paranoia, and problems with impulse control.[25]

More recently, Dr. Stuart Grassian has extensively studied the psychological effects of solitary confinement and sensory deprivation.
He maintains that it produces a unique blend of symptoms found in
no other illness. These symptoms include hypersensitivity to external
stimuli, illusions and hallucinations, panic attacks, obsessions, memory and concentration problems, and paranoia.[26] Grassian notes that
it "appears that sensory restriction produces perceptual disturbances
and illusions, which are analogous to those produced by hallucino-
genic drugs—and clearly, while there are some individuals who could
be said to have volunteered to undergo such hallucinatory, psychotic-
like experiences, it must be almost uniformly terrifying to be forced
involuntarily to undergo an experience similar to that induced by hal-
lucinogenic drugs."[27] Solitary confinement and sensory deprivation
produce "persistent symptoms of post-traumatic stress (such as flash-
backs, chronic hyper vigilance, and a pervasive sense of hopelessness)"
and "lasting personality changes—especially including a continuing

pattern of intolerance of social interaction, leaving the individual socially impoverished and withdrawn, subtly angry and fearful when forced into social interaction."[28] In sum, sensory deprivation can produce terrible psychological effects on the person.

Undoubtedly, these effects have organic origins in the brain, but sensory deprivation also radically assaults our spiritual nature. If human beings were purely spiritual creatures, sensory deprivation would have no effect on them. However, we cannot know simply by contemplating eternal ideas.[29] We know initially through the senses, and therefore, sensory deprivation deeply disturbs us. Although some people may find it refreshing for a few hours, a welcome relief from everyday routine, few can withstand sensory deprivation for more than a day. Without the senses, we cannot perform complex intellect operations. Cut off from its initial source of knowledge, our intellect can only work with what it has already received. Normally, the intellect can process sensory input, focusing on what is important and disregarding the inessential. It can shift its attention organizing reality into wholes. When denied adequate sensory stimulation, however, the person experiences a "kind of dissociative stupor" in which he cannot focus his attention.[30] A being naturally suited to live in the material and immaterial worlds gradually experiences deeply diminished powers without the senses. In fact, under sensory deprivation, "humans are like fish on dry land and cannot survive."[31] Gradually their fragile soul/body unity begins to unravel.

A person deprived of sense perception also experiences extreme difficulty relating to extramental reality. He is forced inward and must rely increasingly on mental objects. Those in solitary confinement or deprived of their senses often obsessively fixate on a thought or bodily sensation, "tortured by it, unable to stop dwelling on it."[32] The KUBARK interrogation manual captures this phenomenon well, noting that a person "cut off from external stimuli turns his awareness inward, upon himself, and then projects the contents of his own unconsciousness outwards, so that he endows his faceless environment with his own attributes, fears, and forgotten memories."[33] Timerman eloquently describes how, when isolated, he desperately struggled to reconstruct his experiences, asking "how can a blind architect fit into his unknown edifice that structure he can neither see nor touch—the fact of his wife, the taste of two candies, his wedding anniversary? Anywhere I place them, the structure collapses."[34] He feels thrown into a precarious world of imagination and concepts and gradually loses touch with reality.

Sensory deprivation also disrupts our experience of time. Torturers often remove devices for measuring time and prevent victims from having access to the sun. For example, the KUBARK manual recommends the "persistent manipulation of time, by retarding and advancing clocks and serving meals at odd times."[35] It also suggests that interrogators avoid establishing any routine with their subjects. Such tactics effectively prevent us from measuring motion and telling time. Without this capacity, we experience a confused state mixing temporality and atemporality. As embodied spirits, we naturally relate to time, but when torturers deprive us of access to it, we gradually begin to disintegrate.

By disorienting someone's sense of time and motion, sensory deprivation obstructs spiritual movements. Our intellectual activity "must be activated from without, first by a movement outward toward the material world, then, actuated by the stimulus of incoming sense knowledge and intellectual responses to it, it returns back to its spiritual source within, and lights up with conscious self-presence."[36] A person lacking sense information cannot initiate or complete this movement. She is completely at the mercy of what her interrogators want her to perceive. As Scarry notes, an interrogator possesses an imposing world that contrasts with "the small and shredded world objectified in the prisoner's answers, answers that articulate and comment on the disintegration of all objects to which he might have been bonded in loyalty or love or good sense or long familiarity."[37] Put spatially, the victim's world shrinks as the torturer's expands, powerfully impeding spiritual movement.

In fact, as Scarry also argues, a torture room often objectifies a constricted spiritual universe. Torture victims find themselves in rooms stripped of familiar items: "barred, sealed, guarded" with "little of the larger world" allowed to enter.[38] Objects that normally spatially orient a person disappear replaced by barren walls or doors. Torture rooms "are often given names that acknowledge and call attention to the generous, civilizing impulse normally present in the human shelter."[39] Called "safe houses" or "guest rooms," they dramatize the destruction of normal existence. For example, in Iraq, the CIA maintained safe houses at Camp Nama, each painted in different colors. Equipped with boom boxes and strobe lights, they became the site of horrible torture.[40] Likewise, interrogators at Abu Ghraib learned to "speak of the place they house their prisoners as an 'inn,' and to call their prisoners 'guests.'"[41] Unlike those at motels or hotels, however, detainees confronted an instable and threatening environment unlike any they had ever encountered.

The Jose Padilla case vividly illustrates how sensory deprivation undermines human transcendence. Padilla was a troubled American with a history of criminal activities. Deeply committed to Islam, he traveled frequently throughout the Middle East. In 2002, he was arrested at Chicago's O'Hare International Airport and was charged with plotting to ignite a "dirty bomb" (a radioactive explosion potentially killing hundreds or thousands of people). He was eventually classified as an "enemy combatant" and was imprisoned in South Carolina. For several years, he was charged with no crime, but was finally indicted for crimes unrelated to the dirty bomb charges. Eventually, he was convicted on terrorism conspiracy charges and sentenced to seventeen years in prison.[42]

Padilla was subjected to twenty-one months of solitary confinement and sensory deprivation. Military officials created "hermetic isolation from any human contact other than with the interrogators."[43] When transported, he was blindfolded and had his hearing blocked by earphones. Americans became aware of Padilla's condition when he appeared in a photo on the front page of the *New York Times*.[44] He had no contact with other inmates and little communication with guards. He briefly saw a lawyer after twenty months of imprisonment. Moreover, his isolation was aggravated by the efforts of his captors to maintain

> complete sensory deprivation. His tiny cell nine feet by seven feet had no view to the outside world. The door to his cell had a window, however, it was covered by a magnetic sticker, depriving Mr. Padilla of even a view into the hallway and adjacent common areas of his unit. He was not given a clock or a watch and for most of the time of his captivity, he was unaware whether it was day or night, or what time of year or day it was.[45]

Many elements of spiritual destruction appear here; interrogators isolated Padilla from his normal way of knowing, disrupted his temporal awareness, and constricted his universe. Padilla's treatment became a public issue when his lawyers claimed it destroyed his competency to stand trial. He was found competent but undoubtedly suffered profound aftereffects from isolation. An examining psychiatrist, Dr. Angela Hegarty, wrote that Padilla suffered from "post-traumatic stress disorder, complicated by the neuropsychiatric effects of prolonged isolation."[46] Dr. Stuart Grassian (who examined Padilla) also reports that well after his conviction, Padilla continued to evidence deep paranoia, a profound sense of helplessness, and "physiological reactivity when reminded" of his trauma.[47] Sadly, few Americans protested such a radical assault on Padilla's transcendence.

Torture and Self-Possession

In addition to undermining transcendence, torture targets a person's delicate and precarious self-possession. Our unity is a "marvelous connection" of diverse elements that coalesce.[48] The person's self-possession is even more remarkable because it unifies a "complex of differing factors, each bound to operate in its own distinctive way."[49] The person must "give a face to the turbulent multiplicity that dwells within him" and "freely seal it with the seal of his radical ontological unity."[50] Physical deformations easily upset internal unity, reminding us that that we are embodied spirits rather than disembodied souls. The person is also subject to spiritual loss, despair, apathy, loneliness, and other ills threaten the person's fragile integrity. Confronting these powerful disunities, we must "learn to exercise enough self-mastery over the significant choices of our lives to be called moral persons, however imperfectly and incompletely."[51] Self-possession is never complete but requires continual cultivation.

Torture ruptures self-possession by creating deep internal conflicts. Torture puts the person in the "unavoidable position of betraying or colluding against himself, an experience the victim undergoes whether or not he actually informs or confesses."[52] A torturer produces internal conflict by carefully administering pain. As philosopher David Sussman perceptively notes, the torturer seeks to "take his victim's pain" and "make it begin to express the torturer's will."[53] The victim may remain silent, but "now experiences within him something quite intimate and familiar that speaks for the torturer, something that pleads a case or provides an excuse for giving in."[54] Torture invades the personality with a foreign presence expressing someone else's will.[55] In some cases, the victim even welcomes it, actively participating in his own violation. Torture, then, is "not just an assault on or violation of the victim's autonomy, but also a perversion of it, a kind of systematic mockery of the basic moral relations an individual bears both to others and herself."[56] It pits the person's will against her body or her will against itself, perniciously dividing her.

Such a divided person experiences extreme difficulty cultivating self-possession. He cannot control pain and what others do to him. Moreover, torturers often deliberately undermine self-possession by trying to reduce a person to infantile states. Through his spiritual center, a person unifies the matter of his body, but this unity can easily collapse under torture. Rather than persisting as a center of cognitive and affective activity, he disintegrates into competing physical and emotional forces. Rather than transcending matter, he begins to resembles it. The CIA's 1983 Honduran interrogation manual vividly describes this process, maintaining that

> [t]he purpose of all coercive techniques is to induce psychological regression in the subject by bringing a superior force to bear on his will to resist. Regression is basically a loss of autonomy, a reversion to an earlier behavioral level. As the subject regresses, his learned personality traits fall away in reverse chronological order. He begins to lose the capacity to carry out the highest creative activities, to deal with complex situations, to cope with stressful interpersonal relationships, or to cope with repeated frustrations.[57]

The authors of the manual are no philosophers, but they recognize how torture ruptures the personality. Someone may spend years cultivating virtues and good habits, gradually taking responsibility for actions and a personality. He may understand himself as a "distinctive person among other persons in the world."[58] Under torture, however, he can easily lose much of what he has accomplished.

Timerman vividly depicts how torture destroys self-possession. When released from prison, he found himself inescapably reverting to his torturer's anti-Semitism. A complex and cosmopolitan man, he embraced vicious and stereotypical images of himself as a Jew.[59] Similarly, witnessing a family's torture, Timerman notes that "the entire effective world, constructed over the years with utmost difficulty, collapses with a kick in the father's genitals, a smack on the mother's face, an obscene insult to the sister, or the sexual violation of a daughter. Suddenly an entire culture based on familial love, devotion, the capacity for mutual sacrifice collapses. Nothing is possible in such a universe, and that is precisely what the torturers know."[60] The family nurtures and develops the person, but torture mocks its attempts to cultivate humanity.

"Stress positions" operate very effectively against self-possession. Rejali details their different forms demonstrating how they have appeared in many societies. Sometimes, they include ropes or other devices to suspend victims in painful positions. For example, the British military used rope techniques on soldiers and sailors in the eighteenth and nineteenth centuries. Likewise, American slave owners punished slaves by suspending them by the wrists and yanking them with pulleys. They favored this technique because it left no permanent marks, thus ensuring that slaves would retain monetary value on the slave market.[61] Other torturers employed stress positions requiring no instruments. Such "positional tortures" require victims to "assume normal human positions, but for abnormal periods of time."[62] They include standing, kneeling, sitting, squatting, bowing, or lying. For example, in the 1970s, the British forced suspected Irish Republican Army members to stand for hours. They stood "spread-eagled against the wall, with their fingers put high above the head against the wall, the legs spread apart and the feet back, causing them to stand on their toes with the weight of the body mainly on the fingers."[63] Those standing quickly experienced horrible pain and suffered serious circulatory problems.[64] Such positions break the will by putting tremendous stress on the body.

Like sensory deprivation, stress positions gained a certain scientific panache in the twentieth century. As McCoy demonstrates, in the 1950s, the CIA asked psychologists at Cornell University to explore "self-inflicted" pain.[65] They concluded that techniques like forced standing undermine a detainee' will to resist. Their research found its way into the KUBARK interrogation manual, which comments that it has "been plausibly suggested that, whereas pain inflicted on a person from outside himself may actually focus or intensify his will to resist, his resistance is likelier to be sapped by pain which he seems to inflict upon himself."[66] With self-inflicted pain, "the motivational strength of the individual is likely to exhaust itself" in an "internal encounter."[67] Rather than futilely pitting interrogator against detainee, it turns the detainee against himself, making him feel responsible for his suffering. Identical conclusions and language appear in CIA interrogation manuals of the 1980s.[68]

The United States used stress positions widely in the War on Terror. For example, in late 2002, interrogators at Guantánamo requested permission to use "stress positions (like standing), for a maximum of four hours."[69] In an appalling memo, Defense Secretary Rumsfeld approved this request, but sarcastically scrawled, "However, I stand for 8–10 hours a day. Why is standing limited to 4 hours?"[70] It goes without saying that standing on the job bears no relationship to a stress position. Even a fit human being would experience difficulty maintaining a stress position for long. However, responding to intense criticism from lawyers in the services, in December 2002, Rumsfeld halted the use of stress positions to allow the Pentagon Working Group to develop interrogation policy.[71] In its memo, however, the working group discussed prolonged standing (up to four hours) and allowed the secretary of defense to use "exceptional techniques."[72] This opened the door for military and intelligence officials to employ stress positions. The defense secretary walked right through it, telling interrogators that "if in your view, you require additional interrogation techniques for a particular detainee, you should provide me, via the Joint Chiefs of Staff, a written request describing the proposed technique, recommended safeguards, and the rationale for applying it with an identified detainee."[73] Secretary Rumsfeld thus allowed interrogators wide latitude to employ stress positions.

Official legitimacy produced significant abuse at Guantánamo. In 2002 and 2003, prisoners were shackled in stress positions for hours. One such position, a detainee reported, was

"short shackling" where we were forced to squat without a chair with our hands chained between our legs and chained to the floor. If we fell over, the chains would cut into our hands. We would be left in this position for hours before an interrogation, during the interrogations (which could last as long as 12 hours), and sometimes for hours while the interrogators left the room.[74]

FBI documents, interviews with released detainees, and legal briefs all confirm that U.S. officials at Guantánamo frequently used such stress positions to break detainees' wills.[75] Once interrogators received the green light from Donald Rumsfeld, they embraced this form of torture.

In secret CIA prisons, interrogators also avidly embraced stress positions. *Washington Post* reporters Dana Priest and Barton Gellman (two reporters who worked tirelessly in the early years of the War on Terror to expose torture) reported that at a CIA prison at Bagram, Afghanistan, detainees

are sometimes kept standing or kneeling for hours, in black hoods or spray-painted goggles, according to intelligence specialists familiar with CIA interrogation methods. At times they are held in awkward, painful positions and deprived of sleep with a 24-hour bombardment of lights—subject to what are known as "stress and duress" techniques.[76]

Khalid Sheikh Mohammed was likely subjected to such treatment. He was reportedly imprisoned in a cell where he "was unable to stand upright, to sit comfortably, or to recline fully."[77] In these and other cases, the CIA used self-inflicted pain to break the will of its high-value detainees.

Finally, in Iraq, soldiers and intelligence officials also employed stress positions. In September 2003, General Sanchez, commander of Coalition Ground Forces in Iraq, approved positions that included extended kneeling, sitting, and standing.[78] In early 2004, the ICRC reported that detainees were "forced to remain for prolonged periods in stress positions such as squatting or standing with or without the arms lifted."[79] In particular, it found that at Camp Cropper near the Baghdad International Airport (a site for high-value detainees), interrogators used "stress positions (kneeling, squatting, standing with arms raised above the head) for three or four hours."[80] Similarly, military reports about the Abu Ghraib scandal note how interrogators used stress positions. The Taguba Report (the investigation of the Abu Ghraib scandal conducted by General Antonio Taguba) describes how a detainee "was placed on a box with wires attached to his fingers, toes and penis."[81] One such episode was captured in the infamous photo of a hooded man at Abu Ghraib standing on a box and attached to electrodes. The detainee was "led to believe" that "if his legs gave way, and he fell off the perch, he would be electrocuted. His hood was lifted briefly to see the wires leading from the wall to his body. They were false electrodes that aimed at inducing anxiety, not physical pain. How long he shuddered in absolute fear of his life we don't know, but we can readily imagine the trauma of his experience and empathize with this hooded man."[82] Such torture created physical and spiritual disintegration that few people can withstand.

Torture and Communication without Loss

When reacting to this horror, people often say that torture harms both victim and perpetrator, but this seems like a meaningless cliché. Am I really harmed if I subject someone to stress positions or sensory deprivation? We can understand such harm better, however, if we explore how torture destroys communication without loss. Any interrogation threatens the spiritual communion between persons. It detains people against their will, demands something from them, and creates an uneasy relation of giving and taking. The detainee may lose elements of her identity by betraying country or comrades. Additionally the interrogator has much to gain in terms of prestige and career advancement.

In sum, interrogation is a zero-sum game challenging people to retain elements of their spirituality.

Torture, however, devastates communication of any kind. As Scarry notes, severe pain often renders its sufferers mute.[83] It seems ineffable, leaving victims struggling to express themselves. Severe pain shatters language rendering it ineffective and inoperative. Often, others speak for torture victims, a morally ambiguous responsibility. Because torture ruptures speech, we have difficulty holding perpetrators responsible for crimes. Torture victims often cannot articulate what happened to them, and political leaders manipulate their experiences for selfish gain.

Torture also creates a horrible mirror image of spiritual communication. A strictly utilitarian relation, it produces distinct winners and losers. Rather than welcoming another, the torturer treats him as an object to be used for specific ends. Instead of a copresence, possessiveness, acquisition, and competition reign. In the War on Terror, where "actionable intelligence" was vital, interrogators had no incentive to consider detainees as persons. They resolved to obtain limited information, rather than encountering unexpected gifts from others. They deliberately diminished rather than shared the experiences of others. Because communication without loss is an intersubjective good, their action necessarily diminished them. It robbed them of an extraordinary relationship open only to persons.

In such a world, active receptivity quickly disappears. Deliberately stripped of parts of their identity, torture victims often cannot respond positively to others. A personal being can "impregnate its environment with its own quality, thereby recognizing itself in its surroundings and entering into an intimate relationship with it."[84] In contrast, a torture victim often views his environment as a threat. As Scarry notes the torture room "is not just the setting in which the torture occurs; it is not just the space that happens to house the various instruments used for beating and burning and producing electric shock. It is itself literally converted into another weapon, into an agent of pain."[85] Baths and pools, normally inviting, become nightmarish sites of potential drowning. Chairs or beds, usually items for resting, become the locus of hours of stress positions. Useful tools suddenly threaten harm. For example, Rejali details the horrible history of the magneto, the electrical device many countries adopted in the twentieth century to administer electrical shocks. It originated with the military field telephone that torturers adapted to torture.[86] Rejali's detailed study illustrates Scarry's thesis that torturers often convert everyday objects into threatening devices. These threats may also occur in contexts where torturers deliberately mock detainees by using words such as inn or guest. In Iraq, soldiers allegedly brutalized prisoners in a place near Mosul called "the Disco," a perverse reference to the music that played there night and day.[87]

Forced nudity vividly illustrates how torture damages both the torturer and the tortured and destroys communication without loss. Often, soldiers or interrogators must strip prisoners to properly search them. However, this practice differs from using nudity to break a person's will. Sadly, such a practice has a long history. Given public documents, we cannot easily pinpoint when it began reemerging after the September 11 attacks. Reports indicate that some interrogators used forced nudity at the military bases at Kandahar and Bagram in Afghanistan in early 2002.[88] Also in 2002, commanders at Guantánamo requested permission to remove detainees' clothes.[89] In 2003, the Pentagon's Working Group considered "potential removal of all clothing; removal to be done by military police if not agreed to by the subject. Creating a feeling of helplessness and dependence. This technique must be monitored to ensure the environmental conditions are such that this technique does not injure the detainee."[90] In a chart describing the costs and benefits of interrogation techniques, the working group gave forced nudity a "high" in its "contribution to Intelligence Collection."[91] It recommended that interrogators use it against "unlawful combatants outside the United States."[92] This technique soon appeared often at Guantánamo.[93] Under General Miller's command, detainees were stripped of clothes for long periods of time.[94] Similarly, the CIA "used forced nakedness as a psychological weapon" in its secret black sites, providing detailed instructions about how to strip clothing off to maximize humiliation.[95]

Forced nudity migrated to Iraq, appearing in a brutal form at Abu Ghraib and elsewhere.[96] In 2003, General Sanchez adopted new and harsh interrogations techniques that included forced nudity.[97] Soon, it "was pervasive in the military intelligence unit of Abu Ghraib," and from what we can tell, some soldiers saw it as an acceptable form of interrogation.[98] As the Schlesinger Report (the report on the Abu Ghraib scandal released by James Schlesinger in 2004) put it, "the widespread practice of stripping detainees...evolved into something much broader, resulting in the practice of groups of detainees being kept naked for extended periods of time at Abu Ghraib."[99] Soldiers commonly saw naked detainees, a scene horribly captured in the Abu Ghraib photographs. They show naked detainees in pyramids and sexually humiliating positions. Written accounts of what happened at Abu Ghraib only add to the horror. For example, in a sworn statement in the Taguba Report, a detainee reported that "they stripped me from my clothes and the stuff that they gave me and I spent 6 days in that situation."[100] Lacking adequate understanding of interrogation techniques and confused about the chain of command, soldiers used forced nudity to "soften up" detainees for interrogation. Prisoners were "stripped naked for several days while held in solitary confinement," or "paraded naked outside cells in front of other persons deprived of their liberty and guards, sometimes hooded or with women's underwear on their head."[101] When ICRC personnel intervened to stop forced nudity, they were informed that it was "part of the process."[102]

I find such a response deeply disturbing because forced nudity violently dehumanizes us. It "seems to induce a sense of helplessness and danger in the face of imminent danger by depriving the detainee of the sense of protection and illusory security that clothing affords."[103] Studies of those who have experienced forced nudity reveal that "merely being stripped naked implies the breaking of a strict taboo, which leaves victims feeling extremely exposed and humiliated."[104] The exposed person has good reason to worry because others quickly dehumanize him. In Iraq, for example, nudity "gave military police officers the idea that the detainees were in some way less than human and allowed for the normal guidelines of human interaction to deteriorate."[105] The Schlesinger Report notes that "the wearing of clothes is an inherently social practice, and therefore stripping away of clothing may have had the unintended consequence of dehumanizing detainees in the eyes of those who interacted with them."[106] Far from being unintended, forced nudity became an intentional device for dehumanizing detainees to break their wills.

A person forced into nakedness no longer seems to have an interior life. A being without a body might be immediately transparent to others.[107] In contrast, human beings must gradually learn about each other. They freely decide what to reveal and protect and hide elements of their personality. They reveal them as gifts to those they trust. However, for "giving to be truly personalized, a gift must proceed from the deeper levels of the person as person, that is, as intellectually self-conscious and free."[108] Clothing retains a realm of secrecy important for self-giving. Forced nudity, in contrast, violently divulges my secrets to everyone. People now measure and quantify my body. I am treated as "essentially absent," and my body becomes an object of use, rather than a gift I freely share.[109]

In the War on Terror, those using forced nudity also adopted vicious stereotypes about Arab or Muslim sensibilities about sexuality. Arab or Muslim males were allegedly particularly vulnerable to forced nudity. For example, at Guantánamo, interrogators repeatedly played on supposed Arab or Muslims attitudes about women. The log of al-Qahtani's interrogation describes how

> [t]he detainee was stripped searched. Initially he was attempting to resist the guards. After approximately five minutes of nudity the detainee ceased to resist. He would only stare at the wall with GREAT focus. His eyes were squinted and stuck on one point on the wall directly in front of him. He later stated that he knew there was nothing he could do with so many guards around him, so why should he resist. He stated that he did not like the females viewing his naked body while being searched and if felt he could have done something about it then he would have.[110]

The interrogation log records how female interrogators invaded al-Qahtani's personal space knowing that this invasion particularly upset him.[111] It also shows that interrogators harbored crude ideas about Arabs or Muslims. By manipulating supposed cultural attitudes, they justified a terrible violation. Similarly, some MPs who ended up at Abu Ghraib reportedly received "cultural awareness" training teaching them about supposed Arab attitudes toward sexuality.[112] They deliberately linked torture to (supposed) religious convictions, once again demonstrating how torture spiritually assaults the person.

The spiritual perversion of forced nudity becomes clearer if we think about shame. Those forced to submit to the looks of others experience terrible shame. Shame testifies to our spiritual nature and "arises when something which of its very nature or in view of its purpose ought to be private passes the bounds of a person's privacy and somehow becomes public."[113] It shields important values from harm. Shame may include fear, but differs from it by revealing an interior dimension of the person she must protect. This, in turn, testifies to the person's self-possession. We are not to be possessed by another through a look, but we can cultivate a unique self-possession. The naked human body is beautiful, but when it is forced into public view, it becomes subordinate to sexual or other values losing its personal dimension. Shame powerfully reminds us of our spiritual nature.

Shame also shows that when interrogators use forced nudity to break the will, they torture. A person forced into nudity is reduced to "a raw datum, devoid of any meaning and moral values."[114] Guards and interrogators stripping him have little regard for his value as a person. In societies where people are clothed, clothing provides an indispensable protection against utilitarian uses of the human body. By removing it from thousands of prisoners, the United States exposed them to mere use, profoundly violating the personalist norm. It also assaulted their self-possession to break their will. The natural shame that victims experienced reflected a human need to protect dignity. In considering this horror, I prefer to conclude with the voice of a victim. Here is a narrative from the Taguba Report on Abu Ghraib. In a sworn statement, a detainee described how soldiers came "in the morning shift with two prisoners and they were father and son. They were both naked. They put them in front of each other and they counted 1, 2, 3, and then removed the bags from their heads. When the son saw his father naked, he was crying. He was crying because of seeing his father."[115]

A Spiritual Assault? A Recent Challenge

In his book *Torture and Democracy*, Darius Rejali rejects the notion that stress positions and sensory deprivation constitute psychological torture. In fact, he maintains that such techniques (which he calls clean torture) are "not psychological techniques at all."[116] Instead, they are physical targeting their victims' physiology. For Rejali, we gain no understanding of stress positions by considering their "self-inflicted" character. They target our bodies and contain no distinct psychological element. Clean torture, he insists, is torture, and we err by pretending it is merely psychological.

Rejali also strongly rejects the idea of a science of torture. When moderns discuss torture, he maintains, they "see an intelligent design, and that design speaks to them of an evil scientist."[117] For them, modern torture originates "in acts of hidden conspiracy beyond our reach, a misrepresentation that is as antidemocratic and disempowering as it is misleading."[118] By positing scientific perversions, scholars make an irrational leap of faith that ignores social scientific research. The real story of modern torture, Rejali maintains, is that modern democracies invented clean torture to evade detection by human rights monitors. It originated in police departments and torture chambers in the United States, France, and Great Britain. We serve the cause of clarity and justice better by ceasing to blame science for modern torture.

Rejali has authored a remarkable work demonstrating how modern democracies have tortured. Too often, we use Nazi or Communist examples, forgetting that American and European police forces tortured in stationhouses and prisons. Rejali also persuasively shows that despite pretensions at being a science, torture often resembles a craft. Torturers adopt techniques for contingent reasons reproducing what seems to work or acting on recommendations from others. Finally, Rejali constructs valuable typologies of torture preventing us from carelessly grouping diverse techniques together.

Nevertheless, I find Rejali strangely tone deaf to spiritual matters. For example, when defining torture, he mentions only physical torment or pain, arbitrarily ignoring spirituality.[119] Similarly, he misunderstands the significance of self-inflicted pain. Naturally, it is physical, but to the *subject* it may appear self-inflicted. It thus creates internal battles that differ from a fight against external torture. Stress positions effectively break the will because they undermine our fragile internal unity. By ignoring torture's spiritual character, Rejali thus overlooks important elements of modern torture.

Similarly, Rejali criticizes those promising a science of torture, but never considers why they promised it. Such a science may be illusionary, but many people *think* it exists. Modern science both probes nature's secrets and seeks to control them and often includes a "technological spirit, a desire and disposition rationally to understand, order, predict, and (ultimately) control the events and workings of nature, all pursued for the sake of human benefit."[120] In the twentieth century, this spirit found its way into the torture chamber. Torture techniques in the War on Terror not only have many (often banal) sources, but also reflect an impulse to control the human mind. Rejali seems unaware of this feature of modernity.[121]

By considering scientific perversions, we need not conclude that science causes all modern evil. Instead, we draw attention to troubling elements of the modern technological spirit. Some scientists and their allies see in the behavioral sciences opportunities to manipulate human nature. They seek to fundamentally alter it by modifying "the human material itself."[122] Historian Rebecca Lemov carefully demonstrates how this impulse moved from psychological laboratories to the national security arena. Numerous psychologists embraced the idea that if we "could quantify and control the internal arena of the personal self," we could reduce the need for "brutal external force" in societies.[123] For example, in his horrific experiments, Cameron promised the CIA that he could remake a person's personality. He aspired to radically change society by subjecting people to electroshock and other treatments. Fortunately, Cameron failed in his promethean aspirations, but he held them nevertheless. Similarly, William Sargant, a British psychologist, penned a well-known book in which he claimed to develop a science of brainwashing and interrogation.[124] Sargant and Cameron were only two of many twentieth-century scientists who sought to develop a science of interrogation and torture. Some viewed sensory deprivation and self-inflicted pain research as particularly appealing ways to control the mind. Modern science's prestige led them to think it could scientifically produce good intelligence.

In the War on Terror, psychiatry and psychology once again contributed to torture. As I have already mentioned, BSCTs evaluated detainees' psychological health, locating weakness for interrogators to exploit. Psychologists reportedly brought insights from the SERE programs first to the CIA and then to the military at Guantánamo.[125] Some interrogators found them valuable because of their supposed scientific character. Psychologists touted their scientific expertise, finding a willing audience among interrogators.[126] For example, according to Jane Mayer, psychologist James Mitchell advised the CIA on its interrogation of Abu Zubaydah. Reportedly, he insisted that Zubaydah be treated like a caged dog in an experiment. When FBI agents objected to treating a human being this way, Mitchell reportedly responded by saying, "Science is science."[127] Other psychologists eagerly assured interrogators that interrogation techniques were medically safe. For example, in July 2002, Air Force Major Jerald F. Ogrisseg, chief of Psychological Services at Air Education and Training Command, wrote a memorandum about the SERE program. Remarkably, he maintained that although he lacked long-term studies of service personnel subjected to its training, he could be "reasonably certain" that it produced few negative psychological effects.[128] SERE instructors also taught in Iraq in 2003, reportedly helping TF-20 (a secretive commando group that hunted al-Qaeda members and insurgents) in its interrogations.[129] In December, 2008, U.S. Senator Carl Levin of Michigan released a thorough report detailing the links between the SERE program and interrogations.[130] Importantly, we should remember that not all psychologists approved of using their science to torture. In fact, some of them in the CIA and the psychological profession strongly opposed torture.[131] For example, the American Psychological Association (APA) erupted in controversy for several years over torture. When its leadership appointed a panel to discuss the issue, six out of nine of its members were military psychologists, some of whom had participated in interrogations. The result was a predicable whitewash and a refusal to adequately regulate psychologists involved in interrogations. However, a group of psychologists rebelled against this charade, battling to ensure that their profession would remain out of the torture business.[132] Despite opposition, in 2008, members of the APA voted in large numbers to exclude psychologists from future involvement in torture.[133]

We should also be aware that governments continue to research scientific ways to manipulate the mind. The CIA experimented with mind control drugs in the 1950s, but failed miserably to harness them for interrogations. Despite this history, contemporary researchers see the biological sciences as allies in matters of national security. Jonathan Moreno documents how defense and intelligence agencies are working in the booming field of neuroscience.[134] The Defense Advanced Research Projects Agency (DARPA) is a science agency funding neuroscientific research for military use. It supports research into "technologies to enable remote interrogation and control of biological systems at the system/organ/tissue/cellular/molecular scales."[135] Some researchers entertain grandiose ideas about how neuroscience will change modern warfare. Like the LSD experimenters of the 1950s, they may go nowhere merely displaying overactive scientific imaginations. Or, they may yield frightening technologies. We cannot doubt, however, that their work reflects a disturbing modern approach to technology and the mind.

In sum, Rejali rejects the role of science in modern torture because he is inattentive to science's dangers. To recognize them, we need a sophisticated conception of how scientific techniques threaten human nature and how scientific techniques threaten it. Such awareness originates not in blind faith, but in a wise understanding of modernity.

Why Is Torture Wrong? Concluding Comments

Scholars say that torture violates human rights, destroys autonomy, and corrodes institutions. Although helpful, such analyses often presuppose simplistic understandings of the person. By exploring spirituality, we see more clearly why torture is profoundly wrong. The person is more than a rights-bearing creature because he transcends his situation through knowledge. He unites diverse objects to constitute larger wholes. Torture deliberately diminishes this capacity, forcing him to obsessively consider pain or intelligence data. It thus dethrones him from his unique place in the cosmos. Forced to consider a narrow range of objects, he no longer seems to have a power "extending to the infinite."[136]

Similarly, torture not only destroys autonomy but also targets our remarkable self-possession. We can gradually understand ourselves as centers of activity and responsibility. Practices like self-inflicted pain systematically undermine self-possession by creating internal conflicts. A torture victim often cannot order her internal life. Once again, torture assaults a distinctive mark of the person.

Finally, torture spiritually corrupts institutions and individuals. People often pursue self-interest or narrow national concerns. However, as spiritual beings, they can sometimes move beyond utilitarian concerns. They can exchange gifts without losing what they have and welcome others without possessiveness. Torture targets this capacity in turn reducing human relations to a struggle of wills. It prevents people from exchanging spiritual gifts, radically stunting human relationships. In the world of Abu Ghraib, little spiritual communion exists. Torture disfigures a beautiful element of our humanity, thereby diminishing all who employ it.

Some readers may have already lost patience with this talk of spirituality and torture. Mentioning spirituality together with torture seems misplaced. International politics is violent and nasty marked by the naked pursuit of power and interest. In this world, communication without loss seems like an ideal best left to interpersonal relations. As theologian Reinhold Niebuhr famously wrote, "a sharp distinction must be drawn between the moral and social behavior of individuals and social groups, national, racial, and economic; and that this distinction justifies and necessitates political policies which a purely individualistic ethic must always find embarrassing."[137] This divorce between political and interpersonal life appeals to many people thinking about the War on Terror. Al-Qaeda terrorists show no concern for the spiritual lives of Americans. Osama bin Laden once said that "we believe that the worst thieves in the world today and the worst terrorists are the Americans. Nothing could stop you except perhaps retaliation in kind. We do not have to differentiate military or civilian. As far as we are concerned, they are all targets."[138] While confronting this enemy, moral and spiritual niceties seem to disappear replaced by the imperative to survive at all costs. Some politicians and citizens insist that we jettison interpersonal values altogether to protect the common good. To this response, I now turn.

CHAPTER FOUR

Does Torture Work?
Consequentialism's Failures

> Few beliefs have been more destructive of the respect for the rules
> of law and of morals than the idea that a rule is binding only if
> the beneficial effect of observing it in the particular instance can
> be recognized.
>
> Friedrich Hayek[1]

In the aftermath of the September 11 attacks, many Americans began
contemplating torture. People whom we might expect to oppose it
suddenly seemed to change their minds. For example (as I mentioned
in the introduction), in a now infamous proposal, Alan Dershowitz
proposed that judges issue torture warrants specifying precisely when
and how people should be tortured. Stating that he morally opposed
torture, Dershowitz nevertheless argued that because governments
often torture, we should regulate their conduct.[2] Elshtain confessed
that "before the watershed event of September 11, 2001, I had not
reflected critically on the theme of torture. I was one of those who
listed it in the category of 'never.' It did not seem to me possible that
the United States would face some of the dilemmas favored by moral
theorists in their hypothetical musing on whether torture could ever be
morally permitted. Too, reprehensible regimes tortured. End of question. Not so, as it turns out."[3] Finally, journalist Jonathan Alter talked
about suspected terrorists writing

> [c]ouldn't we as least subject them to psychological torture, like
> tapes of dying rabbits or high-decibel rap? (The military has done

that in Panama and elsewhere.) How about truth serum, administered with a mandatory IV? Or deportation to Saudi Arabia, land
of beheadings (as the frustrated FBI has been threatening)? Some
people still argue that we needn't rethink any of our old assumptions about law enforcement, but they're hopelessly "Sept. 10"—
living in a country that no longer exists.[4]

After September 11, many people shared Alter's sentiments about torture.

Terrorism's horror understandably produces such calls for torture. Al-Qaeda brutally murdered almost three thousand people on
September 11. Its attack completely surprised many Americans who
knew little or nothing about terrorism. Moreover, as the War on Terror
continued, further atrocities followed. Suicide bombing became a pop-
ular military tactic; Americans like Daniel Pearl and Nicholas Berg
were brutally executed; al-Qaeda launched terrible attacks in Europe.
In this climate, many people came to believe that absolute prohibitions
against torture were moral niceties suitable only for peacetime.

Although understandable, this response to terrorism is politically
immature and historically ill-informed. The United States is not the
first country to experience terrorism. Israel, Italy, Germany, Sri Lanka,
and many other nations have confronted it in vicious forms. Moreover,
in the Second World War, Korea, and Vietnam, American military
authorities struggled with moral dilemmas over interrogation. For
example, during the Korean War, the North Koreans committed horrific crimes against American soldiers. They forced American military
commanders to think carefully about how to respond.[5] Moreover, torture occurred in American police departments and prisons throughout the past century.[6] Finally, philosophers and theologians have long
reflected on the morality of torture. We are neither the first people to
think about torture nor are we the first to experience terrorism.

To respond to those justifying torture, in this chapter, I reject arguments appealing to its positive consequences. First, I introduce consequentialism, the idea that we define the goodness of an act by considering
its consequences. I also briefly discuss some consequentialists in political philosophy. Second, I describe a pure consequentialist defense of
torture, which maintains that it can produce beneficial consequences.
I also consider several arguments that fail to undermine consequentialism. Third, discussing temporal and measurement issues, I maintain
that consequentialism cannot adequately measure material and spiritual
consequences. To make this case, I discuss Friedrich Hayek and Russell
Hardin, thinkers who brilliantly demonstrate indeterminacy in social

interactions. Fourth, to illustrate the deficiencies of consequentialism, I consider Mirko Bagaric's and Julie Clarke's incendiary consequentialist defense of torture. I note how it entirely neglects measurement issues and falsely assumes that we can quantify happiness. Finally, I discuss how consequentialists respond to measurement issues, focusing particularly on institutional consequentialism. A compelling approach to social issues, institutional consequentialism devises rules with long-range positive consequences. I argue that despite its attractiveness, this strategy cannot protect us against torture because it lacks an adequate theory of value.

Consequentialism: An Old Tradition

When thinking about ethics, people often consider consequences, and such reflection is normal and indispensable in private and public life. In fact, we rightfully condemn someone for undertaking an important venture while disregarding its consequences. Consequentialism, however, is an outlook that systematizes our concern for consequences, making it primary in ethical reflection. Philosopher Elizabeth Anscombe (who originally coined the term consequentialism) states that the consequentialist "acts for the best in the particular circumstances according to his judgment of the total consequences of this particular action."[7] Utilitarianism is the most famous form of consequentialism and it considers consequences in terms of happiness. However, other forms propose maximizing states of affairs like wealth. Each, however, not only considers consequences, but also uses them to define the value of moral acts.

Although the term consequentialism is of recent vintage, it has a long historical pedigree in political theory. Confronted with violence, the pursuit of power, and disorder, many thinkers have counseled rulers to guide their actions by assessing consequences. For example, writing about how Romulus killed his brother Remus at Rome's founding, Machiavelli justifies his act by saying that "it is a sound maxim that reprehensible actions may be justified by their effects, as it was in the case of Romulus, it always justifies the action."[8] Max Weber famously writes that we must "be clear about the fact that all ethically oriented conduct may be guided by one of two fundamentally differing and irreconcilably opposed maxims: conduct can be oriented toward an 'ethic of ultimate ends' or to an 'ethic of responsibility.'"[9] An ethic of ultimate ends considers an agent's moral purity, whereas an ethic of responsibility focuses on an act's foreseeable consequences. Using powerful language and imagery, Weber maintains that politicians must embrace an ethic of consequences. Finally, noted American political scientist Hans Morgenthau insisted that the "character of foreign policy can be ascertained only through the examination of political acts performed and of the foreseeable consequences of these acts."[10] Famously, Morgenthau warned against adopting utopian foreign ventures that disregard consequences. He and many other illustrious political thinkers have endorsed consequentialism.

Consequentialism and Torture

Consequentialism has import for many ethical issues, but holds particular significance for torture debates. Those advocating torture frequently justify themselves by appealing to consequences. To see their basic argument, let me return to Machiavelli. Famously, he extols the brutal action of Cesare Borgia, the son of a Renaissance pope. Confronting disorder in Romagna, Borgia appointed Messer Remirro de Orca to suppress it. A "cruel and efficient man," de Orca soon stamped out chaos.[11] Pretending to be shocked at his action, Borgia publicly executed de Orca by having him "placed one morning in Cesena on the piazza in two pieces with a piece of wood and a bloodstained knife alongside him. The atrocity of such a spectacle left those people at one and the same time satisfied and stupefied."[12] With this example, Machiavelli recognizes torture's expressive power, its capacity to simultaneously intimidate and fascinate a populace. Borgia's action may appear cruel, he notes, but is really compassionate because it creates order and protects the innocent. Machiavelli insists, in fact, that a person or nation failing to employ such cruelty acts irresponsibly.

Machiavelli powerfully captures the consequentialist approach to torture, and his ideas have appeared often during the War on Terror. Politicians, radio talk show hosts, and journalists appealed to consequences to justify torturing terror suspects. For example, Judge Richard Posner (who has long defended a form of consequentialism) argues that with interrogation, "what is required is a balance between the costs and the benefits of particular methods of interrogation."[13] Employing this standard, he argues that torture is morally justifiable in extreme circumstances because "there is such a thing as a lesser wrong committed to avoid a greater one. There is such a thing as fighting fire with fire, and it is an apt metaphor for the use of torture and other extreme measures when nothing else will avert catastrophe."[14] Posner concludes that anyone opposing torture in such circumstances "should not be in a position of responsibility."[15] Here we have Machiavelli's argument repackaged in the language of contemporary legal thought.

Columnist Charles Krauthammer mounts an even stronger consequentialist defense of torture. Refusing to condone it on the battlefield, he endorses traditional protections for POWs. However, when discussing a captured terror suspect who might possess valuable intelligence, he says that "not only is it permissible to hang this miscreant by his thumbs. It is a moral duty."[16] Commenting on his reaction to Khalid Sheikh Mohammed's torture, Krauthammer notes that "I myself have not gnashed a single tooth. My garments remain entirely unrent. Indeed, I feel reassured."[17] He repeatedly says that a "rational moral calculus" supports torturing known terrorists in select and highly regulated situations. Krauthammer guides his judgments by considering consequences, thus revealing a commitment to consequentialism.

Must We Be Consequentialists?

Confronting such arguments, some opponents of consequentialism say that torture fails to "work." Forced confessions, they maintain, are highly unreliable because a person will say anything to stop torture. For example, Joshua Dratel argues that "the justifications of torture all presuppose the efficacy of torture as compared with traditional, nonabusive methods of interrogations—a conclusion reached without the slightest discussion or empirical proof."[18] Supporting this judgment with a patina of scientific respectability, Randy Borum writes that

> [t]he potential mechanisms and effects of using coercive techniques or torture for gaining accurate, useful information from an uncooperative source are much more complex than is commonly assumed. There is little or no research to indicate whether such techniques succeed in the manner and contexts in which they are applied. Anecdotal accounts and opinions based on personal experiences are mixed, but the preponderance of reports seems to weigh against their effectiveness.[19]

Borum and other researchers point out difficulties in garnering scientific data about torture. Governments cannot conduct controlled experiments to ascertain its efficacy. During the cold war, the United States and the Soviet Union experimented on foreign agents, inmates, and other vulnerable populations. They also used data from German scientists who had experimented on prisoners in the Second World War concentration camp Dachau and elsewhere.[20] These terrible experiments yielded some knowledge of torture's powers, but little systematic assessments of its efficacy. For Borum and others, then, claims about torture's efficacy are unscientific and exaggerated.

Those defending torture often respond to such criticism by making unsupported assertions. For example, Posner states that "it is possible in principle that torture, through resorted to frequently, is a completely inefficacious method of obtaining true information. But this is very unlikely; the practice is too common."[21] Krauthammer argues that it

> simply will not do to take refuge in the claim that...torture never works anyway. Would that this be true. Unfortunately, on its face, this is nonsense. Is one to believe that in the entire history of human warfare, no combatant has ever received useful information by the use of pressure, torture, or any other kind of inhuman treatment? It may indeed be true that torture is not a reliable tool. But that is very different from saying that it is *never* useful.[22]

Rather than providing scientific evidence for their claims that torture works, these torture proponents offer uninformed historical and medical speculations. As Rejali perceptively notes, "whenever apologists claim empirical insight, everyone should simply ask them repeatedly for evidence, check the sources, and then double-check the claim with other sources."[23] Rather than empirical evidence, those claiming torture works usually offer little more than anecdotes.

Some torture proponents, however, describe specific cases that supposedly demonstrate torture's effectiveness. For example, the Bush administration repeatedly argued that enhanced interrogation produced important information from Khalid Sheikh Mohammed and others. Similarly, Posner, Dershowitz, and Yoo all cite the 1995 case of Abdul Hakim Murad, who was tortured by Philippine authorities. Hakim Murad was involved in a plot to kill the late pope John Paul II and to blow up commercial airlines. Dershowitz and Yoo argue that torture forced a confession before the plot could succeed, saving thousands of lives. Other scholars cite French torture in the Algerian War, and American torture in the Vietnam War's Phoenix Program, maintaining that both demonstrate torture's efficacy.

Scholars have subjected such claims to withering criticism. For example, McCoy, an expert on Philippine politics, shows that torturing Hakim Murad provided little important intelligence data. Instead, "the Manila police got all the important information in the first few minutes, when they seized his laptop with the bomb plot and evidence that led the FBI to World Trade Center bomber Ramzi Ahmed Yousef in Pakistan."[24] Murad's subsequent torture yielded very little important information. Similarly, journalist Ron Suskind verified some claims of the Bush administration about Khalid Sheikh Mohammed and other detainees but maintains that others remain unsubstantiated. For example, he details how President Bush made extravagant and misleading claims about Abu Zubaydah's intelligence value.[25] Recall that Zubaydah was captured by the CIA and FBI in 2002. Wounded, he was nursed back to health only to be tortured using waterboarding and other techniques. A psychologically unbalanced person, he not only produced some useful information, but also gave false testimony leading to wild goose chases. Officials have also conveniently ignored cases where torture produced false information with detrimental consequences. For example, in late 2001, the United States captured Ibn al-Shaykh al-Libi, the first important al-Qaeda representative caught in the War on Terror.[26] Under the U.S. program of "extraordinary rendition," where detainees were sent to other countries to be tortured, al-Libi was sent to Egypt where Egyptian authorities tortured him. He confessed to knowing about close connections between Saddam Hussein and al-Qaeda. This information became one piece of evidence that the Bush administration used to justify going to war against Iraq. When received, many intelligence officials doubted its reliability. Nevertheless, U.S. officials continued using it in public statements about the war. The American public later learned that al-Libi's information was false, a product of a desperate man under torture.

Considering such complex cases and history, what can we conclude about consequentialism and torture? First, it is indeed foolish to claim that torture never works in the narrow sense of obtaining useful intelligence. We have too many examples where people succumb to it and provide truthful testimony. Second, however, we should distinguish between short- and long-term efficacy. The French succeeded with torture in Algeria in the short term but their conduct may have cost them the war.[27] Third, we should carefully scrutinize public claims about torture's efficacy. Obviously, citizens cannot access classified information, but should demand that public officials provide minimal evidence that torture has worked. Fourth, because interrogators can employ sophisticated, noncoercive interrogation methods, we ought to know if they tried them before torturing. Proponents of torture rarely provide such evidence. Fifth, empirically, consequentialists cannot easily establish torture's reliability as a practice. Without controlled experiments, they cannot ascertain if it produces reliable information most of the time. Perhaps it yielded such information with Khalid Sheikh Mohammed but not with al-Libi. How, then, can we know when it is reliable? Ignoring this problem, Dershowitz, Posner, Krauthammer trade on colorful anecdotes, which others can counter with different anecdotes. They appeal to controversial intuitions about pain to establish torture's effectiveness, and others respond by describing how terrible pain produces false information. Such intuitions and anecdotes cannot establish torture's reliability as a practice.

Nevertheless, those opposing torture should avoid focusing too much attention on whether it is efficacious. Suppose we somehow show historically and scientifically that torture produces reliable information most of the time? We would then be forced to concede that it is morally justifiable. By concentrating on the *empirical* question of whether torture worked, its opponents play the consequentialist game. Whether we ought to torture becomes a matter of measuring its efficacy. Once in this empirical game, those opposed to torture weaken their position and may end up losers.

How Well Can We Measure Consequences?

To further see what's wrong with the consequentialist approach to torture, we must think more carefully about consequences. Any consequentialist requires a standard or currency for measuring consequences. Historically, standards have included pain and pleasure, happiness, money, welfare, and utility. Since utilitarianism's popularity in the nineteenth century, consequentialists have confronted measurement problems. How can we measure goods or values? In the early years of utilitarianism, debates about measurement focused on the meaning of pleasure, with Jeremy Bentham and John Stuart Mill offering differing conceptions of it. Mill's critics challenged him to explain how moral agents could measure consequences. William Whewell, Henry Sidgwick, and Mill all debated how individuals could understand an act's consequences. Critics of classical utilitarianism pointed out that measurement depends on how others act, and we often cannot predict their behavior. They also noted that despite pretences to scientific objectivity, utilitarians provide little scientific evidence for their utility claims. Instead, they appeal to the general utility of certain rules, using limited historical data to establish it.

In the twentieth century, the measurement problem emerged in disputes about rule and act utilitarianism. Rule utilitarians argue that we should avoid calculating every act's consequences and instead rely on general rules. No one, they maintain, can know enough about the consequences of an act to adequately calculate them. Therefore, we need "rules of thumb" that tell us which kinds of acts have utility value. Act utilitarians, in contrast, insist that we calculate every act. In a well-known book written some decades ago, philosopher David Lyons powerfully rejected the act/rule utilitarian distinction. He maintained that rule utilitarianism invariably becomes act utilitarianism in particular cases.[28] For example, a person uncertain whether a general rule produces positive consequences should calculate her act's consequences. To revert to a rule in such a case amounts to adopting an irrational "rule worship."[29] Lyons convinced many utilitarians to abandon the once-popular rule/act distinction.

Twentieth-century economists and social theorists greatly enhanced our understanding of consequentialism and measurement problems. They focused particularly on strategic interactions, actions involving multiple actors or institutions. For example, they debated ordinal versus cardinal utility. Cardinal utility measures the strength of particular desires or preferences, whereas ordinal utility measures only their ranking. A cardinal measurement would seek to ascertain precisely how much I like ice cream as opposed to fruit. It might then make what are called interpersonal comparisons, measuring exactly how much I like ice cream against how much you like fruit. In contrast, ordinal measurement simply finds out that I prefer ice cream over fruit. Moreover, it generally refuses to make interpersonal comparisons, claiming they are hopelessly subjective. In the twentieth century, Italian economist Vilfredo Pareto initially embraced cardinal measurement, only to turn against it in favor of its ordinal cousin. For example, discussing national power, he asks how we measure it. He considers whether we can say that a nation's power has increased without precisely quantifying it. Often lacking precise calculations, we "get around the difficulty by substituting rough approximations for the precise numerical data that we cannot have."[30] Such measurements are ordinal and teach us much without requiring precise quantification.

Some thinkers insightfully link measurement problems to strategic interactions. In particular, the economist Friedrich Hayek famously analyzed cognitive shortcomings in modern societies. He argues that we can know little about an act's future consequences because it is "impossible for any mind to comprehend the infinite variety of different needs of different people, which compete for the available resources and to attach a definite weight to each."[31] What someone knows depends on local variables and opportunities. To completely comprehend an act's consequences, we would need to understand other people's talents, background, and opportunities. Additionally, we would have to know how they would respond to our action. Neither social institutions nor individuals possess such information and, therefore, cannot predict the full consequences of actions or policies.

Hayek uses a sophisticated account of information to criticize utilitarianism. He distinguishes between utility of means and utility of ends. We can measure an act's utility as a means for dealing with diverse situations unknown to us. Or, we can apply it to ends for action, seeking to precisely measure their utility. The former approach, Hayek argues, is plausible, whereas the latter is impractical. Like Lyons, he argues that rule utilitarianism eventually breaks down to become act utilitarianism. However, he also rejects act utilitarianism, arguing that for it to work we would have to "always presuppose that some other rules were taken as given and generally observed and not determined by any known utility."[32] Other agents are acting when we act, thus preventing us from precisely predicting the consequences of our acts.

For Hayek, utilitarianism particularly fails to comprehend how rules reflect our ignorance. Rules "are an adaptation" to the "inescapable ignorance of most of the particular circumstances which determine the effects of our actions."[33] They serve as general purpose tools rather than as guides to the precise utility of acts. They identify kinds of actions in terms of their "probable effect which need not be foreseeable by the individuals" adopting them.[34] Summarizing his criticism of utilitarianism, Hayek states that we "may of course aim at the 'greatest happiness of the greatest number' if we do not delude ourselves that we can determine the sum of this happiness by some calculation, or that there is a known aggregate of results at any one time."[35] All we can do is appeal to how a system of rules deals with information disadvantages.

Hayek bolsters his case against utilitarianism by considering forms of knowledge not amenable to quantification.[36] People employ local knowledge they often cannot articulate or rationalize. For example, someone experienced in the plumbing trade possesses knowledge garnered from years of labor. It allows her to constantly adapt to changing technological circumstances. If asked about it, she might be inarticulate but can display her knowledge when repairing an appliance. Writing about her, an economist could develop a theoretical account of plumbing without ever capturing its local knowledge. In fact, his theory operates at a level of abstraction that invariably neglects such knowledge. Obviously, this account of local knowledge holds import for consequentialism. A consequentialist can identify general patterns of action and consequences. In a small society, he can possess considerable local knowledge and can quantify consequences. However, in a large society, he cannot hope to possess the local knowledge of thousands or millions of people. He will thus be unable to calculate a policy's precise consequences.

Rational choice theorist Hardin strengthens Hayek's argument by accentuating indeterminacy in social and political life. Strategic interaction often renders actions indeterminate. I cannot know how others will respond to my actions, and as a result,

> all that I determine with my strategy choice is some constraints on the possible outcomes I might get. To narrow this array to a single outcome requires action from you and perhaps many others. I cannot commonly know what the best strategy choice is for me unless I know what strategy choice others will make. But if all of us cannot know what all others are going to do, then it is not coherent to say that thereafter we can alter our choices in the light of that knowledge.[37]

Hardin carefully details failed attempts to deny indeterminacy in economics and international relations. In light of such failures, he urges us to accept indeterminacy and to devise policies recognizing it. Hardin recommends that we adopt general rules that may harm future unknown individuals. For example, he insightfully discusses vaccination programs that immunize millions of children. With them, we not only save many lives, but we also know that vaccinations will harm a small percentage of unknown children who are allergic to them. Nevertheless, we adopt a vaccination policy knowing about its possible future harm.

We can enhance Hardin's and Hayek's arguments by considering an action's scope and temporality.[38] How do we decide for whom consequences matter? Pareto wrestles with this problem when noting that we can measure both individual and communal utility.[39] Far from neatly coinciding, they often "stand in overt opposition."[40] One act can maximize my utility, at the same time damaging that of my community. Although Pareto thinks we can arrive at a rough calculus of utility, he resists reducing all utilities "down to one."[41] He concludes that how we calculate them depends on prior ethical commitments, which he attributes to sentiment rather than reason. Unfortunately, Pareto's appeal to sentiment offers no guidance for calculating consequences.

Political actors often restrict consequence to fellow citizens and their nation. For example, the Bush administration showed little concern for international law, embracing a unilateralism that many countries found frightening. John Yoo, Jack Goldsmith, David Addington and others in the administration rejected the claim that international law or norms bind U.S. foreign policy. This restriction may be politically justifiable but is morally arbitrary. Once we admit that torture policies affect international institutions, norms, and regimes, measuring torture's consequences becomes very difficult. For example, in 2002–2003, Donald Rumsfeld and General Geoffrey Miller might have believed that their interrogation techniques produced good intelligence. However, they showed no recognition that their decision might detrimentally impact countries victimized by declining international ethical standards. This example illustrates the difficulties in ascertaining consequentialism's proper scope.

Temporally, consequentialism fares no better. When considering torture's consequences, how far in the future should we project them? Anglican theologian Kenneth Kirk, a keen student of ethics, once wrote that "the consequences of any action continue to all eternity; neither good nor bad can be summed up in such a way as to make effective moral accountancy possible."[42] Pareto also notes that we can consider various utilities "with reference to time—in reference to the present, that is, and to one point or another in the future."[43] He again resolves this problem by appealing to sentiments about action. Confronted with questions about time, consequentialists either make absurd claims about long-term consequences or consider only immediate consequences. For example, philosopher J.C. Smart argues that normally, "the utilitarian is able to assume that the remote effects of his actions tend rapidly to zero, like the ripples on a pond after a stone has been thrown on it."[44] However, he offers no serious defense of this odd claim. Powerful technologies affect future generations, and we have every reason to believe our actions affect them. Smart never explains at what temporal slice our acts begin to have no effect. Shall we consider policy in light of five, ten, or more years? Similarly, some years ago, philosopher

Richard Brandt offered a utilitarian justification for rules of war.[45] He maintained that noncombatant immunity has long-range utilitarian value. However, his case reads like a "just so" story with little historical reliability. How do we know that the principle of noncombatant immunity always produces positive outcomes? Over what period of time should we measure its effects? Perhaps intentionally killing non-combatants quickly ends wars, thus preventing long-term suffering, a claim some military historians make. Without empirical evidence, Brandt's case remains highly speculative. Thinkers like Brandt suffer from the illusion of "immediate success."[46] Torture and other horrors may work in one or two instances, but may be "a disaster according to the duration proper to state-vicissitudes and nation-vicissitudes."[47] Unfortunately, those devising public policy rarely consider more than immediate advantage.

Measurement problems become particularly acute if we consider spiritual values. With material realities, measurement may seem unproblematic (even when it is not!). If I want to feed thousands of people, I measure food and consider how to distribute it. My task may be largely technical, and I can consult economists or development specialists to help me. Recall Marcel's statement that if I "have four things and give two away, it is obvious that I only have two left, and that I am correspondently *impoverished*."[48] However, if we introduce spiritual goods, measurement becomes difficult to understand. How, for example, can we measure "communication without loss"? We have a sense of how to enhance or destroy it, and may cultivate it through reflection and spiritual practices. Such practices involve tacit knowledge we cannot easily describe. We cannot quantify it, but it is essential for understanding spiritual communication. Similarly, we can roughly gauge how social practices affect the person's transcendence through knowledge. We might, for example, come to believe that playing video games all day harms transcendence. Yet, we cannot compute such an effect. Finally, we can consider self-possession in ourselves and others. We gradually learn about which practices enhance it, but cannot create self-possession algorithms.

Our spiritual, but imperfect, way of knowing casts further doubt on the prospect of quantifying consequences.[49] We know slowly and sometimes painfully. We possess some sense of thing's unity, but must investigate it further, perhaps beginning a lengthy inquiry. At any given time, we can declare we know something, but our knowledge may be incomplete. As Aquinas vividly notes, "our knowledge is so weak that no philosopher was ever able to investigate perfectly the nature of single fly. Hence we read that one philosopher passed thirty years in solitude in order that he might know the nature of a bee."[50] When we understand something, therefore, we do not gain complete knowledge of its being. For example, I knew my wife when I married her, but I have learned more about her in the years of marriage. No formula can capture this knowledge, and yet I surely possess it. In fact, it is vital for my spiritual growth and interaction with my wife. Nevertheless, I may be unable to precisely articulate my knowledge.

When consequentialists defend torture, they rarely consider such epistemological issues and can thus easily disregard measurement problems. For example, various hypothetical scenarios about mad bombers focus almost entirely on material realities. The national interest, number of lives, a city—we can measure all these realities. Yet, intangible spiritual values are absent from this analysis. This is no accident because consequentialists need technical tools appealing to bureaucracies and politicians. Once spiritual values enter the picture, precise measurement becomes a fantasy. How can the CIA compute the spiritual impact of sensory deprivation? How can the military quantify how forced nakedness destroys spiritual communication? How can the president gauge the damage that stress positions inflict on the human spirit? Faced with such difficult questions, most politicians simply ignore spiritual realities altogether.

Thus, if we consider spiritual values and strategic interaction, consequentialism confronts deep measurement difficulties. Spiritual values block easy agreement on a standard for measuring consequences. Once we admit them into our calculus, we lose the capacity to precisely measure and must rely on less technical ways of knowing. Finally, even if we could measure spiritual consequences, we confront extreme problems with strategic interaction and indeterminacy.

Consequentialism and Torture: An Impoverished Debate

In light of such sophisticated arguments, contemporary consequentialist defenses of torture appear remarkably impoverished. Those defending torture show almost no awareness of indeterminacy in strategic interaction, offering simplistic examples remote from institutional realities. Let me illustrate this phenomenon by considering a controversial defense of torture offered by Mirko Bagaric and Julie Clarke. Bagaric–Clarke purport to be rationalists in emotional debates about torture. They argue that "torture is indeed morally defensible, not just pragmatically desirable."[51] They insist that by dispassionately analyzing it, we eliminate its pejorative associations. We should locate torture with other unpleasant acts such as responding to hostage takers or performing painful surgery. In such situations, we must act and, therefore, should specify appropriate responses.

Bagaric and Clarke argue that we can justifiably torture to protect the innocent. They confidently maintain that regulated torture will produce positive consequences. They even offer an equation to help policy makers decide when to torture. When considering torture, they write, political leaders should consider

(1) whether the person to be tortured is a wrongdoer,
(2) the number of lives that will be lost if the information is not forthcoming,
(3) the probability that the person to be tortured actually has the relevant information,
(4) the immediacy of the harm,
(5) and the likelihood that other methods will forestall the risk.[52]

Policy makers should calculate these variables, and "torture should be permitted where the application of the variables exceeds a threshold level."[53] Bagaric and Clarke acknowledge imprecision in their calculus, but they believe other legal standards are equally imprecise. To guide the calculus, they embrace a utilitarian standard of happiness. Using survey research, they identify happiness as "fit and healthy bodies, realistic goals, self-esteem, optimism, an outgoing personality, a sense of control, close relationships, challenging work, and active leisure, punctuated by adequate rest and a faith that entails communal support, purpose, and acceptance."[54] Establishing a hierarchy of interests, Bagaric and Clarke list them (in their order of importance) as life, physical integrity, food, shelter, health care, liberty, and education.[55] With this hierarchy, they can justify torture when it protects life at the expense of the lesser value of physical integrity.

This defense of torture suffers from severe shortcomings and should appeal only to those uninformed about utilitarianism's history. First, Bagaric–Clarke display remarkable ignorance of the great utilitarian debates about measurement. For example, they never discuss cardinal versus ordinal measurement, assuming instead a simplistic ordinal standard. Many twentieth-century utilitarians explored such a standard only to abandon it as hopelessly subjective. Second, Bagaric–Clarke focus entirely on short-term consequences. They never mention domestic and international institutions. If we consider them, measurement problems become acute. For example, to evaluate whether torture enhances overall happiness, we must know how other nations would react to an official U.S. torture policy. Would they abandon international institutions and embrace torture policies? How would countries with diverse cultural norms institutionalize torture? Bagaric and Clarke never consider such complexities, completely ignoring cultural factors. Responding to slippery slope arguments, they note how much torture occurs in the world and maintain that their proposal would reduce it. However, this is purely speculative relying on uninformed intuitions and anecdotes. Bagaric and Clarke offer little scientific, historical, or empirical evidence to support their claims.

Such disregard for strategic interaction is particularly troubling given what happened in the War on Terror. For example, with the intense need for actionable intelligence in November 2001, the CIA might have believed that torture would produce beneficial consequences. However, looking back at its fateful decisions, we see their negative effects. They include the United States' loss of international reputation for moral decency, its disgrace in the eyes of many Muslims, and the numerous innocent lives that U.S. policy destroyed. Similarly, in 2002, the Defense Department proclaimed that its interrogation techniques applied only to prisoners at Guantánamo Bay. However, as we have already seen, they quickly migrated to Iraq with horrific results. A more careful analysis of military institutions would consider such possibilities, yet Bagaric and Clarke proffer only optimistic assertions about how institutions ideally behave. Finally, as Joseph Margulies details, after Guantánamo opened tyrants like Charles Taylor of Liberia and Robert Mugabe of Zimbabwe attacked journalists and others using the concept of "enemy combatant."[56] When criticized, they cited U.S. policy to excuse their crimes. Naturally, we cannot expect tyrants to protect human rights simply because the United States does. However, U.S. torture undermined international efforts to respect moral norms. Guilty of terrible acts, the United States robbed itself of the capacity to credibly enforce moral norms.

Perhaps, however, legalized torture would expose abuses, allowing us to hold evildoers accountable for their crimes.[57] Given the many actors in international relations, however, we cannot know if such a result would obtain. To assess its possibility, we would need to understand how hundreds of diverse countries and millions of people would respond to legalized torture. Surely, Hayek and Hardin are correct in saying that we simply lack such information. Often, we cannot even predict how citizens within one government will respond to policies. How can we expect to understand how others in the international arena will react when the world's most powerful country legalizes torture? Strategic interaction creates huge measurement problems in international relations, but Bagaric and Clarke seem blissfully unaware of them.

Bagaric and Clarke also completely overlook spiritual values. Their conception of happiness reverses the hierarchy of values that many religious people affirm. Theists identify a proper relationship to God as the most important good in their lives. Buddhists may emphasize that *nirvana* (ultimate peace or the final goal of the Buddhist life) guides all they do. Socrates embraced moral integrity over life choosing to ingest the poison hemlock rather than compromise his ideals. Instead of such noble ends, Bagaric and Clarke offer empirical studies of what some people think constitutes happiness. Like many consequentialists, they reduce complex spiritual ends to trite ideas like a "faith community." In fact, Bagaric and Clarke never acknowledge that millions of people might value spiritual goods over material ones. If they considered this possibility, they would realize that they are entirely overconfident in their utilitarian calculus. How, for example, can their formula measure communication without loss? How can it quantify self-possession and how it relates to physical integrity? In sum, Bagaric and Clarke assume a shallow value theory. Unfortunately, in its brashness, it resembles many consequentialist approaches to torture.[58] Public discussion of torture since September 11 has been marred by superficial understandings of consequences and endless renditions of ticking bomb scenarios. In light of important developments in economics and social thought, such analyses are deeply flawed.

Consequentialist Responses

To some people, the demand for precisely measuring consequences seems excessive. We often make family or work decisions by roughly gauging consequences. Should I accept a job that increases my salary but takes me away from my family? Should I subject my children to vaccinations given the small risk they present? If we cannot precisely measure consequences, we seem hopelessly at sea in our personal lives. Yet, somehow we make decisions and therefore, something seems amiss in the demand to precisely measure consequences.

Hayek and Hardin, in fact, see measurement problems as reason to embrace consequentialism. They insist that because we lack complete information about actions, we must rely on institutions and rules to guide decisions. As I have already noted, Hayek resists the label utilitarianism, but argues that rules are "a device for coping with our constitutional ignorance" about our acts' consequences.[59] Customs, traditions, and moral rules arise for complex reasons that we often cannot understand. However, they play an indispensable role in reducing ignorance, and without them, we would be paralyzed. John Gray calls Hayek's argument "indirect utilitarianism," because with it, "the proper role of utility is not prescriptive or practical, but rather that of a standard of evaluation for the assessment of whole systems of rules or practices."[60] We evaluate a rule system by considering whether it would help an anonymous person maximize her pursuit of unknown future purposes.

Hardin provides a similar analysis that he calls "institutional utilitarianism." It "establishes rules for conduct in typical cases and leaves some freedom to the relevant parties to work out their own better solutions or to recur to political institutions to prevent others from violating the rules."[61] Contracts, rights, and principles of justice all exemplify institutional utilitarianism. Hardin distinguishes his view from rule utilitarianism by emphasizing institutional force. Rule utilitarianism affirms rules of thumb that guide action, but which we discard when they lack utility. It often adopts a highly individualist conception of social rules. In contrast, institutional utilitarianism assumes that institutions enforce rules for the general welfare. Moreover, we alter them only with great care because alterations carry significant costs, and we often cannot know whether new institutional arrangement will be beneficial. We must, then, never carelessly discard rules. Thus, institutional utilitarianism adopts a long-term and piecemeal approach to rules.

To illustrate institutional utilitarianism, let me return to vaccinations. A government worried about bioterrorism might vaccinate against smallpox, thus preventing an epidemic that would kill millions. However, it knows that some people will be allergic to the vaccine and be harmed by it. As a child, I was one of these victims and became very ill after receiving the smallpox vaccine. Considering such cases, Hardin maintains that we "cannot know in advance who will be losers from it. Government acts, therefore, as if from a principle of insufficient reason and supposes it cannot distinguish differences between citizens or the targets of its policies in advance."[62] In some cases, it possesses enough information about how policies will affect particular individuals or groups. It can then devise policies with this knowledge in hand.

However, in cases like vaccination, a government may never know precisely whom the policy will affect, knowing only its overall beneficial consequences. For Hardin, this mixture of knowledge and ignorance characterizes much of social and political life.

Hardin applies institutional utilitarianism to topics such as rights. Going back to Mill, utilitarianism has often justified rights by appealing to utility. Hardin adopts this strategy, arguing that rights are "institutional devices for reducing the burden of gathering information and calculating consequences."[63] They are not absolute, but instead constitute important rules supported by institutional force. For example, in a particular case, we may discover that respecting private property yields a poor outcome. We retain a right to it because it helps us deal with incomplete information and enables agents to make optimal choices. We abandon it only if we discover that it systematically harms people. We are not, then, compelled to adhere to rights in a changing society. They will be effective in some societies and ineffective in others. We may change rights, but we should never suddenly overturn an entire legal system. On this understanding, rights originate not in the person's nature, but in the role they play in promoting general welfare.

Similarly, Hayek proposes "immanent criticism" of social rules, maintaining that the "test by which we can judge the appropriateness of a particular rule will always be some other rule which for the purpose in hand we regard as unquestioned."[64] Thus, we criticize a rule from within a tradition always considering how people will respond to changes. We "frequently know that a certain kind of action will be harmful, but neither we (nor the legislator) nor the acting person will know whether that will be the case in a particular instance."[65] Hayek thus proposes that we change rules by carefully considering how they relate to other rules.

Hardin and Hayek provide a sophisticated defense of institutional utilitarianism that those in the torture debate should consider. Rights, rules, norms, and regimes enable us to cope with the information gaps arising from strategic interactions. Institutional consequentialism is well suited for dealing with contemporary institutions. Because of their size and scope, they create numerous information problems. Many indispensable rules arise spontaneously to meet these problems. We often forget how they originated and cannot expect a full consequentialist defense of them. Simplistic appeals to maximizing happiness cannot explain what happens when millions of people interact. In sum, Hayek and Hardin enrich our understanding of rules and social interactions in a complex world.

No Protection against Torture

Unfortunately, institutional consequentialism cannot protect us from torture. Let us consider, for example, Hayek's immanent criticism. It cannot explain which rules to embrace within a system. We operate not within hermetically sealed rule systems, but in a legal environment with domestic and international law. International law strongly opposes torture, but some American jurists and politicians take guidance only from American law. They insist that American politicians should avoid drawing on international law. Others see this approach as profoundly myopic because it prevents us from learning from other societies. How should we adjudicate between these different approaches to the law? Both appeal to existing systems of rules guiding our conduct. Hayek offers no clear criterion for deciding between bodies of law or for dealing with conflicts between them. Second, even assuming we know which system to embrace, we will experience difficulty ascertaining which rules to adopt. Sadly, torture appeared prominently in many European societies for centuries.[66] Europeans and Americans also tortured in Algeria, Vietnam, Kenya, and elsewhere. Like private property and liberty, torture is a part of the Western tradition. Given its long historical pedigree, why not revive it? Confronting terrorism, some Americans are perfectly willing to take this step to protect themselves. Immanent criticism offers no protection against their demand for security at all costs.

We can see further dangers of institutional utilitarianism by considering what Hayek says about human value. Later in life, he authored a powerful critique of socialism that emphasized cultural evolution.[67] In it, he insists that "mere existence cannot confer a right or moral claim on anyone."[68] For Hayek, human rights arise entirely because of social rules or practices. Unless a person participates in a web of social relations, she possesses no moral value. Such a position ignores our value as spiritual beings, which no social rule or institution creates. Rules recognize an already existing value inherent in human nature. Without such a conception, we will have great difficulty resisting calls to torture.

Similarly, Hardin offers little defense against torture. He maintains that in the War on Terror, we cannot retain absolute rules about civil liberties. For him, act-based moral theories refuse to make moral trade-offs, and therefore, cannot respond adequately to terrorism. They are "irrelevant for the judgment of devices for dealing with terrorism in its new international, world-wide high tech form in which the costs of delivering pain can be dwarfed by the scale of the pain delivered."[69] For Hardin, we must adapt our ethic to changing circumstances and cannot hold that torture is always evil. On institutional utilitarian grounds, it may not pass moral muster because we know so little about its efficacy. Nevertheless, in some (albeit rare) circumstances, we might need to torture, and the morally responsible leader concedes this possibility.

Ultimately, Hardin and Hayek provide no defense against torture because they embrace subjectivist theories of value. Hardin repeatedly makes statements like "we commonly assert, with Hume, and rightly so, that values are not objective."[70] For him, no value resides in objects, and utility is "a coherent notion only at a subjective level. It is utility to you or to me that interests us."[71] Hayek embraces a similar value subjectivism stating that value, is "not an attribute or physical property possessed by things themselves, irrespective of their relations to men, but solely an aspect of these relations that enables men to take account opportunities others might have for their use."[72] Values gradually develop over time, guided by needs and emotions, and do not adhere in persons or objects.

Hardin and Hayek defend value subjectivism by discussing phenomena like prices, but fail to sustain their thesis. For example, Hardin criticizes Bentham for vacillating between subjectivist and objectivist value theories. He should have recognized, Hardin maintains, that no value resides in physical objects. Gold, for example, is no more inherently valuable than bronze. People pay different prices for metals depending on markets and social expectations. This example cannot, however, establish a subjectivist theory of value. Many artifacts have conventional value differing from society to society. Modern economists convincingly demonstrate profound difficulties with grounding price theory in objects. Nevertheless, we need not conclude that all value is subjective. For example, notwithstanding the price people might pay, a person's value exceeds that of even the most exquisitely made chair. Someone valuing the chair more than the person suffers from a profound value perversion. Thus, Hardin errs by moving from the conventional value of artifacts to value subjectivism. For measurement purposes, economists might assume value subjectivity. They might also object to introducing metaphysical conceptions of the person into a social science. Such responses are legitimate subjects for debate among economists, but philosophically, we are under no obligation to endorse value subjectivism.

By adopting value subjectivism, moreover, Hardin and Hayek abandon a clear conception of the person's value. They draw on sources like

David Hume, neo-Kantianism, and evolutionary theory, all of which lack a metaphysical defense of the person's value.[73] Of course, a person operates within a tradition of rules, customs, or laws, but she can transcend it and inquire about larger wholes. She can not only consider the good for one society, but also inquire about the human good per se. We are not, as Hayek falsely suggests, condemned to believe that we must "always stop with our criticism at something that has no better ground for existence than that it is the accepted basis "of a tradition."[74] As spiritual beings, we can seek goods transcending particular traditions. This capacity enables us to recognize the person's value and use it as a norm to evaluate social rules. Hayek offers no convincing reason to deny our transcendence, instead making unconvincing appeals to ethical subjectivism.

Hardin also robs himself of critical resources by neglecting the spiritual person. For example, he acknowledges that for "any theory of human welfare, a fundamental issue is the nature of the individual person."[75] However, like many utilitarians he embraces a shallow conception of the person whose identity is a "matter of constancy of personal character and preferences in the face of constantly renewed molecular structure, and more interestingly, of slowly changing experience."[76] Rather than recognizing the person as a spiritual–physical center of activity, he describes how she weakly or strongly identifies with herself over time. A being willingly to sacrifice future interests for immediate gain possesses weak identification, whereas one considering future interests has strong identification. Hardin also discusses integrated and motley conceptions of the self. A motley self is a disordered collection of desires or reasons, whereas an integrated one links desire and reason into coherently. In these discussions of the self, Hardin displays no recognition of the valuable elements of our interior life. He leaves us with only a subjective sense of self, a precarious unity that easily disintegrates under torture.

With their deficient theories of value, Hardin and Hayek reveal why we need a proper conception of the person. I have focused on them at length because they offer a compelling ethic that withstands the standard criticisms of consequentialism. Nevertheless, despite their insights, they resemble many contemporary thinkers who have lost a rich sense of human nature. They fail to recognize that the person is valuable regardless of subjective preferences or particular social rules. His value originates in a spiritual–material nature, and without recognizing it, we cannot hope to protect people from torture.

Conclusion

Many citizens, intellectuals, and politicians find consequentialist approaches to torture attractive. They seem responsible and rational, unlike the emotional outbursts erupting in torture debates. However, if we explore consequentialism carefully, its rationality crumbles. Despite hypothetical, historical, or contemporary examples, we have little evidence that torture is a reliable social practice. Undoubtedly effective in some cases, we have scant evidence of its long-range effectiveness. This paucity of evidence seems endemic to the subject. Despite horrific twentieth-century human subject research, we have few controlled torture experiments. Other than using detailed studies of torture's efficacy, we cannot measure its overall utility. Perhaps it was effective in the Italian Renaissance, but ineffective in ancient China. Instead of intellectual responsibility, then, torture advocates offer anecdotes or pretenses to scientific objectivity.

Consequentialist defenses of torture also display remarkable naïveté about measuring consequences. Hayek, Hardin, and others demonstrate how strategic interaction creates quantification problems. Because an act's consequences depend on how others behave, a consequentialist must predict how multiple agents will act. Undoubtedly, in small communities we can measure consequences fairly easily. With intimate knowledge of neighbors and their needs, we can predict how they will respond to our actions. However, once we move beyond small communities, we confront considerable ignorance about consequences. We cannot dispel it by inventing better computer software or producing more rigorous social-scientific research. Instead, it remains irremediable, present as long as we have complex agents interacting.

Measurement difficulties become more acute if we think about spiritual realities. We cannot divide and measure them. Religious traditions have for centuries developed practices for enhancing them, but they bear little resemblance to quantification. Instead, they rely on reflection, prayer, or meditation. Through them, the person, her loved ones, and community ascertain spiritual progress or regression. Policy makers have only general awareness of such practices, and those claiming greater precision merely display their ignorance.

We can mitigate this ignorance by embracing institutional consequentialism, but by itself it cannot adequately ground morality. Any responsible moral agent must consider consequences and should learn from institutional consequentialism. However, it ignores the person's remarkable value and embraces mistaken epistemological and metaphys-ical ideas. Consequently, institutional consequentialism cannot protect us against torture, particularly when terrorism tempts us to use it.

Perhaps, however, we must torture even if we affirm the person's value. For some, torture presents an inescapable choice between evils. Choices in such circumstances seem fundamentally irrational or tragic. On this understanding, neither absolute opposition to torture nor utili-tarian calculus aids us. To this possibility, the problem of "dirty hands," I now turn.

CHAPTER FIVE

No Reason to Torture: Dirty Hands and Spiritual Damage

Such methods are exceedingly cruel, and are repugnant to any community, not only to a Christian one. It behooves, therefore, every man to shun them, and to prefer rather to live as a private citizen than as a king with such ruination of men to his score. None the less, for the sort of man who is unwilling to take up this first course of well doing, it is expedient, should he wish to hold what he has, to enter on the path of wrong doing. Actually, however, most men prefer to steer a middle course, which is very harmful: for they know not how to be wholly good nor how to be wholly bad.

Machiavelli[1]

Many people find pure consequentialism calculating and insensitive. They may sometimes support torture, but feel it is still wrong. They may also reject the demand for precision in political life viewing it as hubristic. Political actors operate in a confusing world of imperfect information and demands for immediate action. Unlike academic theorists, they make no pretence to possessing perfect knowledge and cannot calculate all consequences of their action. Given the dangerous arena of politics, how can politicians completely justify their actions? All they can do is make rough estimates of consequences hoping to protect spiritual and material goods. They often confront intense clashes of obligations admitting of no easy resolution. They must act, but any action yields tragedy.

The position I just sketched is known as the "dirty hands" approach to political ethics and has received considerable support in recent years.

In this chapter, I explore and reject it. First, using Michael Walzer's work, I outline the main features of the dirty hands approach. I supplement Walzer's account with Jean Bethke Elshtain's recent theological defense of dirty hands. Second, I describe how dirty hands theorists presuppose a universe marked by irresolvable moral conflicts. Third, I maintain that the dirty hands approach captures important elements of our experience with torture. It acknowledges political and spiritual conflicts and shows how political leaders confront terrible choices. Fourth, however, I argue that like pure consequentialism, the dirty hands approach cannot measure consequences and relies on ill-defined conceptions of political prudence. I also show how its appeal to moral emotion provides no reason to torture. Fifth, I maintain that the dirty hands approach ignores how torture ruptures the person's being and damages communities. To illustrate this damage, I discuss how the Bush administration abandoned Common Article Three of the Geneva Conventions. Although this decision seemed sound on dirty hands grounds, it disregarded the person's value and yielded devastating consequences. Finally, I call for an absolute ban on torture rejecting arguments that it is morally self-indulgent and hypocritical. I illustrate this ban's importance by discussing a torture case in Germany arguing that it helps us distinguish between objective wrongness and subjective culpability.

The Dirty Hands Approach

The dirty hands approach maintains that in politics, some actions are "justified, even obligatory, but nonetheless wrong and shameful."[2] Long part of political thought, its advocates include Max Weber, Jean Paul Sartre, Walzer, and others. Unlike pure consequentialists, dirty hands thinkers make no pretence about resolving our revulsion at torture. Instead, they acknowledge torture's wrongness, at the same time recognizing its necessity and moral legitimacy.

Let us listen to Walzer's well-known and eloquent defense of the dirty hands position. In politics, Walzer tells us, no one can remain morally pure. A politician confronts a world in which some actions are clearly wrong, and we cannot dispel their wrongness through utilitarian calculus.[3] This means that "a particular act of government (in a political party or in the state) may be exactly the right thing to do in utilitarian terms and yet leave the man who does it guilty of a moral wrong."[4] Rejecting utilitarianism, Walzer notes that the moral life is "constituted at least in part by rules, the knowing of which (and perhaps the making of which) we share with our fellows. The experience of coming up against these rules, challenging their prohibitions, and explaining ourselves to other men and women is so common and so obviously important that no account of moral decision-making can possibly fail to come to grips with it."[5] When breaking moral rules, agents can offer excuses. Excuses acknowledge wrongdoing but not justifications and differ from justifications, which constitute a "denial of fault and an assertion of innocence."[6] Walzer blocks the easy exit of justification, insisting instead that dirty hands politicians can only excuse themselves.

In defending excuse over justification, Walzer maintains that breaking moral rules leaves a moral residue. Broken rules "still stand and have this much effect at least: that we know we have done something wrong even if what we have done was also the best thing to do on the whole in the circumstances."[7] Responding to this moral residue, agents should feel guilt and remorse. The dilemma of dirty hands, then, arises because political actors must sometimes break rules, but know they commit wrongdoing. They experience the anguish of an unavoidable, tragic choice.

Analyzing works by Machiavelli, Weber, and Albert Camus, Walzer proposes a public response to torturers. We want politicians to feel anguish when they torture, but cannot leave the problem of dirty hands "entirely within the confines of the individual conscience."[8] Like those engaging in civil disobedience, leaders violating moral norms "go beyond a moral or legal limit, in order to do what they believe they should do. At the same time, they acknowledge their responsibility for the violation by accepting punishment or doing penance."[9] However, the state rarely punishes an agent for moral violations. Consequently, we must subject him to public approbation and condemnation. We should "honor him for the good he has done," and punish him for breaking moral norms.[10] Walzer, thus, insists that dirty hands politicians should both feel remorse and undergo public penance.

Walzer's account of political ethics has obvious implications for contemporary torture debates. In extreme situations, a politician may decide to torture an al-Qaeda suspect. We should not render this decision easy by removing its awful character. Moreover, we should avoid absolving him of responsibility for his terrible act. We hold that torture is wrong, but recognize that leaders sometimes must use it to protect the common good. We also develop institutional mechanisms for acknowledging the rightness and wrongness of the torturer's acts.

Endorsing Walzer's account of dirty hands, Elshtain adds theological dimensions to it. Discussing those who torture in extreme situations, she argues that "within Christian moral thinking, and the tradition of casuistry that arose from it, the statesman or stateswoman has another chance. He and she can stand before God as a guilty person and seek forgiveness."[11] Rather than rigidly adhering to absolute prohibitions against torture, a Christian politician must grapple with moral ambiguity. Unlike Dershowitz, Elshtain opposes legalizing torture arguing that legal sanction removes its horrible character and encourages people to torture. However, a politician may be forced to torture if the alternative is catastrophe because "neighbor-regard in Christian moral thinking ranks concrete responsibility ahead of rigid rule-following."[12] Those refusing to torture adopt a legalistic "code-fetishism" or "pietistic rigorism" that values moral purity over people's lives.[13] In contrast, neighbor-regard "involves concern for forms of life and how best to make life at least slightly more just or, to cast it negatively, slightly less unjust."[14] One should incur moral guilt "when the lives of others are at stake."[15] Elshtain thus departs from the idea that torture is always wrong, maintaining instead it might be necessary in rare circumstances.

A Universe of Irresolvable Conflicts

In addition to defending the occasional recourse to torture, dirty hands theorists embrace a particular conception of moral conflict. Despite their many differences, Machiavelli, Weber, Reinhold Niebuhr, Thomas Nagel, and Bernard Williams all maintain that moral conflict reveals contingency in political life. For example, Machiavelli famously depicts Fortune's power. Confronting violence and continual change, he maintains, we are lucky if we can control half our actions.[16] Most of the time, we find ourselves swept up like flotsam on Florence's Arno river, completely unable to control our destiny. In this world, we should expect terrible conflicts of values. Similarly, in Weber, we see a clash of irrational forces. A politician "lets himself in for the diabolic forces lurking in all violence," knowing he will often commit horrible acts.[17] He anguishes over the wrongs he must do, and "one cannot prescribe to anyone whether he should follow an ethic of absolute ends or an ethic of responsibility, or when the one and when the other."[18] Each individual must choose how to resolve moral dilemmas. Reinhold Niebuhr describes a "constant and seemingly irreconcilable conflict between the needs of society and the imperatives of a sensitive conscience."[19] A group leader feels this tension and knows that she cannot eliminate it. For Niebuhr, politics is a tragic arena of conflict and contingency.

Philosopher Thomas Nagel also emphasizes irresolvable moral conflict. Discussing absolutist and utilitarian approaches to war, he suggests we "face the pessimistic alternative that these two forms of moral intuition are not capable of being brought together into a coherent moral system, and that the world can present us with situations in which there is no honorable or moral course for a man to take, no course free of guilt and responsibility for evil."[20] He calls these situations a "moral blind alley," emphasizing that it appears often in political life. For Nagel, the world is structured in a way that places us in irresolvable conflicts.[21]

Similarly, Williams argues that human beings often confront an intense conflict of values. Such conflict, he maintains, "is not necessarily pathological at all, but something necessarily involved in human values."[22] Williams links value conflict to a powerful conception of contingency in human life. For example, in a well-known essay on moral luck, he denies that the "disposition to correct moral judgment and the objects of such judgment" are "free from external contingency."[23] Dirty hands conflicts reveal the bankruptcy of attempts to completely avoid contingency because "there is a plurality of values which can conflict with one another and which are not reducible to one another" and "we cannot conceive of a situation in which it was true both that all value-conflict had been eliminated, and that there had been no loss of value on the way."[24] For Williams, value conflicts constantly threaten to undermine our internal coherence.

Dirty Hands: An Attractive Position

At first glance, the dirty hands approach to torture is deeply attractive. First, it avoids utilitarianism's shallow and technological approach to ethics. Posner, Yoo, and others think we can do simple cost–benefit analyses of torture. For them, a torturer may find her task unpleasant, but should have a clear conscience. Such a position is cold and inhumane and ignores difficult moral conflicts. In contrast, Walzer, Elshtain, and others retain our normal horror at torture. Second, the dirty hands approach captures the complexities of political life. It is too easy to stand outside of politics and condemn political actors for their actions. The president of the United States has access to intelligence reports of constant threats against the United States. He must act quickly and decisively with imperfect information. For example, after September 11, a climate of fear gripped the federal government. Politicians confronted situations in which "whether and how aggressively to check the terrorist threat" was rarely obvious.[25] They faced "blizzards of frightening threat reports" and were often "blinded by ignorance and desperately worried about not doing enough."[26] In this environment, moral purity seems like a luxury.

The emphasis of the dirty hands approach on conflict should also appeal to those aware of our spiritual nature. Dirty hands thinkers often aspire to overturn simplistic conceptions of moral agency that supposedly resolve all value conflicts.[27] Few thinkers aware of our spirituality would adopt such a bizarre idea. We may not be aliens trapped between spirit and matter, as Plotinus sometimes suggests. However, because we are embodied spirits, we experience profound and seemingly irresolvable conflicts. The body rebels against the spirit refusing to accept its influence. The spirit may be divided, torn by anguish, or unable to accomplish its moral and spiritual goals. Spiritual perversions like pride and distrust separate people, creating intense political and social conflicts. Thus, with a proper conception of the human person, we should expect politics to be conflictual. Dirty hands thinkers deserve credit for illuminating this conflict.

The dirty hands approach also offers a noble picture of political life. Undoubtedly, leaders get their hands dirty, but do so for the common good. As Machiavelli once put it when commenting about Florentine citizens battling Pope Gregory XI in 1375, so much higher did those citizens value their city than their souls![28] Weber agrees emphasizing that despite its tragic character the political vocation retains a noble quality. Politicians often do what the rest of us will not or cannot do. In a world where so many despise politics, the dirty hands approach reminds us of its dignity.

Dirty Hands Confusions

Despite these attractions, scholars criticize the dirty hands approach in several ways. First, they maintain that it holds that moral agents must perform an incoherent act. A dirty hands politician it seems "must do wrong to do right. But that, if not a contradiction, is at least a paradox. It would seem that *one cannot logically do what is right by doing what is wrong.*"[29] Second, critics of the dirty hands conception target its claims about remorse. Remorse is "constitutive of the reflection, 'I ought not to have acted in that wrongful way' placing the primary focus on the agent's voluntary role in performing, or participating in, or allowing a particular action that results in moral violation."[30] Remorse in dirty hands circumstances seems irrational and inappropriate. If torturing a terrorist is necessary and morally legitimate, why should I feel remorse? I might regret that evil people force me to torture or feel sad because I must violently stop terrorists. However, these emotions differ from remorse, which implies I have done something wrong. Walzer seems particularly confused when calling for public acts of penance for dirty hands politicians. If the politician has done the right thing to protect the common good, why punish her? Similarly, Elshtain's invocation of God's forgiveness disconcerts. Undoubtedly, *after* a person has sinned, she may seek divine forgiveness. However, Elshtain seems to counsel a person to *knowingly* sin, and then seek forgiveness. How can such a position be coherent?

In what follows, I assume the dirty hands approach is logically coherent and that remorse is appropriate. Williams works out the logic of moral conflicts emphasizing technical matters in deontic logic that I pass over.[31] More importantly, he carefully analyzes moral emotions describing why remorse is sensible in dirty hands situations. For example, he develops the concept of agent-regret, an emotion we experience when doing something terrible but unavoidable. Agent-regret implies that it would be better if things had been otherwise, and it comes in different forms. A lorry (taxi) driver "who through no fault of his own runs over a child, will feel differently from a spectator next to him in the cab."[32] He will want to compensate his victim somehow. Williams convincingly shows that such emotions are perfectly rational. Others like philosopher Stephen De Wijze bolster his case arguing for the "tragic remorse" that comes with "violating both a cherished moral value and being part of the causal process of furthering the immoral projects of others."[33] These treatments of dirty hands remorse cannot entirely dispel its paradoxical character but go a long way toward explaining it.

Rather than tackling these well-worn topics, I maintain instead that the dirty hands approach offers little guidance for politicians or citizens because it cannot coherently measure consequences. Walzer may think it self-evident that a colonial police chief should torture a terrorist with a bomb, but many people disagree. They might insist that he accept the consequences of his refusal to torture. With such differences, Walzer must demonstrate why torture is the preferable option. How does he calculate consequences? Over what period of time does he consider them? Walzer never seriously addresses these problems, instead constructing examples based on intuitions and emotions. We see a similar problem in Weber's ethic of responsibility. At one point in his remarkable essay on politics as a vocation, he says that a politician "is aware of a responsibility for the consequences of his action and really feels such responsibility with heart and soul. He then acts by following an ethic of responsibility, and somewhere he reaches the point where he says: 'Here I stand; I can do no other.'"[34] Unfortunately, Weber never explains how politicians make such decisions. Are they entirely a subjective matter, or do we have public criteria for them? No answer is forthcoming from Weber. Finally, Elshtain never explains how an American politician acting in complex institutions can calculate the consequences of torture. Instead, she plays on our emotions and intuitions and tags dissenters with various unpleasant labels.

Dirty hands proponents also rarely discuss the difficulties in measuring spiritual consequences. How do they calculate spiritual values or goods? Walzer and others never mention this problem and seem oblivious to the problem of quantifying immaterial realities. In most cases, they simply ignore them. Without a more serious treatment of this issue, however, they leave politicians and citizens bereft of resources for thinking about torture. Rather than ethical clarity, we have muddled thinking that leaves our consciences confused.

Too often, dirty hands theorists also mistakenly believe that by itself a phenomenology of dirty hands can justify torture. However, given uncertainties about consequences, I may resolve moral conflict by refusing to torture. When confronted with terrorism, I may experience terrible internal conflicts. I may deeply regret failing to bring an evil person to justice. I may wonder if I have done the right thing or feel agent-regret because something terrible happened. Finally, I may recognize potential moral and material losses for my country. However, without greater precision about consequences, I have no overriding reason to torture. I will experience deep conflicts no matter how I choose. Appealing to intuitions or emotions cannot help me in this situation. Dirty hands proponents devise sensational examples about innocents who will die unless we torture. However, those opposing torture can respond with equally sensational stories about how torture produces disastrous results. Once again, we have appeals and counter-appeals to intuition and anecdote that give us no reason to torture.

Perhaps, however, we can rely on political prudence to tell us when to torture. The prudent person needs no formulae or rules because she understands when to act in the right circumstances. Prudence determines "the proper roads" to practical goals.[35] Perhaps by demanding precision we fundamentally misunderstand political prudence. This is the force of Machiavelli's famous and deeply controversial argument about *virtù* (variously defined as "ingenuity" or "will"). The person of *virtù*, Machiavelli maintains, uses violence decisively, possesses foresight and an understanding of Fortune (*fortuna*), and changes his character with the times.[36] For Machiavelli, politics requires its own prudence, and we cannot artificially prejudge situations requiring its exercise.

Undoubtedly, political actors require prudence and cannot develop detailed blueprints for political action. However, in matters as serious as torture, we cannot disengage prudence from a proper conception of the person. Too often, Machiavelli, Weber, and others ask us to trust leaders to magically do the right thing. Even assuming politicians of the highest moral character, such trust is neither justified nor desirable. Torture unleashes terrible consequences on victims and institutions. Unlike Weber's tragic hero or Walzer's torn colonial administrator, modern politicians operate within institutions requiring rules and virtues. When a leader acts or speaks, she influences an entire chain of command. In such contexts, we cannot allow her freedom to torture. Most importantly, prudence cannot undermine what we owe persons as spiritual beings. For example, we do not rely on prudence to decide when to rape because rape is so horrific that we should avoid deliberating about it altogether. Aristotle recognized this point long ago when he noted that some actions "have names that already imply badness," and "it is not possible, then, ever to be right with regard to them; one must always be wrong."[37] Torture so demeans the person that we cannot leave it to ill-defined prudence to define its moral legitimacy. Instead, we must demand justification from our leaders. Large institutions and societies must be "governed by an explicable order which allows those agencies to be answerable. In a public, large and impersonal forum, 'intuition' will not serve."[38] We also cannot use prudence as an excuse for relying on private and subjective judgments.

Ill-defined prudence also leads leaders dangerously astray because they delink it from goodness. However, he "alone can do good who knows what things are like and what their situation is."[39] The political leader disregarding the person's value loses her moral compass. She makes short-term moral judgments offering an "arbitrary, short-circuiting resort to 'faith' or some other magical capacity."[40] Such irrationality often produces disaster masquerading as true prudence. Theologians and philosophers have long recognized the dangers of such a counterfeit.

Americans battling terrorism must work particularly hard to link prudence and the person's value. In his account of his tenure at the Office of Legal Counsel during the Bush administration, Jack Goldsmith captures the challenges facing a contemporary U.S. president. Public support for tough action against terrorism is likely to be short lived in democratic regimes. In fact, ironically, the more successfully a president fights terrorism, the more complacent the public may become. However, the battle against al-Qaeda and its affiliates will continue to be "characterized by unremitting fear of devastating attack, an obsession with preventing an attack, and a proclivity to act aggressively and preemptively to do so."[41] The U.S. president's "most fundamental challenge" will be to "establish adequate trust with the American people to allow the American President to take the steps needed to fight an enemy that the public does not see and in some respects cannot comprehend."[42] Often, the president will need to quickly and decisively respond to threats. Confronting such difficult decisions, he must justify his actions, rather than asking the public to irrationally follow him. More importantly, he cannot lose a moral compass grounded in the person's dignity. Otherwise, he will succumb to pressure to use torture and other immoral means.

Dirty Hands and Spiritual Damage

By ignoring spiritual values, the dirty hands proponents also fail to see how torture damages spiritual beings. Refusing to torture may result in negative consequences, but the will to torture diminishes the person. It "destroys itself by destroying the good which is its subject."[43] Recall, we shape our character through intransitive acts remaining within us. When we deliberately undermine another's transcendence and self-possession, we create an internal absence or fissure. The torturer "frustrates, nihilates, renders sterile" the good in her.[44] We have difficulty articulating this inner sterility because of its emptiness but can recognize its unstable character. Those sensitive to their crimes may confront them years after they tortured and struggle to make recompense. Others may simply ignore their internal poison, rationalizing it away with appeals to duty or their important place in history. However, the fissure in their being "remains latent" within them and is bound to appear in some manner.[45] Once we have tortured, our action "is there and will be there as the core for all later interpretations and reactions; we cannot interpret it any way we like, and only some reactions are appropriate to it"[46] Dirty hands proponents rarely acknowledge such a profound spiritual destruction.

A torturer also introduces a pernicious instability into the body politic that may fester for years. Undoubtedly, with immediate success, "evil and injustice enjoy a seemingly infinite power," but this success eventually yields disorder.[47] Unstable forces may not appear to those perpetuating evil, particularly if they stubbornly proclaim their own righteousness. Spiritually, however, we know that an evil will unleashes unwanted and undesirable forces. In fact, evil may pass from one person to another through a perverse kind of transitive action.[48] Unless a person rejects it, it retains a "power of reproduction by which it must always bring forth more evil."[49] Those harmed are "stirred to react in more or less crafty ways of evil-doing."[50] This reaction may appear in torture victims long after they have been tortured. For example, in the Iraq War, the United States arrested and abused thousands of Iraqis generating profound resentments. Sometimes, those tortured ended up aiding the insurgency against the United States. In other cases, torture produced an abiding hatred of the United States that may appear in future generations. We cannot calculate exactly how these spiritual perversions will affect institutions in Iraq but know they will likely appear. Such a dynamic has played itself out in countries such as Israel and Northern Ireland.

Given how little we know about future consequences, we cannot ascertain precisely how much evil torture produces. Perhaps good forces and choices will heal its destruction. Nevertheless, when thinking about torture, we know that it often produces pernicious tendencies. Maritain calls such fruition the "historical fructifications of good and evil," meaning that good acts have a tendency to enhance communities, whereas evil ones tend to undermine them.[51] Inductively, we can collect historical evidence of how evil poisons institutions, but understand its instability primarily by considering the spiritual personality. A being turning against the good cannot avoid infecting others with his perverted acts.

Spiritual Damage: A Case Study

The language of historical fructification may seem too abstract, so let me illustrate it with the example of how the Bush administration abandoned the Geneva Conventions. As Mayer notes about this decision, "of all the complicated legal arguments made by the Bush Administration in the first months after September 11, none more directly cleared that way for torture than this."[52] In the immediate aftermath of September 11, President Bush convened an interagency group to consider how to handle suspected terrorists. A small number of administration officials cut short its deliberations by secretly composing memoranda authorizing military commissions to try suspected terrorists.[53] Excluding National Security Advisor Condoleezza Rice and Secretary of State Colin Powell, this group presented a military commissions document to President Bush, who immediately signed it. When he later requested advice about the Geneva Conventions, military lawyers (JAGs) and Secretary Powell strongly opposed jettisoning them. Secretary of State Powell warned that doing so would "reverse over a century of U.S. policy and practice supporting the Geneva Conventions" and produce "immediate adverse consequences for our conduct of foreign policy."[54] William Taft, legal advisor to the State Department, cautioned that "any small benefit from reducing" the U.S. commitment to the Geneva Conventions "will be purchased at the expense of the men and women in our armed forces we send into combat."[55] Nevertheless, Attorney General John Ashcroft and then legal counsel to the president Alberto Gonzales opposed Taft and Powell. Infamously, Gonzales declared that the War on Terror ushered in a "new paradigm" that "renders obsolete Geneva's strict limitations on questioning enemy prisoners and renders quaint some of its provisions requiring that captured enemy are afforded such things as commissary privileges, scrip (i.e. advances of monthly pay), athletic uniforms, and scientific instruments."[56] Other Bush administration officials held similar views about the Geneva Conventions.

Despite opposition, President Bush decided that the Geneva Conventions offer no protection to al-Qaeda members. Rather than considering captured prisoners on a case-by-case basis to ascertain their combatant status, he stated that "none of the provisions of Geneva apply to our conflict with al-Qaeda in Afghanistan or elsewhere throughout the world because, among other reasons, al-Qaeda is not a High Contracting Party to Geneva."[57] Fatefully, he also maintained that "the relevant conflicts are international in scope and Article 3 applies only to 'armed conflict not of an international character.' "[58] He urged Americans to treat prisoners humanely even if they lacked Geneva protections.

On dirty hands grounds, we can develop a strong case that President Bush made a good decision. Jack Goldsmith, Ron Suskind, and others capture the tremendous fear gripping leaders and federal agencies after the September 11 attacks. The president had little accurate intelligence about al-Qaeda and anticipated further attacks. He needed to act decisively on very limited information. In such an atmosphere, secrecy seemed a necessary means for protecting the nation. A president who went through all bureaucratic hoops might encounter crippling obstacles to stopping terrorists. Deception was also vital because modern bureaucracies leak information to the press. It might also enable the president to address the constant legal challenges impeding swift action against terrorists. Finally, a president who uncritically adhered to the Geneva Conventions would be guilty of rule worship and would favor his own moral integrity over the country's safety. In sum, it seems that a responsible politician would act exactly as President Bush did.

For some Americans, President Bush's decision also made sense because al-Qaeda rejects the Geneva Conventions. Some legal scholars maintain that the conventions demand reciprocity, and those rejecting them should receive no treaty protections. For example, legal scholar Eric Posner writes that "treaties are flexible instruments that change with the times or lose their value. States enter into treaties when doing so is in their interests; and they withdraw from them, violate them, or interpret them out of existence when the pacts no longer serve their interests."[59] Although opposing the decision to abandon the Geneva Conventions, Secretary Powell and Senator John McCain also emphasized their reciprocal character. They maintained that by abiding by them, the United States encourages others to treat captured American soldiers humanely. However, reciprocity is unlikely to obtain with al-Qaeda. As Gonzales put it when responding to Powell in 2001, "our adversaries in several recent conflicts have not been deterred by GPW [the Geneva Conventions] in their mistreatment of captured U.S. personnel, and terrorists will not follow GPW rules in any event."[60] Posner agreed, noting that there is "no reason to think that if the Bush administration improves or worsens the conditions of detention it will have any effect on al Qaeda's behavior toward captured Americans or other westerners. Nor is there any reason to think that al Qaeda will appreciate the improvement in military commissions commanded by the Supreme Court, and reciprocate by offering 'regularly constituted' trials to its victims before beheading them as enemies of Islam."[61] In sum, it seems we should abandon the Geneva Conventions if our adversaries reject them.

Al-Qaeda's character and tactics lend further credibility to this interpretation of the Geneva Conventions. Why should we extend the norms of civilized warfare to vicious adversaries who reject them entirely?

Why should they receive treaty protection when they brutally murdered almost three thousand innocent people in one day? Al-Qaeda uses irregular tactics and should not expect protection from the Geneva Conventions. They regulate conduct only between nations or specified groups in international politics.

Unfortunately, although initially plausible, such discussions of the Geneva Conventions interpret them simplistically. In fact, one "mistake commonly made is to assume that" if a "combatant does not qualify as a POW, then he has no rights under the Geneva Conventions. This is clearly not correct."[62] Some Geneva provisions protect only certain kinds of combatants and depend on how they behave. Some rights that Geneva grants may also be reciprocal requiring two parties to embrace them. Others, however, obtain regardless of how detainees act. In particular, Geneva's Common Article Three (so-called because it appears in all four Geneva Conventions) expresses a moral minimum protecting detainees not covered by other parts of the conventions. Because of its importance, let me quote this article in its entirety:

Article 3

In the case of armed conflict not of an international character occurring in the territory of one of the High Contracting Parties, each party to the conflict shall be bound to apply, as a minimum, the following provisions:

1. Persons taking no active part in the hostilities, including members of armed forces who have laid down their arms and those placed hors de combat by sickness, wounds, detention, or any other cause, shall in all circumstances be treated humanely, without any adverse distinction founded on race, colour, religion or faith, sex, birth or wealth, or any other similar criteria.

   To this end the following acts are and shall remain prohibited at any time and in any place whatsoever with respect to the above-mentioned persons:

   (a) Violence to life and person, in particular murder of all kinds, mutilation, cruel treatment and torture;
   (b) Taking of hostages;
   (c) Outrages upon personal dignity, in particular, humiliating and degrading treatment;
   (d) The passing of sentences and the carrying out of executions without previous judgment pronounced by a regularly

> constituted court affording all the judicial guarantees which are recognized as indispensable by civilized peoples.

2. The wounded and sick shall be collected and cared for.

> An impartial humanitarian body, such as the International Committee of the Red Cross, may offer its services to the Parties to the conflict.

> The Parties to the conflict should further endeavor to bring into force, by means of special agreements, all or part of the other provisions of the present Convention.

> The application of the preceding provisions shall not affect the legal status of the Parties to the conflict.[63]

Many nations have long considered Common Article Three a minimal protection for detainees.[64] Historically, the United States often demanded that its prisoners be afforded its protections.[65] For many people, it ensured a minimally humane treatment for detainees not covered by other parts of the Geneva Conventions.

Aware of its importance, the Bush administration specifically repudiated Common Article Three. As I have already noted, President Bush decided that it applies only to conflicts "not of an international character." He and his advisors maintained that this phrase means that Common Article Three obtains only in civil wars or forms of domestic conflicts. Because al-Qaeda operates internationally, it cannot claim protection under Common Article Three. Critics rejected this interpretation insisting that "not of an international character" means a conflict not between states. They pointed out that Common Article Three's drafters considered and rejected an interpretation like that of the Bush administration. States, they also argued, repeatedly demonstrated their awareness of Common Article Three's meaning when insisting that it protect their soldiers.

Instead of addressing these complex interpretative questions in international law, I want to suggest that those rejecting Common Article Three overlook its moral import.[66] Rather than a contract that parties can break under certain circumstances, it expresses a nonnegotiable obligation to acknowledge the person's value. It also conveys the idea that even the worst evildoers retain value. Neal Katyal, one of the heroic lawyers defending detainees in the *Hamdan* case, eloquently captured the moral import of Common Article Three during oral testimony before the Supreme Court. He noted that "We're not talking about, you know, Miranda rights or something like that. We're talking about just a set of core ideas that every country on the world—every country in the world is supposed to dispense when they create war-crimes trials. And, even that minimal standard, the Government says they don't want to apply here."[67] Common Article Three thus articulates a duty to respect the person regardless of his or her behavior.

Common Article Three also obliges nations to acknowledge human value when they are most inclined to disregard it. The Geneva Conventions "in this sense establish minimum rules that apply even when arguably no other law does, shining the light of law, however dim, into the darkness of war."[68] When rejecting them, President Bush promised to treat detainees humanely, but his promise was hollow. The person's value *requires* our acknowledgment, and humane treatment is no option we grant merely out of moral largesse. In fact, it is remarkably naïve to think that in terrible times, parties in a conflict will voluntarily adhere to humane treatment. Instead, we need institutional policies protecting the person's value. Otherwise, we depend on the goodwill of weak human beings who commit evil in the absence of rules and laws. Under institutional or political pressure, leaders, interrogators, and soldiers will often embrace evil unless restrained by law. For example, the ICRC provision in Common Article Three hold particular importance because it prevents detainees from disappearing. During the 1970s and the 1980s, tens of thousands of Latin and South Americans simply disappeared, were kidnapped, or killed by military governments. Common Article Three reaffirms the duty to monitor the location of detainees to prevent the worst abuses. Without it, in the War on Terror, we saw at least one hundred (perhaps more) "ghost detainees" vanish into secret U.S. prisons throughout the world.

Those claiming that Common Article Three is a reciprocal agreement ignore its moral import. They fail to realize that some elements of international law originate not in contracts or conventions, but in the moral demands that human nature makes upon us. Nations may legitimately abandon particular treaties when others disregard or violate them. In an international arena dominated by the pursuit of power and interest, they make difficult choices about which agreements to maintain. However, some elements of international law codify moral principles existing independently of the actions or existence of states.[69] Common Article Three is one such code because it recognizes a person's special value. Those rejecting it often display a disdain for this value or adhere to some ethical theory that holds that legal agreements create human value. They ignore the value inherent in spiritual beings, falsely concluding that contracts or agreements create it.[70]

By disregarding this moral minimum, the Bush administration unleashed terrible consequences on detainees and others. Let us assume that a dirty hands case for this decision in 2002 was persuasive. Whatever its immediate benefits, it created a climate of official indifference toward supposed legal niceties. Secretary of Defense Rumsfeld repeatedly made public statements casting doubt on whether suspected terrorists were entitled to Geneva Convention protection.[71] As we have already seen, he authorized harsh interrogation techniques for Guantánamo Bay, only to rescind them after intense opposition from military lawyers.[72] Despite this opposition, his Pentagon Working Group deliberately excluded important JAG and civilian lawyers, and went ahead with its recommendations for harsh treatment.[73] Deception and secrecy dominated many administration decisions.[74] As Goldsmith notes, the decision to reject Common Article Three "was very vague, it was not effectively operationalized into concrete standards of conduct, and it left the hard issue about 'humane' and 'appropriate' treatment to the discretion of unknown officials."[75] Such a defective policy produced terrible consequences. As both Schlesinger and Taguba reports detail, policies intended solely for use at Guantánamo Bay quickly migrated to Iraq. General Geoffrey Miller seemed to be the key conduit for this flow of brutality. Author of a cruel interrogation regime at Guantánamo, he went to Iraq in August 2003, right before the Abu Ghraib horrors began. From what we know from numerous reports and press accounts, he prepared the way for interrogators to employ extreme brutality in Iraq. Soldiers at Abu Ghraib reported deep confusion about proper interrogations and the Geneva Conventions. The result was predictable abuse and torture.

The decisions to suspend the Geneva Conventions also created years of litigation that stalled justice for detainees. For example, in the *Hamdan* decision, the U.S. Supreme Court strongly rejected the Bush administration's claims about Common Article Three.[76] *Hamdan* held that it protects al-Qaeda suspects, and affirmed that the president must grant minimal protection to even the worst terrorists. It returned the military commissions issue back to the U.S. Congress, which eventually passed a disturbing act removing habeas corpus from detainees (the 2006 Military Commissions Act). The dispute over the Military Commission Act lasted for several years. In the meantime, hundreds of detainees languished at Guantánamo Bay, waiting for the administration to develop a coherent military commissions system. Despite administration rhetoric about the evil people occupying Guantánamo, it contained hundreds of people whose guilt or innocence was entirely unclear. Many were released after years of torture and isolation. Some were innocent victims of a profoundly disorganized and confused system. Others may have been guilty of crimes but were never punished because incompetent interrogations made it impossible to ascertain their guilt. Many of these events resulted from the initial decision to unilaterally disregard the Geneva Conventions.

Despite its eventual victory with the 2006 Military Commissions Act, the Bush administration's decision to reject the Geneva Conventions was very costly. If "it had earlier established a legislative regime of legal rights on Guantánamo Bay, it never would have had to live with the Court's Common Article 3 holding."[77] Here, we see the fundamental danger of the dirty hands approach, its bias toward short-term consequences. Too often, it appears reasonable if we restrict our attention to immediate consequences. Once we consider long-term consequences, particularly spiritual ones, the dirty hands position seems far less rational.

The Geneva Conventions example also illustrates the abstract and noninstitutional character of much of dirty hands thinking. Walzer, Elshtain, and others say almost nothing about how dirty hands decisions infect institutions. In actual cases, leaders act within a web of rules, regulations, and mores. They play official roles requiring character traits cultivated over many years. For example, when the Office of Legal Counsel gave the Bush administration its justification for torture, its decision profoundly affected multiple actors. It particularly damaged the military, which subsequently struggled to recover from the administration's cavalier attitude toward the Geneva Conventions. Finally, politicians operate in an international arena where reputation matters. For better or worse, Abu Ghraib and Guantánamo Bay symbolized an immoral hegemon arrogantly disregarding international public opinion. The damage to U.S. reputation has been immense, and if it can be corrected, it will take years to do so. In this regard, the dirty hands approach profoundly misleads because it rarely considers reputation, a vital element of political success.

Perhaps the United States could have avoided this damage. A dirty hands approach to torture might not always produce as much harm as the Bush administration did. Nevertheless, we can predict that by disregarding the values expressed in Common Article Three, we will damage persons and institutions. This treaty embodies a minimal respect for persons, and repudiating it produces a moral fissure. In the Bush administration's case, officials also used considerable deceit, which in turn produced additional spiritual perversions. We cannot predict how such distortions will play themselves out because evil and good interact in complex ways, and it is as "easy to disentangle these remote causations as to tell at a river's mouth which waters come from which glaciers and which tributaries."[78] We can only hope the Bush administration's damage to domestic and international institutions will eventually dissipate.

The Self-Indulgence Charge

By considering torture's spiritual damage, we can also reject the charge that refusing to torture is morally self-indulgent. Dirty hands advocates lack precision about consequences but rarely hesitate to hurl the self-indulgence charge. For example, as we have seen, Elshtain maintains that those refusing to torture are guilty of "rule-mania," and "moralism." We want leaders, she says, to "rank their moral purity as far less important in their overall scheme of things" than eliciting information that might save lives.[79] Those refusing to torture are guilty of "moral laziness" because they cannot respond properly to evil.[80] Although she is particularly strong in her charges, Elshtain differs little from others in the dirty hands tradition. Many level the charge that a person refusing to do evil acts "displays a possessive attitude toward his own virtue."[81] Combined with colorful examples of children threatened or cities destroyed, the self-indulgence charge carries considerable emotional weight.

Dirty hands thinkers capture the dangers of self-indulgence but ignore how it appears in many approaches to ethics. Some people exhibit squeamishness about violence and are excessively attached to their virtue. Their attachment blinds them producing a dangerous indecisiveness. They have the "fear of soiling" themselves by "entering into the context of history."[82] A person prone to such fears should stay out of politics. International politics, in particular, often requires moral compromises because it requires us to ally ourselves with evil and corrupt people. However, excessive moral indulgence is not the sole property of those refusing to torture. Torturers may believe they are morally pure agents of a just cause. For example, Mark Osiel describes how Alfredo Astiz, a leader of Argentine death squads in the 1970s, occupied a military role "that dictated that commands from superiors were never to be questioned, much less challenged."[83] He clung to a sense of moral purity while committing terrible atrocities. A dirty hands politician may also succumb to excessive preoccupation with anguish or moral heroism. Such indulgence "can arise with any moral motivation whatsoever."[84] It implies undue reflexivity, where someone focuses entirely on the self while diverting attention from other objects. Dirty hands theorists, thus, wrongly imply that those refusing to torture are *necessarily* guilty of self-indulgence.

More importantly, the self-indulgence charge ignores how someone refusing to torture can be a witness to moral truths. She can express a commitment to a community that recognizes the person's value. She can refuse to torture because torture produces evil that eventually appears in the social order. Such acts reflect not self-indulgence but a deep concern for a community's spiritual health. They look to the future knowing that evil acts produce detrimental long-term consequences. We cannot, then, claim that those refusing to torture always care excessively for their moral integrity.

To summarize what I have said about spiritual damage, dirty hands advocates ignore it, using sensational examples driven by a short-term vision. They neglect a sophisticated analysis of our spiritual personalities. Despite its imprecision about consequences, the dirty hands position continues to appeal to people frightened by terrorism. Yet, with its impoverished conception of the human person, it offers little guidance in difficult times.

Maintaining an Absolute Ban on Torture

I want to end this chapter by calling for a complete ban on torture. Even the worst terrorists remain embodied spirits who are uniquely valuable in the universe. Terrorism challenges this conception of human value. Those who attacked the United States on September 11 seemed utterly without conscience. Those who brutally beheaded Americans in Iraq seemed subhuman. Such circumstances test our commitment to human value, and a torture ban institutionalizes and reinforces this commitment. It also prevents us from succumbing to fear or desperation leading to horrific crimes. A torture ban, thus, not only has expressive value, but also contains our worst impulses. It creates a bright line that political actors dare not cross, hopefully protecting us from our own barbarism.

A torture ban also reminds us that torture is like few other crimes. Too often, its proponents treat it like self-defense or other acts, falsely maintaining that it is "not special at all."[85] However, because it uniquely assaults the person, torture differs from other acts. It is akin to genocide or rape—acts that are traditionally thought to be always wrong. A torture ban acknowledges its unique horror. With the advent of new media, public discussions of torture have descended to unprecedented lows. Journalists and radio personalities talk blithely about the worst atrocities. In some circles, people have lost any awareness of torture's moral seriousness. A torture ban would renew our sense that is truly something horrible.

We should also adopt a torture ban because consequentialist and dirty hands positions cannot rationally sustain themselves. We know torture ruptures our being and unleashes destructive forces into the world. In contrast, neither pure consequentialism nor the dirty hands approach offers any clear guidance about consequences. Instead, they proffer speculations based on limited historical data, amateur psychological ideas, emotionally charged examples, and false charges about moral self-indulgence. Put together, these arguments offer no rational justification for torture.

Those rejecting a torture ban often take refuge in personal experience. For example, they ask if we would torture to protect our children. We should respond to such appeals by acknowledging their emotional purchase. I have twin boys and if terrorists kidnapped them, I would likely want to torture their kidnappers. However, my emotional response cannot justify torture. The moral or civil law exists not to validate my passions, but to promote the common good. Moreover, I cannot expect the law to serve my every emotional need. Finally, we cannot ascertain an act's moral legitimacy by considering emotionally charged situations. In sum, we learn little by considering our powerful impulse to protect loved ones at all costs.

Those opposing a torture ban also maintain, however, that governments will invariably contravene it. Politicians struggling to protect their country from terrorism will torture detainees. This was the force of Dershowitz's call for "torture warrants." Dershowitz claimed that torture "would certainly be employed if we ever experienced an imminent threat of mass casualty biological, chemical or nuclear terrorism."[86] Rather than pretending it will disappear, he argued we should ensure that governments employ it only selectively. We thus retain accountability in public officials, a vital value in a democracy. A torture ban, in contrast, allows torture to exist in the shadows. It produces hypocrisy because leaders publically disavow it while secretly torturing. For Dershowitz, such a policy is unworthy of a democratic people.

Dershowitz raises important points about governments and torture, but fails to distinguish between moral responsibility and moral wrongness. Torture bans will not eliminate torture, and leaders will often torture in extreme circumstances.[87] Nevertheless, torture is objectively wrong regardless of what an agent thinks about it. Objective wrongness exists in all circumstances, whereas subjective culpability differs with them. In extremity, someone may believe she must torture, but it "is never acceptable to confuse a 'subjective' error about moral good with the 'objective' truth rationally proposed to man in virtue of his end, or to make the moral value of an act performed with a true and correct conscience equivalent to the moral value of an act performed by following the judgment of an erroneous conscience."[88] The evil someone commits "though not chargeable to the person in question, does not cease to be evil and disorder in the moral order."[89] By confusing objective wrongness and subjective culpability, Dershowitz suggests that torture may sometime be morally legitimate.

By distinguishing subjective culpability from objective wrongness, we can respond properly to torturers. We might mitigate punishment for someone who tortures out of a profound sense of duty. For example, Osiel describes how some Argentine torturers wavered in their commitment to torture. However, clergymen assured them that their acts were morally justifiable. Navy officers "returning from dropping victims into the sea received comfort from chaplains who would cite parables from the Bible about separating the wheat from the chaff."[90] In such cases, judges trying torturers might recognize a confused conscience, and hand out lighter sentences. However they should never concede that the torturer's act was morally justifiable.

Judges often encounter significant difficulties in ascertaining subjective culpability for torture. As Osiel demonstrates in his careful studies of torture in 1970s Argentina, moral agents may be fully convinced of their moral uprightness. They may honestly believe that torturing terrorists will save Western civilization or protect the innocent.[91] In such cases, judges must carefully analyze their state of mind. They must decide complex issues, like whether we should presume defendants know the wrongfulness of their action, or whether we should allow them to rebut this presumption. Such matters render decisions about subjective culpability very difficult.

Future jurists may find this task particularly hard with the architects and executors of torture policy in the War on Terror. The torture memos deliberately created legal cover for public officials accused of torture. Because the Office of Legal Counsel rescinded them only at the end of 2004, the CIA and other interrogators may have assumed their actions were morally and legally justified. Moreover, Supreme

Court decisions, Congressional legislation, and new military law all render it difficult to hold people responsible for torture in the early days of the War on Terror. Interrogators or administration officials might claim that domestic law was unclear until the 2005 Detainee Treatment Act, the 2006 Military Commissions Act, or President Bush's 2007 Executive Order on torture. Operating in a legal limbo, they might argue that they did their best in difficult circumstances. Finally, top Bush administration officials made deliberately ambiguous statements about the Geneva Conventions. They were well aware of the legal dangers of their policies, but future prosecutors will have to carefully ascertain their state of mind.

All these matters bear on discovering subjective culpability and will occupy future jurists, human rights activists, and legal scholars. We need sophisticated legal tools to ascertain subjective culpability, but we cannot forget that torture is objectively wrong. Despite his state of mind, a torturer has committed wrongdoing. Too often, dirty hands theorists fail to grasp the key distinction between subjective culpability and objective wrongness.

By exhibiting sensitivity to the subjective culpability/objective wrongness distinction, we may also avoid hypocrisy. I agree with Dershowitz that the dirty hands approach encourages it. We tell torturers it is both right and wrong to torture and excuse them if they show sufficient contrition. This approach offers no comfort to torture victims. A man whose psyche has been destroyed by sensory deprivation may care little about a politician's remorse. However, I am not proposing we ban torture, but simultaneously absolve agents of wrongdoing. Instead, I maintain that torture is always wrong, but acknowledge that politicians may use it out of moral weakness and institutional pressures. This is not, as Dershowitz maintains, a "don't ask, don't tell" policy, but one recognizing human frailty and political realities.[92] We demand accountability from military officers and intelligence agents by prohibiting torture. If they contravene this prohibition, we use military and civilian justice systems to evaluate their moral responsibility. We must not, under any circumstances, legitimize their actions judicially or politically.

Let me offer a concrete example to illustrate this approach to torture. In 2003, Germans confronted a difficult torture case.[93] Eleven-year-old Jacob von Metzler, the son of a prominent banker, was kidnapped in 2002. His parents agreed to pay a million dollar ransom, which was collected by the kidnapper, Magnus Gaefgen. The Frankfurt police observed him collecting it and arrested him. He refused to reveal where he hid Jacob and toyed with the police by relaying false information about the crime. Believing the boy was in imminent danger, Frankfurt

Police Vice President Wolfgang Dascher threatened Gaefgen with torture. Putting his threat into writing, he scared Gaefgen into revealing Jacob's location. Sadly, the boy was already dead, his body stuffed in plastic, and located under a dock.

When it became public, Dascher's threat to torture provoked a storm of controversy. Some public officials argued that he acted justifiably in a dirty hands situation. Others roundly condemned him citing Germany's ugly history of torture. Dascher himself created controversy by denying he was guilty of torture. He described his action as coercion, rather than torture, and some German officials echoed the Bush administration's rhetorical contortions about torture. Dascher was arrested and charged with employing the threat to torture, a crime under German law. He faced up to ten years in prison, but in 2004, he was convicted of a lesser offense and given one year's probation.[94] On its face, this seems like a classic dirty hands case with a clash of obligations. Someone must not only protect the innocent, but also avoid torturing. Dascher chose to override one obligation in favor of another and accepted the price for his action. We might punish him for wrongdoing, but on dirty hands grounds, he did the right thing.

However, we can look at this case differently, a way adopted by those prosecuting Dascher. The German court refused to absolve him of his crime. It rejected both necessity and self-defense arguments, insisting that Dascher could legitimately claim neither. It did not, as the dirty hands theorists hold, argue that Dascher was justified in threatening torture. Instead, the judge maintained that he acted immorally and assessed his culpability.[95] We can understand this response better by recalling the moral act's structure of object, intention, and circumstances. Dascher's object was to threaten torture, and it defines his act as immoral. However, his intentions were complex. The court found that Dascher had a legitimate intention to help the child.[96] Circumstantially, he confronted a "hectic atmosphere, great emotional pressure on the investigating officers and the consequences of the crime."[97] Given these circumstances and intentions, the judge handed down a lesser sentence. By keeping these dimensions of the moral act in mind, we avoid the sloppy thinking often exhibited by dirty hands thinkers. Dascher's act was objectively wrong, but intention and circumstances diminished his subjective culpability.

Dascher's case exemplifies how best to respond to torture in extreme circumstances. We maintain an absolute ban on it, refusing to concede that it is ever morally justifiable. We can distinguish between justification and excuse here. A torturer can never *justify* her action but may be able to *excuse* it. Legal scholar Kent Greenwalt drew this distinction well some years ago, stating that

> [j]ustified action is warranted action; similar actions could prop-
> erly be performed by others; such actions should not be interfered
> with by those capable of stopping them; and such actions may be
> assisted by those in a position to render aid. If action is excused,
> the actor is relieved of blame but others may not properly perform
> similar actions; interference with such actions is appropriate; and
> assistance of such actions is wrongful.[98]

In many areas of the law, we may avoid codifying rigid distinctions
between justification and excuse. We may allow judges and juries considerable latitude in defining the boundaries between them. However,
with torture, judges, juries, and citizens must never erase the justification/
excuse distinction. However, acknowledging human frailty, we mitigate moral responsibility for torture. We unequivocally adhere to the
justification/excuse distinction, placing the burden of excuse on those
who torture.[99] In some cases, we choose not to impose draconian punishment for immoral decisions. Sentencing will depend on intention
and circumstances, matters best left to juries, judges, and courts-martial.
Legal systems will need to develop this response to torture so that it dis-
courages torturers from trying to evade punishment for their crimes. By
recognizing excuses, they risk encouraging torture, and how they proceed depends on the details of their law. Ethically, what matters is that
they codify the basic idea that torture is always objectively wrong.[100]

The Costs of Refusal

Those of us insisting on a torture ban must acknowledge its possible costs.
Often, torture opponents argue that nonviolent interrogation obtains the
best intelligence data. Whether this is true is an empirical matter best
left to professional interrogators. We know that FBI interrogators often
prefer nonviolent interrogations over torture.[101] We also cannot know
whether torture is a reliable social practice. Nevertheless, occasionally it
might be more efficacious than nonviolent interrogation. Without access
to classified information, we must admit that refusing to torture might
harm people. Sometimes, "police officers, soldiers and other state agents
may face a bitter choice if all legally available means of interrogation
are exhausted: to make themselves guilty of a crime or to risk innocent
lives."[102] On this matter, dirty hands proponents correctly remind us that

political choices often yield tragic outcomes. No politician should deny responsibility for what happens under her leadership. As Weber puts it, it is "immensely moving when a *mature* man [or woman]—no matter whether old or young in years—is aware of a responsibility of the consequences of his conduct and really feels such responsibility with all of his heart and soul."[103] Rather than embracing conceptual escape valves, we should honestly recognize the possible costs of refusing to torture.

Torture opponents should also recognize the contingency that dirty hands thinkers depict so brilliantly. In some circumstances, soldiers and intelligence officers may feel overwhelmed by moral conflict, acutely experiencing Nagel's moral blind alley. At times, contingency may powerfully threaten their integrity and self-possession. They may believe that "world affairs are in a way governed by fortune and by God, that men with their wisdom are not able to control them, indeed that men can do nothing about them."[104] Institutional structures or personal virtues cannot completely protect them from contingency. Those who repudiate torture and risk harm to others may feel profound remorse and guilt lasting a lifetime.

Conclusion

For many people, the dirty hands position represents a compromise between absolute opposition to torture and consequentialism. It depicts real and seemingly irresolvable conflicts between obligations. It refuses to adopt utilitarianism's simplistic and excessively rational approach to torture. Finally, it brilliantly captures the experiences of leaders forced to respond to those bent on destruction.

Despite its attractiveness, I have maintained that the dirty hands position is conceptually unstable. It cannot explain how to measure consequences, asking us instead to trust in a politician's intuitions. It also ignores spirituality, thus underestimating the damage torture inflicts on persons and communities. Finally, the dirty hands position exhibits a profound moral blindness because it seeks to "cultivate and exalt evil in order to fight against evil."[105] Such a position is highly dangerous in our troubled times.

Rather than self-indulgence, those refusing to torture witness to the person's value. Rather than acceding to evil under extreme circumstances, they reveal the "true face" of torture as "a violation of the person's humanity."[106] Rather than deriding them as self-indulgent idealists or moralists, we should celebrate their courage.

Conclusion: Machiavelli's Challenge—Torture and Memory

> Purifying the memory means eliminating from personal and collective conscience all forms of resentment or violence left by the inheritance of the past... This occurs whenever it becomes possible to attribute to past historical deeds a different quality, having a new and different effect on the present, in view of progress in reconciliation in truth, justice, and charity among human beings.
> International Theological Commission, *Memory and Reconciliation*[1]

In the *Prince*, Machiavelli writes a disturbing passage about memory and truth. Men, he writes

> judge more according to their eyes than to their hands; since everyone is in a position to observe, just a few to touch. Everyone sees what you appear to be, few touch what you are; and those few do not dare oppose the opinions of the many who have the majesty of the state defending them; and with regard to the actions of all men, and especially with princes where there is no court of appeal, we must look at the final result.[2]

Political memory, Machiavelli assumes, is short and success easily dazzles a populace worried about its own security. Some people show concern for victims of political crimes, but governments easily neutralize them through force and propaganda. In most cases, those harmed disappear from memory and history.

I have always found these remarks deeply disturbing and think they make it difficult to defend Machiavelli against charges that he is the "teacher of evil."[3] Nevertheless, rather than viewing them as cynical manipulation, I think they have great significance for torture debates. Machiavelli describes how governments willfully manipulate memory. He also understands that people desperate to protect themselves often forget terrible crimes if guaranteed security. These realities confront those of us who oppose torture. To conclude this book, I respond to Machiavelli's powerful challenge by reflecting on torture and memory. I first consider legal attempts to hold torturers' responsible, recognizing their importance, but arguing that they often cannot rectify injustice. Torture victims may appear unsympathetic and powerful people with legal and financial resources easily undermine their credibility. Second, I urge us to carefully preserve the memory of torture. Public discussions and education may be legally inefficacious but prevent us from forgetting torture victims. Finally, after detailing the damage U.S. torture has unleashed, I consider repentance as a vital component of responding to torture. I once again emphasize the importance of a spiritual approach to torture.

Law and Torture in the War on Terror

Human rights activists and military lawyers seek to hold torturers legally responsible for their crimes. For example, in 2005, the American Civil Liberties Union and Human Rights First initiated a lawsuit against Defense Secretary Donald Rumsfeld. They amassed impressive evidence of his complicity in torture and also named Colonel Thomas Pappas and General Ricardo Sanchez as defendants. The U.S. military successfully prosecuted some soldiers involved in the Abu Ghraib scandal. Convicted of various offenses, they received sentences ranging from dishonorable discharge to ten years' imprisonment. Members of the U.S. Army Criminal Investigative Command (CID) and the Naval Criminal Investigative Service (NCIS) often courageously investigated allegations of torture in Iraq and Afghanistan. Finally, civilian lawyers have sued the United States and other governments on behalf of torture victims. For example, they took the case of Maher Arar, a Canadian falsely accused of terrorism. Arar was "rendered" to Syria by U.S. authorities and tortured by Syrian intelligence. He later received monetary compensation from the Canadian government and an official apology. Lawyers have represented other detainees seeking reparations from the U.S. government.[4]

For some scholars, legal remedies are a vital tool for responding to torture. For example, Mark Osiel argues that criminal trials shape collective memory and undermine destructive narratives about war crimes.[5] Although he studies transitional democracies such as Argentina (governments transitioning to democracy from authoritarian rule), he nevertheless illustrates the import of a legal response. Trials hold perpetrators responsible for crimes and express important values. They demonstrate that democratic regimes support human dignity, can admit mistakes, and hold political agents morally responsible. If conducted properly, they also allow for honest discussions of why crimes occurred. Legal remedies thus play an important role in rectifying torture's destruction.

Other torture opponents focus on legislative, military, and political prohibitions. For example, several years after September 11, military authorities revised the U.S. *Army Field Manual* to ensure that it prohibits torture. Others sought to change CIA policy to prohibit waterboarding and other torture. Finally, legislators like Senator John McCain worked hard to pass legislation prohibiting the military from torturing. They successfully passed the 2005 Detainee Treatment Act despite considerable opposition from the Bush administration.

Those pursuing these political and legal approaches work tirelessly on behalf of torture victims. Their prospects for success, however, may be slim. For example, as of this writing, much of the 2006 Military Commissions Act (MCA) remains law of the land. Defining the procedures to guide military trials of suspected terrorists, it is a deeply disturbing piece of legislation. It stripped detainees of the writ of habeas corpus, the right to have an explanation and justification for their detention. Habeas corpus dates back centuries in Anglo-American law, but in one legislative act, Congress repudiated this fundamental right.[6] In 2008, the U.S. Supreme Court narrowly overturned this element of the MCA, restoring habeas corpus for detainees.[7] This was a welcome repudiation of the Bush administration's unjust denial of an important right. However, the MCA still allows some testimony from torture to enter the courtroom if it was obtained prior to 2005.[8] It also gave military judges wide latitude in deciding which evidence to accept, including various kinds of heresy. Finally, the MCA also retained the category "enemy combatant" for all those so classified before 2006. Thus, those originally detained as enemy combatants under a confused process retained this classification.[9]

Given the dynamics of U.S. domestic politics, Americans may not change the Military Commissions Act. U.S. senators who worked hard on it may only reluctantly revisit it. Others eager to appear tough on terrorism may refuse to risk political capital on behalf of unpopular detainees. The Supreme Court will likely examine further features of the act, but may refuse to overturn it entirely. Hopefully, political and judicial leaders will have the courage to overturn the MCA, but those opposing it may have to wait a long time for this to happen.

Similarly, lawsuits against administration officials may encounter significant difficulties. Courts are notoriously reluctant to hold public officials responsible for war crimes. Internationally, in 1998, Spanish officials indicted former Chilean dictator Augusto Pinochet for war crimes, but never prosecuted him because of his bad health.[10] Similarly, attempts to indict Henry Kissinger for alleged war crimes committed during the Vietnam War went nowhere.[11] In 2006, Chief Judge Thomas A. Hogan of the Federal District Court for the District of Columbia dismissed the American Civil Liberties Union/Human Rights First case against Donald Rumsfeld.[12] Additionally, the Bush administration carefully crafted its legal strategy to avoid prosecution. As I have shown in this book, the Office of Legal Counsel wrote legal justifications for torture that deeply shaped administration policy. Given this legal framework, prosecutors will have great difficulty indicting the architects of torture policy. Finally, administration officials retain enough charisma, financial resources, and legal assistance to vigorously resist prosecution.[13]

Military prosecutions also remain imperfect instruments for pursuing justice for torture victims. Court-martials admirably prosecuted Americans soldiers guilty of torture and war crimes. Moreover, the JAGs were some of the heroes in the battle against torture, representing unpopular defendants at Guantánamo and elsewhere.[14] However, the military justice system rarely touched those in the military's upper echelons. For example, in the Abu Ghraib trials, General Janice Karpinski was never prosecuted, forced instead into retirement with a demotion and pension. General Geoffrey Miller never received judicial punishment for his role in the Abu Ghraib atrocities. He also went into retirement, reportedly turned down for promotion. Finally, General Ricardo Sanchez, under whose command the Abu Ghraib atrocities occurred, never faced careful scrutiny. Although deeply unpopular for mistakes he made in the Iraq War, he received only public disapproval and retired.[15] In sum, despite its successes, the military judicial system failed to hold senior commanders responsible for torture.

Despite their importance, therefore, legal and political responses to torture in the War on Terror may only partially rectify harm. The U.S. legal system seems unable to fully come to terms with the crimes its officials committed. Sadly, other countries have confronted similar difficulties responding to torture. Worldwide "torturers are rarely punished, and when they are, the punishment rarely corresponds to the severity of the crime."[16] Torturers in Argentina, Guatemala, South Africa, and elsewhere have avoided prosecution. Perhaps, as Philippe Sands has recently argued, the architects of U.S. torture policy will face indictments if they travel overseas.[17] Legally, however, the United States may resemble other countries where torturers escape punishment.

Torture Victims: Unsympathetic Characters?

These legal and political failures should not surprise us because torture victims present unique problems for lawyers and judges. In his moving study of torture in three countries, John Conroy discusses how torture victims often appear very unsympathetic, whereas torturers seem like distinguished public servants. Torture victims "may hold political or religious beliefs not in favor in the larger society, or they may come from some lesser class that is viewed as a threat to society at large."[18] Consequently, victims garner little public sympathy. Those tortured may also be victimized again by governments and media outlets eager to undermine their credibility. With such social dynamics, torture victims often receive little public attention and support.

We have seen this problem acutely in the War on Terror. First, many of us have little sympathy for the architects of the September 11 attacks. Responsible for thousands of deaths and seemingly unrepentant, they have few defenders. Second, others, innocent victims of U.S. policy, may appear less than sympathetic. Take, for example, the "Tipton Three," Shafiq Rasul, Rhuhel Ahmed, and Asif Iqbal. Captured in Afghanistan in 2001, they underwent months of stress positions and other torture. They were returned to Britain in 2004 after British authorities conclusively refuted U.S. allegations that they were terrorists. In important details, their stories matched those of others, and we have little reason to doubt they were tortured. Nevertheless, the three men were not ideal candidates to be defendants in a lawsuit. Ahmed had reportedly used drugs. He, Rasul, and Iqbal claimed they went to Pakistan for a wedding in 2001 and then entered Afghanistan via bus. Those interested in discrediting them immediately focused on this behavior. Why did they go to Afghanistan at all? Did they have some sympathies for the Taliban? When the Tipton Three went public with torture allegations, they encountered many such questions.[19]

Ethically, these questions are entirely irrelevant, but they can inflict political damage. Many young men experiment with drugs and other dubious activities. Many seek political adventure, undertaking dangerous and ethically troubling tasks. These activities, however, can never justify torture. Sadly, they hold considerable weight in the court of public opinion. To be sympathetic, a defendant must be above reproach, a modern-day Job. Some Jobs do exist, and hopefully they will pursue legal justice. However, other torture victims have what people think are tarnished biographies. They will be subjected to character assassination by those eager to change the subject or hide crimes. Leaders can, as Machiavelli notes, use the "majesty of the state" to discredit victims, labeling them the dregs of society unworthy of moral concern.

Repentance: A Vital Response

Although vital, legal approaches to torture, thus, cannot adequately respond to political manipulation. Instead, we need cultural recognition about what happened in the War on Terror. In this book, I have maintained not only that torture is always wrong, but also that it corrupts individuals internally. If my analysis is correct, those who ordered, approved of, or ignored torture cannot avoid serious internal examination. Legal trials may provide an impetus for it, but cannot uproot torture's spiritual poison. It destroys the person and damages the torturer, producing negative effects on character and political life. We cannot combat them by relying solely on legal remedies.

Sadly, in the War on Terror, the United States unleashed many destructive consequences it will have to ameliorate. For example, in Iraq, thousands of Iraqis were arrested and imprisoned. Many simply disappeared from their families for months and suffered terrible abuse. Wives, husbands, and children lost not only key family members, but also working adults. Often, their relatives ended up in overcrowded Iraqi prisons, where they were repeatedly tortured and abused. At one point during the Iraq War, conditions in Iraqi prisons were so bad that the United States was unable to transfer prisoners to them.[20] Such treatment creates incalculable psychological damage.

Similarly, the United States tortured hundreds, if not thousands, of detainees at Guantánamo, Afghanistan, and secret sites throughout the world. Many were released while others languished in legal limbo. Torture left psychological scars on them. For example, at Guantánamo Bay, long isolation reportedly produced deep psychological trauma on detainees. They had families who often had no idea about what happened to them. In 2008, Human Rights Watch reported that consequences of torture "for family relationships are devastating. Except for censored letters (which are not much comfort to illiterate detainees), detainees have been cut off from their families for years, having almost no contact with wives, children, parents, and other loved ones. Some detainees have children whom they have not seen or spoken to since their birth, or whom they only saw years ago as infants."[21] Detainees who returned to their own countries undoubtedly shared stories of torture. Their narratives will remain with families well into the next generation. Many are stigmatized or find themselves unable to function normally. They depend on relatives or others to support them because they cannot find work or are incapable of working.[22] Detainees and their families will likely struggle for years with the psychological and physical aftermath of torture.

By torturing, the United States also damaged its international reputation. Public opinion polls reveal that people in many countries no longer see the United States as a force for human rights and justice. For example, Britain and Germany have seen a sharp decline in those believing that the United States can promote human rights. Those polled in other countries think it violated international law in its treatment of detainees.[23] Similarly, people in many countries now see the United States as a selfish and bullying nation promoting only its own interests.[24] Finally, rightly or wrongly, many in the Middle East deeply resent how the United States treated Muslims after September 11. The scandals of Guantánamo Bay and Abu Ghraib negatively affected how they think of the United States.[25] In sum, U.S. conduct in the War on Terror has deeply harmed its international reputation.

Finally, torture in the War on Terror affected how many Americans think about their country. For some, U.S. torture in the War on Terror was par for the course in American history. American history has seen torture of Native Americans, torture in the war in the Philippines in the early twentieth century, torture in police departments and prisons, torture in the Phoenix Program, and CIA torture. On this reading of American history, we should have expected the United States to abuse its power after September 11. Despite its self-image, America is not morally exceptional, but instead acts like any nation-state pursuing its interests. In fact, for some critics, its record on human rights is far worse than that of other countries. Sadly, recent torture has only added people to the ranks of those who see the United States as a force for evil in the world.

If we add up the damage that torture has inflicted, it seems to trap us in a web of evil. Far from disappearing, it will fester in the tortured and torturers. Surveying our history, we might easily conclude that Americans are incapable of acting better. Examining how militaries torture, we might decide that "we do not learn from past behavior when it comes to torture."[26] Despite all our knowledge of torture and genocide in the twentieth century, governments repeat the same mistakes over and over again. Finally, considering international public opinion, we might think we cannot change it. We lack access to state-controlled media in many countries and continue to alienate allies on matters like torture and the death penalty. In sum, we seemed trapped by our past unable to rectify the terrible damage we have done.

The Past and Spiritual Freedom

To resist this outlook, we need considerable help from medical, military, and political institutions. Alone, philosophers and theologians can do little to alter institutions, but can contribute by illuminating philosophical issues about the person and memory. Human rights or utilitarian approaches to torture do little to address the problems I have identified. We might establish that the United States has violated the rights of thousands of people in the War on Terror. We might also recognize that on utilitarian grounds, torture has been a disaster. In neither case, however, will we address the pervasive sense of despair at our inability to alter our circumstances.

Responding to this despair requires that we alter our relationship to the past. Reconsidering past wrongs presents many dangers. Moral agents often deceive themselves by deliberately obscuring the truth. Or, they seek cheap absolution requiring no significant behavioral or character change. Finally, they think they can alter what happened, ignoring the sad reality that we cannot alter past facts. All these dangers caution against superficial approaches to past crimes.

Nevertheless, we cannot escape memory's challenges by retreating into historical fabrication or amnesia. Instead, we should begin by recalling the person's spiritual capacities. As knowing beings, we range across multiple objects, organizing them into hierarchies of being and value. We are also temporal creatures situated in time, but occasionally cognizing atemporal objects. Finally, we can recognize and shape our unique "I." We are not forced to accept the self-understandings of others, but within limits, we can freely shape our characters.

German philosopher Max Scheler uses these spiritual capacities to illuminate repentance.[27] Repentance, he maintains, is a liberating act freeing the person from the guilt accruing from past evil acts. Those who have tortured, authorized torture, or allowed it to occur cannot alter the past or magically eliminate the pain they caused. In fact, to adopt this idea gravely insults torture victims. A torture victim "can no longer feel at home in the world. The shame of destruction cannot be erased. Trust in the world, which already collapsed in part at the first blow, but in the end, under torture, will not be regained."[28] Those who repent should never demand forgiveness from victims but can in limited ways alter the sense or worth of past acts. There is "no part of our past life which—while its component natural reality is of course less freely alterable than the future—might not be genuinely altered in its *meaning* and *worth*."[29] Unlike nonspiritual beings, we can "attribute to past historical deeds a different quality, having a new and different effect on the present, in view of progress in reconciliation in truth, justice, and charity among human beings."[30] We can remember truthfully, rejecting mendacity and propaganda. For example, we can accurately recall what happened at Abu Ghraib, repudiating official versions of what happened there. Rather than accepting the story that a few "bad apples" tortured, we can consider the institutional and personal choices that produced torture.

Repenting, however, requires not simply remembering, but also remembering in a particular way. We consider the past deed not merely as an event, but as an element of our character and identity. Acts are not, as I argued in chapter two, merely physical events, but instead reflect the character of the acting person. We can, thus, not only recall an event, but also "reinhabit the central *attitude* to the world which we adopted, together with the *tendencies* of thought and will, love and hatred."[31] We can also focus on the "total person out of whose roots the deed, the act of will arose."[32] We take up an attitude toward this past person, rejecting those parts of it that produced evil. For example, what kind of people were we when we ignored evidence of torture? How could we have denied it occurred? What ideas produced such ignorance? What aspects of American society and culture contributed to torture policies? With our capacity to range over time and shape our characters, we can try to adopt a new attitude toward a previous self.

By adopting this new attitude, we may slowly transform ourselves recognizing that we were not necessitated to act as we did. Truthfully remembering a past event "is the beginning of *freedom* from the covert power of the remembered thing and occurrence."[33] For example, despite the tremendous fear of another al-Qaeda attack, we were not forced to waterboard Abu Zubaydah. We could have refused to torture him. Why did people succumb to fear? Why did they believe torture was necessary? Through repentance, we address these questions and freely repudiate the self that led to torture. This freedom constitutes a central element of spiritual self-possession, however difficult it may be to realize it. Within limits we can adopt and actualize ideals of conduct and being. Finally, by truthfully considering the past, we battle the "subterranean" elements of the person remaining after we tortured.[34] We prevent them from growing and festering, creating further difficulties in our relations with others. Repentance thus counters torture's negative spiritual consequences.

Repentance also addresses the pervasive sense that Americans are merely a force for evil in the world. By repudiating our evil actions, we recall a commitment to human rights and justice that has played a vital role in our history. We carefully consider why we took past, brutal action but reject its value and the character supporting it. Recall that evil possesses a transitive character passing from person to person. By altering a past deed's present value, we hope to halt its transmission. As a result, we are not compelled to accept a narrative positing America as a brutal power always seeking self-interest.

In sum, we cannot eliminate the damage we have unleashed by automatically healing victims through self-examination. Torture's spiritual damage will remain with us for some time shaping events and future acts. Nevertheless, we can truthfully reconsider the past, rejecting the conduct and attitudes of those who carried out torture in our name. In this way, we may uproot its deepest effects, and hopefully prevent them from appearing in future acts.

Memory and Institutions

These philosophical ideas may seem too abstract for those seeking institutional change. Moreover, they focus primarily on the individual suggesting an easy isomorphism between the individual and complex institutions.[35] In fact, we need institutional mechanisms for recognizing the truth. We can begin by publically acknowledging that the United States has tortured. Many Americans deeply resist this conclusion, flatly denying or evading it by recourse to semantic games. In this book, I have maintained that once we carefully define torture, we must conclude that the U.S. government tortured in the War on

Terror. In light of the evidence, we cannot claim that Americans never torture. We need not morally equate the United States with al-Qaeda, the Nazis, or some other evil entity. Such false comparisons do little to illuminate our action. We also need not we accept an either–or, a world of the worst mass murders or the morally pure. Individuals and nations occupy a scale of wrongdoing, and in the War on Terror, we legally embraced and administered ethically repugnant policies. Our democratic constitution enables us to recognize this truth, an option unavailable in other societies. We should be able to acknowledge crimes without continually claiming credit for virtue.

I recognize difficulties in institutionalizing public examinations of memory and can only offer general suggestions. We might make public apologies, conduct symposia, or sponsor media events. For example, in 2007, the Canadian government officially apologized to Maher Arar for its role in sending him to Syria to be tortured. It also provided him with $10.5 million in compensation.[36] Such public apologies are fraught with moral ambiguity because they may prematurely end inquiries into crimes.[37] They may also provide cheap therapy without requiring difficult institutional change. Finally, enemies and opportunists may misrepresent public apologies for propaganda purposes. However, a public apology is a first step and can go a long way in addressing past wrongs. It can "*set the stage* for rapprochement between estranged groups and for substantive reformulations of group identity."[38] In contrast to the Canadian government, U.S. officials retained Arar on their terrorist watch list. Individual U.S. politicians publically apologized to him, but he received no official apology from the U.S. government.[39] Sadly, we have similarly disregarded hundreds of others, refusing to acknowledge wrongdoing. The Bush administration maintained that it acted legally and ethically and needed to offer no apologies.[40] In contrast, Canada offered an attractive way to address past wrongs.

Future leaders who might apologize for torture will need to carefully consider timing, language, and context. Ill-timed apologies only offend victims producing further anger and enmity. They suggest a willingness to change the subject or absolve perpetrators of responsibility. Leaders must also recognize that "words and deeds often matter as much as (or even more than) the sentiments behind them."[41] In the War on Terror, we will have to be particularly attentive to the language of public apologies. American leaders have carelessly used words like "Crusade" and "Islamo-fascism." Whatever their conceptual coherence, they have deeply offended Muslims. Those apologizing for torture, therefore, must recognize how words may offend. They must also carefully decide on where and how to apologize. Who should be present at a public apology? What symbols should appear? Finally, those apologizing will also need to avoid demanding forgiveness. Forgiveness remains the choice of victims, and no perpetrator can rightfully demand it. The late John Paul II devoted considerable attention to the dynamics of public apologies. He often appeared at places like the Wailing Wall in Jerusalem. Rather than mere theatrics, his attention to context increased the impact of his apologies. Any future leader apologizing for torture would do well to emulate such examples.

Truth commissions also provide useful means for considering past wrongs. In the past 20 years, countries like South Africa and Guatemala have commissioned these bodies to consider the past. Similarly, after the September 11 attacks, the 9/11 Commission carefully examine their causes. Truth commissions can simply investigate what occurred or assess blame and issue apologies. If properly constituted, they can conduct inquiries out of the politicized atmosphere of normal government bodies. Those constructing a truth commission must take great care to ensure its impartiality and respectability. Otherwise, it will degenerate into political recriminations that obscure rather than discover the truth.[42] If properly constituted, it could prevent cheap apologies and offer the possibility of genuine reconciliation. The experiences of other nations suggest that democratic and deliberative truth commissions can "help lay the national groundwork for a public acknowledgement of suffering in the form of a meaningful apology."[43] They thus represent an important institutional means of encouraging repentance and spiritual healing.

We cannot, therefore, respond to Machiavelli's challenge simply by altering institutions or securing legal remedies, no matter how important these approaches are. Machiavelli understands how nations operate with shared memories. He and his modern imitators also recognize how states manipulate them. In fact, modern media techniques offer modes of manipulation unimaginable to sixteenth-century Florentines. Confronting them, citizens may easily forget torture victims, particularly when they remain hidden in secret prisons. They may also succumb to propaganda or mythology that absurdly posits that Americans never torture. Or, they may fall prey to attempts to manipulate memory, ignoring their own powers of self-determination. Machiavelli brilliantly explores these issues, and we can only meet his challenge by recalling and cultivating our spiritual nature.

In 1947, Jacques Maritain gave an address to the United Nations Educational, Scientific, and Cultural Organization (UNESCO). With others of his generation, he hoped that a transnational organization could prevent the horrors of the Second World War from reoccurring. Considering these tragedies, he maintained that the

> [t]rue question concerns a people's awareness or lack of awareness of the evil by which they allowed themselves to be contaminated, and of which the members of a community (even those who remained personally immune, even those who fought against that evil) recognize or do not recognize that the community was guilty.[44]

In an age where politicians arrogantly dismiss the past and claim we face entirely new situations, we might benefit from a previous generation's wisdom. Maritain reminds us that we must counter evil by retaining the deepest elements of our spirituality. With them, we can reject the manipulation of memory prominent in the War on Terror. We can resist torture's assault on the human spirit and display our compassion for those it harms. Above all, we can recall our dignity as embodied spirits capable of seeking what is true and good in our world.

NOTES

Introduction

1. Quoted in Alistair Horne, *A Savage War of Peace: Algeria 1954–1962*. With a new preface by the author (New York: New York Review of Books, 2006), 204; italics in the original.
2. I put War on Terror within quotation marks because like many analysts, I think terrorism is a tactic and that we cannot wage wars against tactics. We are at war with al-Qaeda and its supporters, but not with terrorism in general.
3. For details of Kiriakou's account, see ABC News, "Coming in From the Cold: CIA Spy Calls Waterboarding Necessary but Torture. Former Agent Says the Enhanced Technique Was Used on Al Qaeda Chief Abu Zubaydah," available at http://abcnews.go.com/Blotter/story?id=3978231&page=1. See also Jane Mayer, *The Dark Side: The Inside Story of How the War on Terror Turned into a War on American Ideals* (New York: Doubleday, 2008), 162–179. Mayer challenges the accuracy of Kiriakou's account suggesting that initially Abu Zubaydah successfully resisted waterboarding. He may have been waterboarded repeatedly.
4. Darius Rejali, *Torture and Democracy* (Princeton, NJ: Princeton University Press, 2007), 2.
5. See Alan M. Dershowitz, *Why Terrorism Works* (New Haven, CT: Yale University Press, 2002), chapter 4; Charles Krauthammer, "Truth about Torture," *Weekly Standard*, 11.12 (December 5, 2005), available at http://www.weeklystandard.com/Content/Public/Articles/000/000/006/400rhqav.asp; Jean Bethke Elshtain, "Reflections on the Problem of 'Dirty Hands.'" In *Torture: A Collection*, ed. Sanford Levinson (Oxford: Oxford University Press, 2006), 77–89; Michael Walzer famously presented the dirty hands approach to torture in the 1970s, see "Political Action: The Problem of Dirty Hands," in *Torture: A collection*, ed. Sanford Levinson (Oxford: Oxford University Press, 2006), 61–77.
6. For two works that do focus on religious issues, see William T. Cavanaugh, *Torture and Eucharist: Theology, Politics, and the Body of Christ* (Malden, MA: Blackwell, 1998), and George Hunsinger, ed., *Torture Is a Moral Issue: Christians, Jews, Muslims, and People of Conscience Speak Out* (Grand Rapids, MI: William B. Eerdmans, 2008).
7. Sanford Levinson, "Contemplating Torture: An Introduction," in *Torture: A collection*, ed. Sanford Levinson (Oxford: Oxford University Press, 2006), 33. I have learned a great deal from David Luban's excellent analysis of ticking time bomb cases: see David Luban, "Liberalism, Torture and the Ticking Bomb," in *The Torture Debate in America*, ed. Karen J. Greenberg (Cambridge: Cambridge University Press, 2006), 35–84. Henry Shue also demonstrates the flaws in ticking time bomb scenarios: see "Torture in Dreamland: Disposing of the Ticking Bomb," *Case Western Reserve Journal of International Law*, 37.2/3 (2006), 231–239. Finally, see Bob Brecher's recent book, *Torture and the Ticking Bomb* (Malden, MA: Blackwell, 2007).
8. For an excellent analysis of torture's institutional context, see Herbert C. Kelman, "The Social Context of Torture: Policy Process and Authority Structure," in *The Politics of*

Pain: Torturers and Their Masters, ed. Ronald D. Crelinsten and Alex P. Schmid (Boulder, CO: Westview Press, 1995), chapter 3. This volume contains other illuminating essays. I first learned of it by reading Brecher's book.

9. For these kinds of arguments, see Luban, "Liberalism, Torture and the Ticking Bomb," 37–44, and Seumus Miller, "Is Torture Ever Morally Justified?" *International Journal of Applied Philosophy*, 19.2 (2005), 179–192.

10. John Paul II, "Salvifici Doloris," section 5, available at http://www.vatican.va/holy_father/ john_paul_ii/apost_letters/documents/hf_jp-ii_apl_11021984_salvifici-doloris_en.html.

11. For Elaine Scarry's remarkable book about torture, see Scarry, *The Body in Pain: The Making and Unmaking of the World* (New York: Oxford University Press, 1985). See also David Sussman, "Defining Torture," *Case Western Reserve Journal of International Law*, 37.2/3 (2006), 225–230.

12. John Paul II, "Salvifici Doloris," section 2.

13. For an essay explaining Thomistic personalism, see Karol Wojtyla, "Thomistic Personalism," *Person and Community: Selected Essays*. Translated by Theresa Sandork, OSM (New York: Peter Lang, 1993), chapter 10. For a famous introduction to personalism, see Emmanuel Mounier, *Personalism*. Translated by Philip Mairet (Notre Dame, IN: University of Notre Dame Press, 1970). The first chapter of this work is particularly insightful. For a general survey of different kinds of personalism and an accompanying bibliography, see Kevin Schmiesing, "A History of Personalism," available at the Acton Institute Web site at http:// www.acton.org/research/pubs/papers/history_personalism.html.

14. Thomas Aquinas, *Summa Contra Gentiles*, II, 68, 6; italics in the original. Translated with an introduction and notes by James F. Anderson (Notre Dame, IN: University of Notre Dame Press, 2001). In this book, I use the following standard abbreviations for Aquinas's work: ST for the *Summa Theologica* and SCG for the *Summa Contra Gentiles*. My reading of Aquinas presupposes a metaphysical background that I do not consider in detail. I have been influenced by the following works on twentieth-century Thomism: Joseph de Finance, S.J. *Être et agir dans la philosophie de S. Thomas* (Rome: Universitá Gregoriana, 1960); Cornelio Fabro, *La nozione metafisica di partecipazione secondo S. Tomasso d'Aquino* (Torino: Società editrice internazionale, 1950); Fernand Van Steenberghen. *Ontology*. Translated by the Reverend Martin J. Flynn (New York: J.F. Wagner, 1952); Étienne Gilson, *Being and Some Philosophers* (Toronto, Canada: Pontifical Institute of Medieval Studies, 1952); Gregory Rocca, *Speaking the Incomprehensible God: Thomas Aquinas on the Interplay of Positive and Negative Theology* (Washington, DC: Catholic University of America Press, 2004); Rudi te Velde, *Participation and Substantiality in Thomas Aquinas* (Leiden, The Netherlands, E.J. Brill, 1995); John F. Wippel, *The Metaphysical Thought of Thomas Aquinas* (Washington, DC: Catholic University Press of America, 2000).

15. Josef Pieper, *Living the Truth: The Truth of All Things and Reality and the Good* (San Francisco, CA: St. Ignatius Press, 1989), 89.

16. See Joseph de Finance, S.J., *Essai sur l'agir humain* (Rome: Presses de l'Université grégorienne, 1962), chapter deuxieme.

17. W. Norris Clarke, S.J., *Person and Being* (Milwaukee, WI: Marquette University Press, 1993), 94.

18. Clarke, *Person and Being*, 193.

19. Kenneth L. Schmitz, "The First Principle of Personal Becoming," *The Texture of Being: Essays in First Philosophy* (Washington, DC: Catholic University Press of America, 2007), 194.

20. Alfred W. McCoy, *A Question of Torture: CIA Interrogation from the Cold War to the War on Terror* (New York: Henry Holt, 2007); Michael Otterman, *American Torture: From the Cold War to Abu Ghraib and Beyond* (Ann Arbor, MI: University of Michigan Press, 2007).

21. For a good discussion of how Nazi examples cloud our understanding of torture, see Rejali, *Torture and Democracy*, chapter 24. Philippe Sands also discusses Nazi examples, considering particularly what they mean for the moral responsibility of lawyers, see Philippe Sands, *Torture Team: Rumsfeld's Memo and the Betrayal of American Values* (New York: Palgrave Macmillan, 2008), chapters 24–25.

22. John Paul II, "Salvifici Doloris," section 5.

23. Jean Améry, *At the Mind's Limit: Contemplations by a Survivor of Auschwitz and Its Realities.* Translated by Sidney Rosenfeld and Stella P. Rosenfeld (Bloomington, IN: Indiana University Press, 1980), 39.

One   "The Soul Is Somehow All that Exists": Spirituality and Human Dignity

1. Pieper, *Living the Truth*, 83.

2. Karol Wojtyla, *Love and Responsibility.* Translated by H.T. Willetts (New York: Farrar, Straus, & Giroux, 1960), 21.

3. Ibid.; italic in the original.

4. Ibid.

5. Ibid., 22. For excellent analyses of how we experience persons, see John F. Crosby, *Personalist Papers* (Washington, DC: Catholic University Press of America, 2004); Max Scheler, *Formalism in Ethics and Non-Formal Ethics of Values: A New Attempt toward the Foundation of an Ethical Personalism.* Translated by Manfred S. Frings and Roger L. Funk (Evanston, IL: Northwestern University Press, 1973); and Edith Stein, *On the Problem of Empathy* (Washington DC: ICS, 1989).

6. Plato, *Timaeus*; italic in the original. Translated with an Introduction by Donald J. Zeyl (Indianapolis, IN: Hackett, 2000), 35a. In this section, I draw heavily on two articles: W. Norris Clarke, S.J., "Living on the Edge: The Human Person as 'Frontier Being' and Microcosm," *International Philosophical Quarterly*, 36.2, issue no. 142 (June 1996), 183–199, and Gerard Verbeke, "Man as a 'Frontier' According to Aquinas," in *Aquinas and the Problems of His Time*, ed. Gerard Verbeke and D. Verhults (Leuven, Belgium: Leuven University Press, 1976), 195–233.

7. Plotinus, *The Enneads.* Translated by Stephen McKenna. Abridged with an introduction and notes by John Dillon (London: Penguin Books, 1991), IV, 4, 3.

8. Nemesius of Emesa, "On the Nature of Man," in *Cyril of Jerusalem and Nemesius of Emesa.* Translated by William Telfer (London: SCM Press, 1955), 229.

9. Giovanni Pico della Mirandola, *Oration on the Dignity of Man.* Translated by Robert Caponigni (Chicago, IL: Henry Regnery, 1956), 7.

10. Plotinus, *The Enneads*, IV, 8, 4.

11. For a discussion of Plotinus, see Clarke, "Living on the Edge," 185.

12. Clarke, *Person and Being*, 37.

13. For a discussion of the amphibian status, see Eleonore Stump, *Aquinas: Arguments of the Philosophers* (London: Routledge, 2003), chapter 6.

14. *SCG*, II, 68, 6; italics in the original.

15. *ST*, I, 77, 2, respondio.

16. I owe this point to conversations with W. Norris Clarke, S.J.

17. Verbeke, "Man as a 'Frontier,'" 196.

18. Ibid., 207.

19. *SCG*, II, 68, 6.

20. Verbeke, "Man as a 'Frontier,'" 198.

21. For a wonderful analysis of this dual citizenship, see Joseph de Finance, S.J., *Citoyen de Deux Mondes: La place de l'homme dans la création* (Rome: Universitá Gregorian Editrice, 1980).

22. Kwasi Wiredu, *Cultural Universals and Particulars: An African Perspective* (Bloomington, IN: Indiana University Press, 1996), 55.

23. Ibid.

24. Steven Pinker, *The Blank Slate: The Modern Denial of Human Nature* (New York: Penguin Books, 2002), 224.

25. In what follows, I bypass complex issues in Thomistic thought involving abstraction, forms, formal identity, phantasms, and other matters. For full discussions of them, see Yves R. Simon, *An Introduction to the Metaphysics of Knowledge*. Edited and translated by Vukan Kuic and Richard J. Thompson (New York: Fordham University Press, 1990); John P. O'Callaghan, *Thomist Realism and the Linguistic Turn: Toward a More Perfect Form of Existence* (Notre Dame, IN: University of Notre Dame Press, 2003); Jacques Maritain, *Distinguish to Unite or the Degrees of Knowledge*. Translated by Gerald B. Phelan (New York: Charles Scribner's, 1959); Gyula Klima, "Nulla virtus cognoscitiva circa proprium obiectum decipitur," available at http://www.fordham.edu/gsas/phil/klima/APA.htm; Gyula Klima, "Tradition and Innovation in Medieval Theories of Mental Representation," *Proceedings of the Society for Medieval Logic and Metaphysics*, 4 (2004), 5, available at http://www.fordham.edu/gsas/phil/klima/SMLM/PSMLM4/PSMLM4.pdf; Robert Pasnau, *Theories of Cognition in the Middle Ages* (Cambridge, UK and NY: Cambridge University Press, 1997); John N. Deely, *Intentionality and Semiotics: A Story of Mutual Fecundation* (Scranton, PA: University of Scranton Press, 2007); Robert Pasnau, *Thomas Aquinas on Human Nature: A Philosophical Study of "Summa Theologica" Ia 75–89* (Cambridge, UK and NY: Cambridge University Press, 2002). I am grateful to Gyula Klima and John Deely for conversations about Aquinas's epistemology.

26. Stump, *Aquinas*, 245.

27. For a discussion of this change, see Maritain, *Distinguish to Unite*, 87.

28. Pieper, *Living the Truth*, 85. Pieper uses the concept of *Welt* to distinguish the unique character of the human environment. Drawing on the work of biologist Jakob Johann von Uexküll, he describes an *Umwelt* as a field of relations in which a being engages a limited environment. In contrast, a *Welt* is a field of relations in which a being actively engages a world by transcending particular environments. Pieper maintains that nonhuman animals have only an *Umwelt*, whereas humans have a *Welt*. John Deely offers a good discussion of these terms: see John N. Deely, *What Distinguishes Human Understanding?* (South Bend, IN: St. Augustine's Press, 2002), appendix.

29. *ST*, I, 76, 5, answer to objection 4. Twentieth-century Thomists such as Joseph Maréchal and Joseph Donceel used passages like this to maintain that we have an innate drive to know; see Joseph F. Donceel, *Natural Theology* (New York: Sheed and Ward, 1962) and Joseph Maréchal *A Maréchal Reader*. Edited by Joseph Donceel (St. Louis, MO: Herder & Herder, 1970). For a good discussion of these thinkers, see W. Norris Clarke, S.J., *The Philosophical Approach to God: A New Thomistic Perspective* (New York: Fordham University Press, 2007), chapter 1.

30. Pieper, *Living the Truth*, 80.

31. Ibid., 89.

32. See Finance, S.J., *Essai sur l'agir humain*, chapter deuxieme.

33. Both Aquinas and Thomists try to demonstrate that our intellectual activity cannot be physical. For Aquinas's arguments, see *SCG*, II, 49–50. See also Jacques Maritain, "The Immortality of the Soul," *The Range of Reason* (New York: Charles Schribner's, 1952), chapter 5. For a recent treatment of this topic that touches on philosophical materialism, see Gyula Klima, "Aquinas on the Immateriality of the Human Soul," available at http://www.phil-inst.hu/~gyula/FILES/immat.doc.

34. For a recent attack on dualism, see Patrick Lee and Robert P. George, *Body–Self Dualism in Contemporary Ethics and Politics* (Cambridge, NY: Cambridge University Press, 2007).

35. For example, see Aquinas, *Questions on the Soul*, qq. 8 and 15, and *ST*, II, 59–70.

36. *ST*, I, 85, article 1, respondio.

37. Given what we know from animal studies, a contemporary account of animal cognition would have to be more sophisticated than what Aquinas offers. For one good engagement

with contemporary thought, see Deely, *What Distinguishes Human Understanding?* For a very critical but limited response to Aquinas and environmentalism, see Francisco Benzoni, *Ecological Ethics and the Human Soul: Aquinas, Whitehead, and the Metaphysics of Value* (Notre Dame, IN: University of Notre Dame Press, 2007).

38. *ST*, I, 86, 2, respondio.

39. *SCG*, II, 83. For good discussions of mathematics and cognition, see Simon, *An Introduction to the Metaphysics of Knowledge*, 135, and Husserl, *Logical Investigations*. Translated by J.N. Findlay, with a new Preface by Michael Dummett and edited with a new Introduction by Dermot Moran (London: Routledge, 2001), investigation II.

40. Here, I pass over complex challenges to the atemporality of universals. For an excellent treatment of these issues, see J.P. Moreland, *Universals* (Montreal, Canada: McGill-Queen's University Press, 2001).

41. Aron Gurwitsch, *Phenomenology and the Theory of Science*. Edited by Lester Embree (Evanston, IL: Northwestern University Press, 1974), 233.

42. Pieper, *Living the Truth*, 81.

43. Ibid.

44. For discussions of the intrinsic existence of plants and nonhuman animals, see Finance, *Citoyen de Deux Mondes*, chapter 2, and William A. Wallace, *The Modeling of Nature: Philosophy of Science and Philosophy of Nature in Synthesis* (Washington, DC: Catholic University of America Press, 1997), chapters 1–3.

45. Clarke, *Person and Being*, 94.

46. Ibid., 193.

47. *SG*, II, 66, 5.

48. Karol Wojtyla, "The Constitution of Culture through Human Praxis," in *Person and Community: Selected Essays*. Translated by Theresa Sandok (New York: Peter Lang, 1993), 266.

49. Simon, *An Introduction to the Metaphysics of Knowledge,* 49.

50. Kenneth L. Schmitz, "The First Principle of Personal Becoming," 194.

51. For a definition of reductionism and an account of why it fails, see John Foster, *The Immaterial Mind: A Defence of the Cartesian Dualist Conception of the Mind* (London: Routledge, 1991), chapters 2–5.

52. Kenneth L. Schmitz, "Purity of Soul and Immorality," *The Texture of Being: Essays in First Philosophy* (Washington, DC: Catholic University Press of America, 2007), 202.

53. Schmitz, "The First Principle of Personal Becoming," 193.

54. Ibid.

55. Gabriel Marcel, *Being and Having: An Existentialist Diary.* Translated by Katherine Farrer, with an introduction by James Collins (New York: Harper Torchbooks; 1965), 69; italics in the original.

56. Wojtyla, *Love and Responsibility*, 97.

57. Gabriel Marcel, "Phenomenological Notes," *Creative Fidelity.* Translated by Robert Rosthal (New York: Farrar, Straus, & Co., 1964), 89.

58. Ibid.

59. Schmitz, "The First Principle of Personal Becoming," 194.

60. Marcel develops the concept of *disponibilité*, active receptivity toward others (often imperfectly translated as "availability"). He also famously distinguishes between the attitudes of having and being.

61. Marcel, "Phenomenological Notes," 89.

62. Gabriel Marcel, "Incarnate Being," *Creative Fidelity.* Translated by Robert Rosthal (New York: Farrar, Straus, 1964), 28.

63. Marcel, *Being and Having*, 187–188.

64. Kenneth L. Schmitz, "The Geography of the Human Person," *The Texture of Being: Essays in First Philosophy* (Washington, DC: Catholic University Press of America, 2007), 160. Crosby emphasizes the uniqueness of the person in "A Neglected Source of the Dignity of Persons," *Personalist Papers*, 3–32.

65. Schmitz, "The First Principle of Personal Becoming," 196.

66. Simon, *An Introduction to the Metaphysics of Knowledge*, 5.

67. Schmitz, "The First Principle of Personal Becoming," 198.

68. Maritain, *Distinguish to Unite*. 232.

69. Ibid.

70. Ibid.

71. Wojtyla, *Love and Responsibility*, 28.

72. Crosby, "The Estrangement of Persons from Their Bodies," *Personalist Papers*, 115.

73. Wojtyla, *Love and Responsibility,* 41.

74. Peter Singer and Karen Dawn, "Echoes of Abu Ghraib in Chicken Slaughterhouse," *Los Angeles Times*, July 25, 2004, available at http://articles.latimes.com/2004/jul/25/opinion/oe-singer25. All quotes in this paragraph are to this article. I owe this reference to Tara McKelvey's excellent book, *Monstering: Inside America's Policy of Secret Interrogations and Torture in the Terror War* (New York: Carroll & Graff, 2007), 41.

75. *SCG*, II, 45. For a good discussion of perfection and the universe, see Oliva Blanchette, *The Perfection of the Universe According to Aquinas: A Teleological Cosmology* (Pennsylvania: The Pennsylvania state University Press, 1992), chapters 3–5. Philosophers of science have often challenged Aristotelian and Thomistic conceptions of hierarchy in nature. For an excellent response that informs my work, see Wallace, *The Modeling of Nature*.

76. *SCG*, III, 57, 4.

77. Stump, *Aquinas*, 205.

78. Wojtyla, *Love and Responsibility*, 27.

Two   Breaking the Will: Spirituality and the Definition of Torture

1. Richard Posner, "Torture, Terrorism, and Interrogation," in *Torture: A Collection*, ed. Sanford Levinson (Oxford: Oxford University Press, 2006), 291–299.

2. Thomas Aquinas, *On Being and Essence*. Translated by Joseph Bobick (Notre Dame, IN: University of Notre Dame Press, 1965), introduction, para. 1.

3. George W. Bush," Statement by the President," June 26, 2003, available at http://www.whitehouse.gov/news/releases/2003/06/20030626-3.html.

4. Adam Hochschild, "What's in a Word? Torture," *New York Times*, May 23, 2004.

5. Mark Bowden, "The Dark Art of Interrogation," *Atlantic Monthly*, 293.3 (October 2003), 53.

6. For accounts of the atmosphere after the September 11 attacks, see Ron Suskind, *The One-Percent Doctrine: Deep Inside America's Pursuit of Its Enemies since 9/11* (New York: Simon & Schuster, 2007); John Yoo, *War by Other Means: An Insider's Account of the War on Terror* (New York: Atlantic Monthly Press, 2006); Jack Goldsmith, *The Terror Presidency: Law and Judgment inside the Bush Administration* (New York: W.W. Norton, 2007); Joseph Margulies, *Guantánamo and the Abuse of Presidential Power* (New York: Simon & Schuster, 2007); and Mayer, *The Dark Side*, chapters 1 and 2.

7. Mayer, *The Dark Side*, 4.

8. George W. Bush, "Humane Treatment of al-Qaeda and Taliban Detainees," February 7, 2002, in *The Torture Papers: The Road to Abu Ghraib*, ed. Karen J. Greenberg and Joshua L. Dratel. With an introduction by Anthony Lewis (Cambridge, NY: Cambridge University Press, 2005), 134.

9. Bush, "Humane Treatment," 135. In 2005, the Supreme Court rejected President Bush's claims about Common Article Three maintaining that it applies to all prisoners; see U.S. Supreme Court, *Hamdan v. Rumsfeld, Secretary of Defense, et al.*, available at http://www.supremecourtus.gov/opinions/05pdf/05-184.pdf.

10. Bush, "Humane Treatment," 135.

11. For a disturbing account of the secretive nature of deliberations about interrogations, see Barton Gellman, *Angler: The Cheney Vice Presidency* (New York: Penguin Press, 2008).

12. The Bybee–Yoo memo received sharp criticism from legal scholars. For some of this discussion, see Karen J. Greenberg, ed., *The Torture Debate in America* (Cambridge, NY: Cambridge University Press, 2006). This anthology contains good articles on the memo's legal dimensions. See also David Luban, "The Torture Lawyers of Washington," *Legal Ethics and Human Dignity* (Cambridge, NY: Cambridge University Press, 2007), chapter 5. Philippe Sands traces the pernicious effects of Secretary Rumsfeld's approval of these and other memos: see Philippe Sands, *Torture Team: Rumsfeld's Memo and the Betrayal of American Values* (New York: Palgrave Macmillan, 2008).

13. John Yoo and Jay Bybee, "Standards of Conduct for Interrogation under U.S.C. 2340–2340A," August 1, 2002, in *The Torture Papers: The Road to Abu Ghraib*, ed. Karen J. Greenberg and Joshua L. Dratel, with an introduction by Anthony Lewis (Cambridge, NY: Cambridge University Press, 2005) 183.

14. Ibid., 174.

15. Ibid., 176.

16. Ibid., 178.

17. Ibid., 193.

18. The causal relationship between the memos and the policy is complex because some actors denied knowledge of the Bybee–Yoo memos. The CIA tortured prior to the memos, and some analysts maintain that they were merely *ex post facto* justifications for torture. On this matter, I find Sands's account persuasive: see Sands, *Torture Team*.

19. Daniel Levin, "Legal Standards Applicable under 18 U.S.C. 2340–2340A," December 30, 2004, available at http://www.humanrightsfirst.org/us_law/etn/gonzales/memos_dir/levin-memo-123004.pdf.

20. For an extensive and excellent discussion of these signing statements, see Charlie Savage, *Takeover: The Return of the Imperial Presidency and the Subversion of American Democracy* (New York: Little, Brown, 2007), chapter 10. The American Bar Association issued a report sharply criticizing President Bush's use of signing statements: see American Bar Association, "Task Force on Presidential Signing Statements and the Separation of Powers Doctrine," August 2006, available at http://www.abanet.org/op/signingstatements/aba_final_signing_statements_recommendation-report_7-24-06.pdf.

21. I do not intend this as a complete account of the development of torture policy but simply as a sketch of its main elements. For Congressional legislation, see "Detainee Treatment Act of 2005," December 13, 2005, available at http://www.pegc.us/detainee_act_2005.html. See the *Army Field Manual*, FM 34–52, "Intelligence Interrogation," available at http://www.fas.org/irp/doddir/army/fm34-52.pdf. For President Bush's executive order, see "Executive Order: Interpretation of the Geneva Conventions Common Article 3 as Applied to a Program of Detention and Interrogation Operated by the Central Intelligence Agency," available at http://www.whitehouse.gov/news/releases/2007/07/20070720-4.html. The Obama administration reversed most of President Bush's interrogation policies almost immediately after taking office.

22. In medieval philosophy, Peter Lombard heavily emphasized intention. For a good discussion of his work, see Servais Pinckaers, O.P., "A Historical Perspective on Intrinsically Evil Acts," in *The Pinckaers Reader: Renewing Thomistic Moral Theology*, ed. John Berkman and Craig S. Titus. Translated by Sr. Mary Thomas Noble, O.P., Craig S. Titus, Michael Sherwin, O.P., and Hugh Connolly (Washington, DC: Catholic University Press of America, 2005), 194–198.

23. Although emphasized by the Roman Catholic tradition, others outside of it have embraced similar philosophies of action. For example, see Alan Donagan, *The Theory of Morality* (Chicago, IL: University of Chicago Press, 1977), and Gilbert Meilaender, *Bioethics: A Primer for Christians* (Grand Rapids, MI: William B. Eerdmans, 1996), chapter 7.

24. Jean Porter, *Nature as Reason: A Thomistic Theory of the Natural Law* (Grand Rapids, MI: William B. Eerdmans, 2005), 275. For a good discussion of the Thomistic account of action, see Servais Pinckaers, O.P., "Revisionist Understandings of Actions in the Wake of Vatican II," in *The Pinckaers Reader: Renewing Thomistic Moral Theology*, ed. John Berkman and Craig S. Titus. Translated by Sr. Mary Aquinas Noble, O.P., Craig S. Titus, Michael Sherwin, O.P., and Hugh Connolly (Washington, DC: Catholic University Press of America, 2005), chapter 12.

25. Janet E. Smith, *Humanae Vitae* (Washington, DC: Catholic University of America Press, 1991), 216. In this section, I draw heavily on this work.

26. For a detailed and disturbing account of the circumstances at Abu Ghraib, see Philip Gourevitch and Errol Morris, *Standard Operating Procedure* (New York: Penguin, 2008). This book contains important details about the Abu Ghraib disaster. Unfortunately, Gourevitch and Morris fail to carefully indicate all sources making it difficult to substantiate their claims.

27. United Nations Convention against Torture and Other Cruel, Inhuman, or Degrading Treatment or Punishment, June 26, 1987, available at http://www.unhchr.ch/html/menu3/b/h_cat39.htm. For this and other reasons, I find the CAT definition of torture inadequate. For a very good account of why it is problematic, see Gail H. Miller "Defining Torture," Floersheimer Center for Constitutional Democracy, Occasional Paper #3, available at http://www.cardozo.yu.edu/cms/uploadedFiles/FLOERSHEIMER/Defining%20Torture.pdf.

28. For these kinds of torture, see David Luban, "Liberalism, Torture and the Ticking Bomb," 41–44.

29. For a good discussion of voluntary action, see Robert Sokolowski, *Moral Action: A Phenomenological Analysis,* (Bloomington: Indiana University Press, 1984), 11–17.

30. I take this distinction from Aquinas's discussion of action: see *ST*, I–II, qq. 6, 8, and 18. See also Stump, *Aquinas*, 284–285.

31. To address such cases, legal thinkers have developed the concept of "command responsibility." For a discussion of it, see Dinah Pokempner, "Command Responsibility for Torture," in *Torture: Does it Make Us Safer? Is it Ever OK? A Human Rights Perspective*, ed. Kenneth Roth and Minky Worden. Amy D. Bernstein, contributing editor. Published in conjunction with Human Rights Watch, (New York: New Press, 2005), chapter 14. For an insightful discussion of command responsibility, see Lawrence P. Rockwood, *Walking Away from Nuremberg: Just War and the Doctrine of Command Responsibility* (Amherst, MA: University of Massachusetts Press, 2007).

32. Elizabeth Anscombe, *Intention*, 2nd edn (Ithaca, NY: Cornell University Press, 1957), 9.

33. For example, Aquinas discusses a person who steals to commit adultery. In this case, he is a thief and an adulterer, see *ST*, I–II, q. 18, article 7. See also Smith, *Humanae Vitae*, 217.

34. Marcy S. Strauss, "Torture," January 2003, Loyola-LA Public Law Research Paper No. 2003-7, p. 211, available at SSRN: http://ssrn.com/abstract=370680 or DOI: 10.2139/ssrn.370680.

35. Jeremy Waldron, "Torture and Positive Law: Jurisprudence for the White House," *Columbia Law Review*, 105 (October 2005), 1701.

36. Ibid.

37. Philip Zelikow, "Legal Policy for a Twilight War," April 26, 2007, available at http://hnn.us/articles/39494.html.

38. I have learned a great deal from Steven Miles's excellent book on doctors and torture, see Steven Miles, *Oath Betrayed: Torture, Medical Complicity and the War on Terror* (New York: Random House, 2006). Sands maintains that two BSCTs operated at Guantánamo—one that strongly opposed and refused to participate in harsh interrogation and another that supported it. For this discussion, see Sands, *Torture Team*, chapter 15.

39. For minutes of these meetings, see http://levin.senate.gov/newsroom/supporting/2008/Documents.SASC.061708.pdf.

40. Michael Davis, "The Moral Justifiability of Torture and Other Cruel, Inhuman and Degrading Treatment," *International Journal of Applied Philosophy*, 19.2 (2005), 163.

41. Seumus Miller, "Torture," *The Stanford Encyclopedia of Philosophy*, 2006, available at http://plato.stanford.edu/entries/torture/.

42. Rejali, *Torture and Democracy*, 35.

43. Uwe Jacobs, "Documenting the Neurobiology of Psychological Torture: Conceptual and Neuropsychological Observations," in *The Trauma of Psychological Torture*, ed. Almerindo E. Ojeda (Westport, CT: Praeger, 2008), 164.

44. Some attacks on physicalism focus on the intentionality or the object-directed character of thinking arguing that it is irreducible to scientific language and explanation. Others consider qualia, or what it is like to have certain experiences, arguing that physicalism cannot explain them. I find both approaches convincing but will not defend them in this book. For some important refutations of physicalism, see Roderick M. Chisholm, *Perceiving: A Philosophical Study* (Ithaca, NY: Cornell University Press, 1957), 168–173; Richard Swinburne, *The Evolution of the Soul* (Oxford: Oxford University Press, 1997); Charles Taliaferro, *Consciousness and the Mind of God* (Cambridge, NY and UK: Cambridge University Press, 1994); David A. Chalmers, "Consciousness and Its Place in Nature," 2001, available at http://consc.net/papers/nature.pdf; and Jaegwon Kim, *Physicalism or Something Near Enough* (Princeton, NJ: Princeton University Press, 2007). For a recent discussion of neuroscience and consciousness, see M.R. Bennett and P.M.S. Hacker, *Philosophical Foundations of Neuroscience* (Boston, MA: Wiley-Blackwell, 2003).

45. For an excellent, recent collection of articles on the neuroscientific effects of psychological torture, see Alermindo E. Ojeda, ed., *The Trauma of Psychological Torture* (Westport, CT: Praeger, 2008).

46. American Civil Liberties Union, "FBI Inquiry Details Abuses Reported by Agents at Guantánamo," available at http://www.aclu.org/safefree/torture/27816prs20070103.html. See also Gitanjali S. Gutierrez, Esq., "The Case of Mohammed al-Qahtani," in *The Trauma of Psychological Torture*, ed. Alermindo E. Ojeda (Westport, CT: Praeger, 2008), chapter 11.

47. Quoted in Mayer, *The Dark Side*, 207.

48. Gutierrez, Esq., "The Case of Mohammed al-Qahtani," 195–196.

49. As I will discuss in chapter three, some of these techniques originated in Survival, Evasion, Resistance, and Escape (SERE) programs in the Army, Navy, and Air Force. They have included attacks on trainee's religious beliefs: see Otterman, *American Torture*, 104–105. For a discussion of the links between interrogation in the War on Terror and SERE, see Jane Mayer, "The Black Sites: A New Look at inside the CIA's Secrete Interrogation Program," *New Yorker*, August 13, 2007, available at http://www.newyorker.com/reporting/2007/08/13/070813fa_fact_mayer?printable=true. See also Rejali, *Torture and Democracy*, 383, and Sands, *Torture Team*, 47. In 2008, the Senate held hearings on interrogations at Guantánamo, releasing information that established relationships between interrogation and the SERE programs: see U.S. Senate, "The Origin of Aggressive Interrogation Techniques: Part I of the Committee's Inquiry into the Treatment of Detainees in U.S. Custody," available at http://levin.senate.gov/newsroom/supporting/2008/Documents.SASC.061708.pdf. Defense department officials sent documents to Guantánamo that carefully describe stress positions, isolation, sensory deprivation, and other forms of abusive interrogation.

50. "The Taguba Report: Article 15–6 Investigation of the 800th Military Police Brigade," in *The Torture Papers: The Road to Abu Ghraib*, ed. Karen J. Greenberg and Joshua L. Dratel. With an introduction by Antony Lewis (Cambridge, NY: Cambridge University Press), 524.

51. Davis, "The Moral Justifiability of Torture," 164. In this paragraph, I draw heavily from Davis's article.

52. Améry, *At the Mind's Limit*, 28.

53. David Sussman, "What's Wrong with Torture?" *Philosophy and Public Affairs*, 33 (2005), 6. For empirical evidence that helplessness is important in torture, see Ronald D. Crelinsten, "In Their Own Words: The World of the Torturer," in *The Politics of Pain: Torturers and Their Masters*, ed. Ronald D. Crelinsten and Alex P. Schmid (Boulder, CO: Westview, 1995), chapter 4.

54. Sussman, "What's Wrong with Torture?" 7.

55. Shue, "Torture," 52.

56. Heather McDonald, "How to Interrogate Terrorists," in *The Torture Debate in America*, ed. Karen J. Greenberg (Cambridge, NY: Cambridge University Press, 2006), 85.

57. See Andy Worthington, *The Guantánamo Files: The Stories of the 744 Detainees in America's Illegal Prison* (London: Pluto Press, 2007), 94.

58. Margulies, *Guantánamo and the Abuse of Presidential Power*, 27 italics in the original. For another discussion of the mosaic theory, see David Cole, *Enemy Aliens: Double Standards and Constitutional Freedoms in the War on Terrorism* (New York: New Press, 2003), 20–21.

59. Rejali, *Torture and Democracy*, 465.

60. Shue, "Torture," 55.

61. Ibid.

62. Ibid.

63. Several authors make this point about pain. For example, see Patrick Lee, "Interrogational Torture," *American Journal of Jurisprudence*, 51 (2006), 131–147.

64. Miller, "Torture."

65. Ibid.

66. Lee, "Interrogational Torture," 140.

67. *Interrogation Log, Detainee 0631,* December 11, 2002, available at http://www.americantorture.com/documents/featured/featured_02.pdf.

68. Ibid., December 19, 2002. The U.S. government maintains that al-Qahtani's interrogation yielded valuable intelligence data. However, Sands raises serious questions about its intelligence value: see Sands, *Torture Team*, chapters 18–20. For evidence that labeling detainees contributed to abuse and for other instances where detainees were treated like animals, see Mark Danner, *Torture and Truth: America, Abu Ghraib, and the War on Terror* (New York: New York Review of Books, 2004), 13, 44–45.

69. Yoo, *War by Other Means*, 174.

70. Yoo and Bybee, "Standards of Conduct for Interrogation," 210.

71. Martin Rhonheimer, "Intentional Actions and the Meaning of the Object: A Reply to Richard McCormick," *Thomist*, 59.2 (April 1995), 298.

72. Lisa S. Cahill, "Accent on the Masculine," in *Veritatis Splendor: American Perspectives*, ed. Michael E. Allsopp and John J. O'Keefe (Kansas City, MO: Sheed and Ward, 1995), 58; Richard A. McCormick, "Document Begs Many Legitimate Moral Questions," *National Catholic Reporter*, October 15, 1993, 17; and Charles E. Curran and Richard A. McCormick, *Moral Norms and Catholic Tradition: Readings in Moral Theology No. 1* (New York: Paulist Press, 1979).

73. Robert A. Destro, "Foreword," *Educing Information: Interrogation: Science and Art Foundations for the Future*, Intelligence Science Board, December 2006, available at http://www.fas.org/irp/dni/educing.pdf.

74. Eric D'Arcy, *Human Acts: An Essay in Their Moral Evaluation* (Oxford, England: Clarendon Press, 1965), 10.

75. Finance, *Essai sur l'agir humain*.

76. The twentieth century saw many failed attempts to reduce the third to the first person. For excellent discussions of this issue, see Thomas Nagal, *The View from Nowhere* (New York: Oxford University Press, 1989), and John R. Searle, *The Rediscovery of the Mind* (Cambridge, MA: MIT Press, 1992).

77. Rhonheimer, "Intentional Actions and the Meaning of the Object," 288.

78. Ibid., italic in the original.

79. See Sokolowski, *Moral Action*, 27.

80. See John Paul II, "Veritatis Splendor," 78, available at http://www.vatican.va/holy_father/john_paul_ii/encyclicals/documents/hf_jp-ii_enc_06081993_veritatis-splendor_en.html and Rhonheimer, "Intentional Actions and the Meaning of the Object," 282.

81. Pinckaers, O.P., "Revisionist Understandings of Actions in the Wake of Vatican II," 255.

82. D'Arcy, *Human Acts*, 21.

83. Ibid., 23.

84. To defend the position on act essences that I have adopted, I would need to consider issues about modality, action, and nominalism, which I think are at the heart of many contemporary theories of action. For an excellent historical discussion of nominalism and act theory, see Pinckaers, O.P., "A Historical Perspective on Intrinsically Evil Acts," chapter 11. For a powerful and convincing refutation of nominalism, see Husserl, *Logical Investigations*, investigations I and II. I have also learned much about the philosophy of action by reading Yves Simon and Adolf Reinach's work, see Yves R. Simon, *Practical Knowledge*, ed. Robert J. Mulvaney (New York: Fordham University Press, 1991) and Adolph Reinach, *The Apriori Foundations of the Civil Law*. Translated by John F. Crosby, "Aletheia" III (1983), 1–142.

85. Here, without doing full justice to it, I rely on Sokolowski's insightful analysis of the moral act, see Sokolowski, *Moral Action*, 41–76. With Sokolowski, I reject a purely causal approach to acts that individuate them by their causal origins. For discussions of individuating intentions, see Michael S. Moore, "Intention and *Mens Rea*," in *Placing Blame: A General Theory of the Criminal Law* (Oxford: Clarendon Press, 1997), 449–477. Moore insightfully discusses problems in individuating the purpose or object of intention, but operates with a philosophical framework from analytic philosophy that I reject. Consequently, I depart significantly from his analysis. For another good discussion of intention, see Anthony Kenny, "Intention and Purpose," *Journal of Philosophy*, 63 (1966), 642–651.

86. Cahill, "Accent on the Masculine," 58.

87. Smith, *Humanae Vitae*, 219.

88. For a good analysis of consent in such cases, see Michael S. Moore, "Torture and the Balance of Evil," *Placing Blame: A General Theory of the Criminal Law*, (Oxford: Clarendon Press), 708–711.

89. McKelvey, *Monstering*, 108.

90. Some Thomists make this point technically by distinguishing between a *finis operis* and a *finis operantis*. The *finis operis* is the immediate object the agent wills, whereas the *finis operantis* is the motive or further intention of the agent. Making this distinction, Aquinas describes someone building a house. He may intend to earn a profit but still builds a house. The *finis operis* is building the house, whereas the profit is the *finis operantis*. After finishing the house, a builder cannot coherently claim he sought only profit and never aimed at building a house. Similarly, Private Lynndie English may have intended to protect her fellow soldiers at Abu Ghraib, but she cannot coherently claim that she never tortured. For Aquinas's discussion, see *ST*, I–II, q. 141, a. 6, ad. 1. For a good but slightly critical discussion of these kinds of intention, see Martin Rhonheimer, *Natural Law and Practical Reason: A Thomist View of Moral Autonomy*. Translated by Gerald Malsbary (New York: Fordham University Press, 2000), 430–437. Pinckaers raises questions about whether Aquinas clearly develops this distinction or if it is a development of later Thomists, see Pinckaers, O.P., "A Historical Perspective on Intrinsically Evil Acts," 210.

91. See Suskind, *The One-Percent Doctrine*, chapters 3–6 and CNN, "CIA Director: Waterboarding Necessary but Potentially Illegal," February 7, 2008, available at http://www.cnn.com/2008/POLITICS/02/07/mukasey.waterboarding/index.html?eref=rss_topstories. For a good discussion of George Tenet and the CIA, see James Risen, *State*

of War: The Secret History of the CIA and the Bush Administration (New York: Free Press, 2006).

92. Bowden, "The Dark Art of Interrogation," 4.

93. Elshtain, "Reflections on the Problem of 'Dirty Hands,'" 86.

94. Roman Catholic theology often lists torture as an intrinsically evil act that no circumstance can ever justify. For one example, see John Paul II, "Veritatis Splendor," section 89.

95. For discussions of Communist methods of torture, see Otterman, *American Torture*, chapter 3, and the cold war document written by psychologists Harold Wolff and Lawrence Hinkle, Jr., "Communist Control Techniques: An Analysis of the Methods Used by Communist State Police in the Arrest, Interrogation, and Indoctrination of Persons Regarded as 'Enemies of the State,'" April 2, 1956, available at http://americantorture. com/documents/cold_war/01.pdf. I am grateful to Michael Otterman for making this document available online. Rebecca Lemov provides good background on Harold Wolff: see *World as Laboratory: Experiments with Mice, Mazes, and Men* (New York: Hill & Wang, 2005), 203–211.

96. See *Educing Information: Interrogation: Science and Art Foundations for the Future*, Intelligence Science Board, December 2006, available at http://www.fas.org/irp/dni/educing.pdf, 33–34.

97. See Donald Rumsfeld, "Memorandum for the Commander, Southern Command," April 16, 2003, in *The Torture Papers: The Road to Abu Ghraib*, ed. Karen J. Greenberg and Joshua L. Dratel. With an introduction by Anthony Lewis (Cambridge, NY: Cambridge University Press, 2005), 362.

98. "The most commonly reported technique used by non-FBI interrogators on detainees at GTMO [Guantánamo Bay] was sleep deprivation or disruption," U.S. Department of Justice, Office of the Inspector General, *A Review of the FBI's Involvement in and Observations of Detainee Interrogations in Guantánamo Bay, Afghanistan, and Iraq*, May 2008, conclusion, 355, available at http://www.usdoj.gov/oig/special/s0805/final.pdf.

99. See the "Counter Resistance Strategy Meeting Minutes," October 2, 2002, available at http://levin.senate.gov/newsroom/supporting/2008/Documents.SASC.061708.pdf.

100. Quoted in Levinson, "Contemplating Torture," 28.

101. Suskind, *The One-Percent Doctrine*, 230.

102. John Conroy, *Unspeakable Acts, Ordinary People: The Dynamics of Torture* (Berkley, CA: University of California Press, 2002), 125–137, 185–187. For an extensive discussion of the IRA case, see the European Court of Human Rights, *Ireland v. United Kingdom*, January 18, 1978, available at http://www.echr.coe.int/echr/.

103. See Rejali, *Torture and Democracy*, 339–340.

104. For one recent study of the effects of psychological torture, see M. Basoglu, M. Livanou and C. Crnobaric, "Torture versus other cruel, inhuman and Degrading Treatment: Is the Distinction Real or Apparent?" *Archives of General Psychiatry*, 64 (2007), 277–285.

Three   Assaulting the Spirit:
Why Torture Is Wrong

1. Andrew Sullivan, "The Abolition of Torture," *Torture: A Collection*, ed. Sanford Levinson (Oxford: Oxford University Press, 2006), 318.

2. Physicians for Human Rights, "Break Them Down: Systematic Use of Psychological Torture by U.S. Forces," section IV, 2005, available at http://physiciansforhumanrights. org/library/documents/reports/break-them-down-the.pdf.

3. Miller, "Torture."

4. Luban, "Liberalism, Torture, and the Ticking Bomb," 39.

5. Shue, "Torture," in Levinson, *Torture*, 59.

6. *An Evangelical Declaration against Torture: Protecting Human Rights in the Age of Terror*, section 7:9, available at http://www.evangelicalsforhumanrights.org/Declaration.pdf. For a critical response to this declaration, see Keith Pavlischek, " 'Human Rights and Justice in an Age of Terror": An Evangelical Critique of 'An Evangelical Declaration against Torture,' " *Books and Culture*, September/October 2007, available at http://www.christianitytoday.com/books/web/2007/sept24a.html.

7. Elaine Scarry, *The Body in Pain*, chapter 1. I draw on Scarry's book frequently in this chapter.

8. Jacobo Timerman, *Prisoner without a Name, Cell without a Number*. Translated from the Spanish by Toby Talbot (New York: Alfred Knopf, 1981), 34–35.

9. Rejali, *Torture and Democracy*, 333.

10. For information about these experiments, see Colin A. Ross, M.D., *The CIA Doctors: Human Rights Violations by American Psychiatrists* (Richardson, TX: Manitou Communications, 2006). Ross embraces some controversial psychological theories that I do not endorse, but his book contains a wealth of valuable information about MKULTRA and other programs. For example, he offers a chart of known psychologists at universities who received CIA funding—see appendix C. Some contemporary thinkers maintain that these researchers were unaware that their experiments were unethical. They argue that in condemning them, we anachronistically apply contemporary ethical standards to the past. With other scholars, I reject this interpretation because the Nuremburg Code of 1946 and earlier documents show a clear concern for informed consent. Many psychiatrists and psychologists simply ignored informed consent or manipulated subjects into participating in these experiments. For good articles discussing ethics and human subject research, see George J. Annas and Michael A. Grodin, eds., *The Nazi Doctors and the Nuremburg Code: Human Rights in Human Experimentation* (Oxford, England: Oxford University Press, 1995).

11. Historians differ on how much Hebb supported or was aware of CIA activities. McCoy argues that he was fully aware of the CIA's interest in his work. Richard E. Brown, however, disputes his claim: see Richard E. Brown, "Alfred McCoy, Hebb, the CIA and Torture," *Journal of the History of Behavioral Sciences*, 43.2 (April 2007), 205–213. For McCoy's response, see Alfred W. McCoy, "Science in Dachau's Shadow: Hebb, Beecher, and the Development of CIA Psychological Torture and Modern Medical Ethics," *Journal of the History of Behavioral Sciences*, 43.4 (October 2007), 401–417. I find McCoy's account of Hebb and the CIA persuasive.

12. For a discussion of this episode, see Rejali, *Torture and Democracy*, 368–369.

13. For discussions of this history, see McCoy, *A Question of Torture*; John Marks, *The Search for the "Manchurian Candidate": The CIA and Mind Control* (New York: Times Books, 1979); George Andrews, *MKULTRA: The CIA's Top Secret Program in Human Experimentation and Behavior Modification* (Winston-Salem, NC: Healthnet Press, 2001); and Otterman, *American Torture* and Ross, *The CIA Doctors*.

14. For discussions of the Cameron case, see the sources in note 13. See also Gordon Thomas, *Journey into Madness: The True Story of Secret CIA Mind Control and Medical Abuse* (New York: Bantam Books, 1989). For a moving account of how Cameron ruined a man's life, see Harvey M. Weinstein, *Psychiatry and the CIA: Victims of Mind Control* (Washington, DC: American Psychiatric Press, 1990).

15. *KUBARK Counterintelligence Interrogation*, July 1963, IX, B, available at http://www.americantorture.com/documents/cold_war/03.pdf.

16. McCoy, *A Question of Torture*, 91.

17. For evidence of sensory deprivation in Afghanistan, see Worthington, *The Guantánamo Files*, chapters 8–10, 14.

18. Jerald Phifer, "Memorandum for Commander, Joint Task Force 170," October 11, 2002, in *The Torture Papers: The Road to Abu Ghraib*, ed. Karen J. Greenberg and Joshua L. Dratel.

With an introduction by Anthony Lewis (Cambridge, NY: Cambridge University Press, 2005), 227–228.

19. Physicians for Human Rights, "Break Them Down," section II, C, 1, available at http://www.cageprisoners.com/downloads/psych_torture.pdf?PHPSESSID=ece1209595736e66 6d8f1d9cc563ed28.

20. For a discussion of FBI eyewitness accounts of isolation at Guantánamo, see U.S. Department of Justice, *A Review*, chapter 8, section E, 185; chapter 9, section L, 227; and chapter 11, section C, IV, A, 1–2, 300–301. See also David Rose, *Guantánamo: The War on Human Rights*, New York: New Press, 2006.

21. Physicians for Human Rights, "Break Them Down," section II, C, 1.

22. Several studies of Guantánamo have established that many detainees were swept up in raids or sold to the United States in Afghanistan. Although they had no connection to the Taliban or al-Qaeda, they ended up at Guantánamo. This fiasco originated largely from a grossly incompetent screening procedure in Afghanistan. Worthington offers considerable evidence of this incompetence: see Worthington, *The Guantánamo Files*. For a fascinating look at why many people from around the world ended up in Afghanistan, see Sharon Curcio, "Generational Differences in Waging Jihad," *Military Review*, July-August 2005, 84–88.

23. Council of Europe, Parliamentary Assembly, "Secret Detentions and Illegal Transfers of Detainees Involving Council of Europe Member States: Second Report," Committee on Legal Affairs and Human Rights, Rapporteur: Mr Dick Marty, Switzerland, Alliance of Liberals and Democrats for Europe, June 11, 2007, section 247, available at http://assembly.coe.int/Documents/WorkingDocs/Doc07/edoc11302.pdf. Mayer describes how the CIA decided to operate black sites: see Mayer, *The Dark Side*, chapter 7. Risen also discusses the secret prisons: see Risen, *State of War*, chapter 1.

24. Council of Europe, "Secret Detentions and Illegal Transfers," section 30. Mayer maintains that some CIA officials knew El-Masri was innocent of all charges, but in spite of this knowledge, they continued to imprison and torture him: see Mayer, *The Dark Side*, 282–287. For a systematic account of the CIA secret prisons, see Center for Human Rights and Global Justice, NYU Law School, "On the Record: U.S. Disclosures on Rendition, Secret Detention, and Coercive Interrogation," 2008, available at http://www.chrgj.org/projects/docs/ontherecord.pdf. This report discusses cases that match the details in El-Masri's account. See also Center for Human Rights and Global Justice, *Surviving the Darkness: Testimony from the U.S. "Black Sites"* (New York: NYU School of Law, 2007), available at http://www.chrgj.org/projects/docs/survivingthedarkness.pdf.

25. Physicians for Human Rights, "Break Them Down," executive summary.

26. Stuart Grassian, M.D., "Psychiatric Effects of Solitary Confinement," available at http://www.prisoncommission.org/statements/grassian_stuart_long.pdf.

27. Grassian, "Psychiatric Effects."

28. Ibid., 13.

29. Thomas Aquinas, *Questions on the Soul*, Translated by James H. Robb (Milwaukee, WI: Marquette University Press, 1984), q. 15, 186.

30. Stuart Grassian, M.D., "Neuropsychiatric Effects of Solitary Confinement," in *The Trauma of Psychological Torture*, ed. Almerindo E. Ojeda (Westport, CT: Praeger, 2008), 116.

31. Jacobs, "Documenting the Neurobiology of Psychological Torture," 167.

32. Grassian, "Neuropsychiatric Effects of Solitary Confinement," 116.

33. KUBARK, 88.

34. Timerman, *Prisoner without a Name*, 85.

35. KUBARK, 77.

36. Clarke, *Person and Being*, 45.

37. Scarry, *The Body in Pain*, 36.

38. Ibid., 38.

39. Ibid., 40.

40. See McKelvey, *Monstering*, 157–161, and Otterman, *American Torture*, 174.

41. Gourevitch and Morris, *Standard Operating Procedure*, 47.

42. *New York Times*, "Padilla Is Guilty on All Charges in Terror Trial," August 16, 2007, available at http://www.nytimes.com/2007/08/17/us/17padilla.html?_r=1&oref=slogin.

43. Mayer, *The Dark Side*, 199.

44. See *New York Times*, "Video Is a Window into Terror Suspect's Isolation," December 4, 2006, available at http://www.nytimes.com/2006/12/04/us/04detain.html.

45. Southern District of Florida Miami Division, *United States of America vs. Jose Padilla, Defendant. Motion to Dismiss for Outrageous Government Conduct*, October 4, 2006, available at http://www.discourse.net/archives/docs/Padilla_Outrageous_Government_Conduct.pdf.

46. *New York Times*, "Video Is a Window into a Terror Suspect's Isolation."

47. Grassian, "Neuropsychiatric Effects of Solitary Confinement," 124.

48. *SCG*, II, 68, 6.

49. Maritain, *Distinguish to Unite*, 232.

50. Ibid.

51. Clarke, *Person and Being*, 61.

52. Scarry, *The Body in Pain*, 24.

53. Sussman, "What's Wrong with Torture?" 21. I draw heavily from this article in the next few paragraphs. See also "Defining Torture."

54. Ibid.

55. Ibid., 23.

56. Ibid., 30.

57. *Human Resources Exploitation Training Manual*, section 1-1, available at http://www.gwu.edu/~nsarchiv/NSAEBB/NSAEBB122/CIA%20Human%20Res%20Exploit%20H0-L17.pdf. For an analysis of the KUBARK manual, see Steven M. Kleinman, M.S., "KUBARK Counterintelligence Interrogation Review: Observations of an Interrogator: Lessons Learned and Avenues for Further Research," in *Educing Information: Interrogation: Science and Art Foundations for the Future*, Intelligence Science Board, December 2006, chapter 5. Jennifer Harbury explores CIA torture in Latin America, see Jennifer K. Harbury, *Truth, Torture and the American Way: The History and Consequences of U.S. Involvement in Torture* (Boston, MA: Beacon Press, 2005). John Dinges discusses Operation Condor, the Chilean program of torture and assassination in the 1970s that targeted people in South America, the United States and Europe: see John Dinges, *The Condor Years: How Pinochet and His allies brought Terrorism to Three Continents* (New York: New Press, 2005). For an older but still good account of U.S. torture in Latin and South America, see A.J. Langguth, *Hidden Terrors* (New York: Pantheon Books, 1978).

58. Clarke, *Person and Being*, 46.

59. Timerman, *Prisoner without a Name*, 132–133.

60. Ibid., 148.

61. Rejali, *Torture and Democracy*, chapter 14.

62. Ibid., 316.

63. McCoy, *A Question of Torture*, 55.

64. Conroy offers a full discussion of British torture and the IRA, see John Conroy, *Unspeakable Acts, Ordinary People*.

65. McCoy, *A Question of Torture*, 32, 45–47. See also Otterman, *American Torture*, 14–42.

66. KUBARK, section H. For the original study, see Lawrence Hinkle, Jr. and Harold Wolff, *Communist Control Techniques: An Analysis of the Methods Used by Communist State Police in the Arrest, Interrogation, and Indoctrination of Persons Regarded as "Enemies of the State,"* April 1956, available at http://www.americantorture.com/documents/cold_war/01.pdf. See also Albert D. Biderman, "Communist Attempts to Elicit False Confessions from Air Force Prisoners," *Bulletin of the New York Academy of Medicine*, 33.9 (September 1957), 616–625,

available at http://www.pubmedcentral.nih.gov/picrender.fcgi?artid=1806204&blobtype= pdf. Biderman emphasizes the effectiveness of self-inflicted pain arguing that it pits the person against himself. He also notes how it may leave no marks, thus offering cover for interrogators who want to deny that they have tortured.

67. Ibid.
68. For a full discussion of this history, see McCoy, *A Question of Torture,* chapter 3.
69. Phifer, "Memorandum for Commander, Joint Task Force 170," 227.
70. Donald Rumsfeld, "Action Memo," November 27, 2002, in Greenberg, *The Torture Papers, 237.*
71. See Jane Mayer, "The Memo: How an Internal Effort to Ban the Abuse and Torture of Detainees Was Thwarted," *New Yorker,* February 27, 2006, available at http://www. newyorker.com/archive/2006/02/27/060227fa_fact.
72. "Working Group Report on Detainee Interrogations," in *The Torture Papers: The Road to Abu Ghraib,* ed. Karen J. Greenberg and Joshua L. Dratel. With an introduction by Anthony Lewis (Cambridge, NY: Cambridge University Press, 2005), 342, 347.
73. Rumsfeld, "Memorandum for the Commander," April 16, 2003, 360.
74. Ibid.
75. U.S. Department of Justice, *A Review* chapter eight, section II, B, 179–182. Disturbingly, although the Department of Defense rescinded use of stress positions on January 12, 2003, interrogators continued to use short-shackling at least through May, 2004.
76. *Washington Post,* "U.S. Decries Abuse but Defends Interrogations "Stress and Duress" Tactics Used on Terrorism: Suspects Held in Secret Overseas Facilities," December 26, 2002, available at http://www.washingtonpost.com/ac2/wp-dyn/A37943-2002Dec25.
77. Bowden, *The Dark Art of Interrogation,* 3. For background on Khalid Sheikh Mohammed's torture, see Mayer, *The Dark Side,* 270–280. For evidence of widespread use of stress positions in Afghanistan, see Human Rights Watch, "Enduring Freedom": Abuses by U.S. Forces in Afghanistan," March 2004, available at http://hrw.org/reports/2004/afghanistan0304/.
78. Otterman, *American Torture,* 162.
79. "The ICRC Report: Report of the International Committee of the Red Cross (ICRC) on the Treatment by the coalition Forces of Prisoners of War and other Protected Persons by the Geneva Conventions in Iraq during Arrest, Internment, and Interrogation," February 2004, in *The Torture Papers: The Road to Abu Ghraib,* ed. Karen J. Greenberg and Joshua L. Dratel. With an Introduction by Anthony Lewis (Cambridge, NY: Cambridge University Press, 2005), 393.
80. Ibid., 394.
81. "The Taguba Report," 418.
82. Philip Zimbardo, *The Lucifer Effect: Understanding Why Good People Turn Evil* (New York: Random House, 2007), 325. For an interesting discussion about controversies surrounding this photograph, see McKelvey, *Monstering,* chapter 17.
83. Scarry, *The Body in Pain,* 27–60.
84. Marcel, "Incarnate Being," 28.
85. Scarry, *The Body in Pain,* 40. In this section, I draw heavily from Scarry's book.
86. Rejali, *Torture and Democracy,* chapters 7–9.
87. For the documents detailing this abuse, see the American Civil Liberties Web site, available at http://www.aclu.org/projects/foiasearch/pdf/DODDOACID013960.pdf. In such a world, a detainee is no longer at home with her environment.
88. See Worthington, *The Guantánamo Files,* chapters 8–10, 14, and *Human Rights Watch,* "Enduring Freedom."
89. See Phifer, "Memorandum for Commander, Joint Task Force 170," October 14, 2002, 228, and Diane Beaver, "Memorandum for Commander, Joint Force 170," October 11, 2002, in Greenberg, *The Torture Papers,* 234.
90. "Working Group Report on Detainee Interrogations," 343.
91. Ibid., 353.
92. Ibid., 347.

93. "The Schlesinger Report: Final Report of the Independent Panel to Review DOD Detention Operations," August 2004, in *The Torture Papers: The Road to Abu Ghraib*, ed. Karen J. and Joshua L. Dratel. With an introduction by Anthony Lewis (Cambridge, NY: Cambridge University Press), 941.

94. McCoy, *A Question of Torture*, 129.

95. Mayer, *The Dark Side*, 273.

96. "The Schlesinger Report," 941.

97. Mayer, *The Dark Side*, 242.

98. *New York Times*, "The Reach of War: Sexual Humiliation; Forced Nudity of Iraqi Prisoners Is Seen as Pervasive Pattern, not Isolated Incidents," June 8, 2004, available at http://query.nytimes.com/gst/fullpage.html?res=9E01EFD71E31F93BA35755C0A9629C8B63.

99. "The Schlesinger Report," 973.

100. "The Taguba Report," 505.

101. "The ICRC Report," 392.

102. Ibid., 393.

103. Metin Basoglu, ed., *Torture and Its Consequences: Current Treatment Approaches* (Cambridge: Cambridge University Press, 1992), 204.

104. Physicians for Human Rights, "Break Them Down," executive summary.

105. Ibid., IV, C.

106. "The Schlesinger Report," 973.

107. SG, II, 98. Aquinas considers disembodied understanding when discussing angels, arguing that they lack bodies.

108. Clarke, *Person and Being*, 78.

109. Marcel, "Incarnate Being," 32.

110. *Interrogation Log, Detainee 063,* November 23, 2002 to January 11, 2003, 22:00, available at http://www.americantorture.com/documents/gitmo/13.pdf.

111. For example, "Detainee became irritated with the female invading his personal space. He made several attempts to push her away from him with his back because she was standing behind him. Detainee spit at SGT M and the DOD linguist because he was annoyed by the female behind him and they were seated directly in front of him. Detainee was offered water and food. He did not want water or food," *Interrogation Log, Detainee 063*, 18:00. Mayer discusses the origins of these ideas about Arabs and sexuality: see Mayer, *The Dark Side*, 167–168.

112. See Philip Gourevitch and Errol Morris, "Exposure: The Woman behind the Camera at Abu Ghraib," *New Yorker*, March 24, 2008, available at http://www.newyorker.com/reporting/2008/03/24/080324fa_fact_gourevitch.

113. Wojtyla, *Love and Responsibility*, 186.

114. John Paul II, "*Veritatis Splendor*," section 48.

115. "The Taguba Report," 505.

116. Rejali, *Torture and Democracy*, 381.

117. Ibid., 542.

118. Ibid.

119. Ibid.

120. President's Council on Bioethics, *Beyond Therapy: Biotechnology and the Pursuit of Happiness*, chapter 1, October 2003, available at http://www.bioethics.gov/reports/beyondtherapy/.

121. For a good discussion of modernity and torture, see John T. Parry, "The Shape of Modern Torture: Extraordinary Rendition and Ghost Detainees," *Melbourne Journal of International Law*, 6 (2005), 516–533.

122. Leon R. Kass, "The New Biology: What Price Relieving Man's Estate?" *Toward a More Natural Science: Biology and Human Affairs* (New York: Free Press, 1985), 18–19. Many twentieth-century thinkers raised similar concerns. For a sample of the literature, see Martin Heidegger, "The Question Concerning Technology," in *The Question Concerning Technology and Other Essays*, ed. William Lovett (New York: Harper Torchbooks, 1977), 3–35; Jürgen Habermas, *The Theory of Communicative Action, Volume 1: Reason and*

the Rationalization of Society (Boston, MA: Beacon Press, 1985); and Jacques Ellu, *The Technological Society* (New York: Vintage Press, 1967).

123. Rebecca Lemov, *World as Laboratory*, 3. Lemov is particularly good in discussing Dr. Louis Jolyon West, who received CIA funding for experiments using LSD, sensory deprivation, psychosurgery, and other techniques; see chapter 10.

124. William Sargant, *Battle for the Mind: A Physiology of Conversion and Brain-Washing* (Garden City, NY: Doubleday, 1957). Like Cameron, Sargant believed we could radically alter a person's personality. Ross details the work of many other psychologists and psychiatrists working with the CIA on a science of torture; see Ross, *The CIA Doctors*.

125. See Jane Mayer, "The Experiment," *New Yorker*, July 11, 2005, available at http://www.newyorker.com/archive/2005/07/11/050711fa_fact4. In 2004, the Department of Defense issued the Church Report on detainee treatment (named after Vice Admiral Church). However, the report was heavily redacted. In 2008, the American Civil Liberties Union received unredacted portions that establish that psychologists were deeply involved in interrogations in Afghanistan. According to the report, they "do not function as mental health providers, and one of their core missions is to support interrogations." For this portion of the Church Report, see http://www.aclu.org/pdfs/safefree/church_353365_20080430.pdf. I owe this reference to Michael Otterman.

126. Katherine Eban provides a disturbing account of how psychologists assisted in interrogations, see Katherine Eban, "Rorschach and Awe," *Vanity Fair*, July 17, 2007, available at http://www.vanityfair.com/politics/features/2007/07/torture200707?printable=true&currentPage=all. Scot Shane of the *New York Times* traces how interrogators at Guantánamo used verbatim Albert Biderman's 1957 chart on effective interrogation techniques that North Koreans designed for American POWs in the Korean War; see *New York Times*, "China Inspired Interrogations at Guantánamo," July 2, 2008, available at http://www.nytimes.com/2008/07/02/us/02detain.html?_r=1&hp=&pagewanted=all&oref=slogin.

127. Mayer, *The Dark Side*, 156. Mitchell may have based his advice on the work of psychologist Martin Seligman, who developed the concept of "learned helplessness" in the 1960s. Seligman demonstrated that by shocking dogs, a researcher could reduce them to a condition of complete passivity. Discussing Seligman, Mayer notes that he spoke to the Navy's SERE school in 2002, see Mayer, *The Dark Side*, 164. We do not really precisely know how much he knew about the SERE program.

128. Jerald F. Ogrisseg, "Psychological Effects of Resistance Training," July 24, 2002, available at http://levin.senate.gov/newsroom/supporting/2008/Documents.SASC.061708.pdf.

129. Mayer, *The Dark Side*, 244–246.

130. "Senate Armed Services Inquiry into the Treatment of Detainees in U.S. Custody," December 2008, available at http://levin.senate.gov/newsroom/release.cfm?id=305735.

131. Mayer, *The Dark Side*, 162.

132. For a good discussion of the controversies at the American Psychological Association meetings, see Stephen Soldz and Brad Olson "Psychologists, Detainee Interrogations, and Torture: Varying Perspectives on Nonparticipation," in *The Trauma of Psychological Torture*, ed. Almerindo E. Ojeda (Westport, CT: Praeger, 2008), chapter 4.

133. "Psychologists Vote to End Interrogation Consultations," *New York Times*, September 17, 2008, available at http://www.nytimes.com/2008/09/18/us/18psych.html?fta=y.

134. Jonathan D. Moreno, *Mind Wars: Brain Research and National Defense* (New York: Dana Press, 2006).

135. Ibid., 13.

136. *ST*, I, 76, 5, answer to objection 4.

137. Reinhold Niebuhr, *Moral Man and Immoral Society: A Study in Ethics and Politics* (New York: Charles Scribner's, 1960), xi.

138. *The 9/11 Commission Report: Final Report of the National Commission on Terrorist Attacks upon the United States* (New York: W.W. Norton, 2004), 47.

Four   Does Torture Work? Consequentialism's Failures

1. Friedrich A. Hayek, *The Constitution of Liberty* (Chicago, IL: University of Chicago Press, 1960), 159.

2. Dershowitz, *Why Terrorism Works*, 131–165.

3. Elshtain, "Reflections on the Problem of 'Dirty Hands,'" 77.

4. Jonathan Alter, "Time to Think about Torture," *Newsweek*, November 5, 2001, available at http://www.newsweek.com/id/76304/.

5. For an account of these terrible atrocities, see Philip Chinnery, *Korean Atrocity! Forgotten War Crimes, 1950–1953* (Annapolis, MD: U.S. Naval Institute Press, 2000).

6. Rejali makes this point throughout *Torture and Democracy*, 16–21, 70–74, 124–126, 240–242.

7. Elizabeth Anscombe, "Modern Moral Philosophy," *The Collected Philosophical Papers of G.E.M. Anscombe* (Minneapolis, MN: The University of Minnesota Press, 1981), 33.

8. Niccoló Machiavelli, *The Discourses*. Edited with an introduction by Bernard Crick. Translated by Leslie J. Walker, S.J. With revisions by Brian Richardson (New York: Penguin Books, 1970), I, 9. Machiavelli carefully discusses Romulus's action, and I cannot capture the subtlety of his account here.

9. Max Weber, "Politics as a Vocation," in *From Max Weber Essays in Sociology*. Translated, edited, and with an introduction by C. Wright Mills and Hans H. Gerth (Oxford: Oxford University Press, 1958), 120.

10. Hans J. Morgenthau and Kenneth W. Thompson, *Politics Among Nations: The Struggle for Power and Peace*, 6th edn (New York: Alfred A. Knopf, 1985), 4.

11. Niccoló Machiavelli, *The Prince: A Bilingual Edition*. Translated and edited by Mark Musa (New York: St. Martin's Press, 1964), chapter 6.

12. Ibid.

13. Posner, "Torture, Terrorism, and Interrogation," 293.

14. Ibid., 294.

15. Ibid., 295.

16. Krauthammer, "The Truth about Torture," *Weekly Standard*, 11.12, December 5, 2005, available at htt//www.weeklystandard.com/content/public/articles/000/000/006/400hqav.asp; 309.

17. Ibid., 310.

18. Joshua Dratel, "The Curious Debate," in ed. Karen J. Greenberg, ed. *The Torture Debate in America*, (Cambridge, NY: Cambridge University Press, 2006), 115.

19. Randy Borum, "Approaching Truth: Behavioral Science Lessons on Educing Information from Human Sources," in *Educing Information: Interrogation: Science and Art Foundation*, section I: 713, available at http://www.fas.org/irp/dni/educing.pdf.

20. For a discussion on how the CIA used German data, see Linda Hunt, *Secret Agenda: The United States Government, Nazi Scientists, and Project Paperclip, 1945 to 1990* (New York: St. Martin's Press, 1991). See also Alfred W. McCoy, "Legacy of a Dark Decade: CIA Mind Control, Classified Behavioral Research, and the Origins of Modern Medical Ethics," in *The Trauma of Psychological Torture*, ed. Almerindo E. Ojeda (Westport, CT: Praeger, 2008), chapter 3.

21. Posner, "Torture, Terrorism, and Interrogation," 294.

22. Krauthammer, "The Truth about Torture," 314; italics in the original.

23. Rejali, *Torture and Democracy*, 532.

24. McCoy, *A Question of Torture*, 112. See also Rejali, *Torture and Democracy*, chapters 21 and 22.

25. Suskind, *The One-Percent Doctrine*, chapter 3. See also Rejali, *Torture and Democracy*, 500–512.

26. Suskind, *The One-Percent Doctrine*, 53, 76. Mayer provides good background on the al-Libi case, see Mayer, *The Dark Side*, chapter six.
27. For a well-known discussion of this war, see Horne, *A Savage War of Peace*. Rejali argues that Algerian torture produced false information and harmed thousands of innocent people: see Rejali, *Torture and Democracy*, chapter 22.
28. See David Lyons, *Forms and Limits of Utilitarianism* (Oxford: Clarendon Press, 1965).
29. I take the phrase rule worship from J.C. Smart and Bernard Williams, *Utilitarianism: For and Against* (Cambridge: Cambridge University Press, 1973).
30. Vilfredo Pareto, *The Mind and Society*, Vol. IV. Edited by Arthur Livingston. Translated by Andrew Bongiorno and Arthur Livingston, with the advice and active cooperation of James Harvey Rogers (New York: Harcourt, Brace, 1935), 1457.
31. Friedrich A. Hayek, *The Road to Serfdom*. With a new introduction by Milton Friedman (Chicago, IL: University of Chicago Press, 1994), 66.
32. Friedrich A. Hayek, *The Mirage of Social Justice* (Chicago, IL: University of Chicago Press, 1976), 20.
33. Ibid.
34. Ibid., 22.
35. Ibid., 23.
36. I have learned a great deal from John Gray's work on Hayek: see John Gray, *Hayek on Liberty*, 3rd edn (London: Routledge, 1998).
37. Russell Hardin, *Indeterminacy and Society* (Princeton, NJ: Princeton University Press, 2003), 1.
38. I first encountered this objection to consequentialism as an undergraduate student of the Protestant theologian James Gustafson. For Gustafson's argument, see James M. Gustafson, *Ethics from a Theocentric Perspective: Volume Two, Ethics and Theology* (Chicago, IL: The University of Chicago Press, 1984), chapter 3.
39. Pareto, *Mind and Society*, 1461–1462.
40. Ibid., 1462.
41. Ibid.
42. Kenneth E. Kirk, *Conscience and Its Problems: An Introduction to Casuistry* (Westminster: Westminster John Knox Press, 1999), 375.
43. Pareto, *Mind and Society*, 1462.
44. Smart and Williams, *Utilitarianism*, 64.
45. Richard Brandt, "Utilitarianism and the Rules of War," in *War and Moral Responsibility: A Philosophy and Public Affairs Reader*, ed. T.M. Scanlon, Marshall Cohen, and Thomas Nagel (Princeton, NJ: Princeton University Press, 1974).
46. Jacques Maritain, "The End of Machiavellianism," *The Range of Reason* (New York: Charles Scribner's, 1952), 134–164.
47. Ibid., 149.
48. Gabriel Marcel, *Being and Having: An Existential Diary*. Translated by Katherine Farrer (New York: Harper Torchbooks, 1965), 69; italics in the original.
49. John Gray suggests that an Aristotelian conception of knowing supports Hayek's idea of tacit knowledge, and I have adapted his idea: see Gray, *Hayek on Liberty*, 112–135.
50. Quoted in W. Norris Clarke, S.J., "Action as the Self-Revelation of Being: A Central Theme in the Thought of Thomas Aquinas," in S.J. *Explorations in Metaphysics: Being, God, Person*, ed. W. Norris Clarke, (Notre Dame, IN: University of Notre Dame Press, 1994), 56.
51. Mirko Bagaric and Julie Clarke, *Torture: When the Unthinkable Is Morally Permissible* (Albany, NY: State University of New York Press, 2007), 2.
52. Ibid., *Torture*, 38.
53. Ibid.
54. Ibid., *Torture*, 102.
55. Ibid.
56. Margulies, *Guantánamo and the Abuse of Presidential Power*, 143.

57. Rejali carefully considers and rejects the idea that regulation reduces torture: see Rejali, *Torture and Democracy*, chapter 23.

58. For a similarly impoverished argument, see Eric A. Posner and Adrian Vermeule, "Should Coercive Torture Be legal?" *Chicago: Public Law and Legal Theory Working Paper No. 84*, available at http://papers.ssrn.com/sol3/papers.cfm?abstract_id=690902#PaperDownload.

59. Hayek, *Mirage of Social Justice*, 12.

60. Gray, *Hayek on Liberty*, 57–59.

61. Russell Hardin, *Morality within the Limits of Reason* (Chicago, IL: University of Chicago Press, 1988), 78.

62. Hardin, *Indeterminacy and Society*, 45.

63. Hardin, *Morality within the Limits of Reason*, 79.

64. Hayek, *Mirage of Social Justice*, 25.

65. Ibid., 28.

66. For a good history of European torture, see Edward Peters, *Torture* (New York: B. Blackwell, 1985). See also Rejali, *Torture and Democracy*.

67. Friedrich A. Hayek, *The Fatal Conceit: The Errors of Socialism*. Edited by W.W. Barthley, III (Chicago, IL: University of Chicago Press, 1988). I find many of the arguments in this book philosophically sloppy and morally offensive, but I will not discuss them here. I thank Wolfgang Grassel at St. Norbert College for alerting me to this work.

68. Ibid., 152.

69. Russell Hardin, "Civil Liberties in the Era of Mass Terrorism," *Journal of Ethics*, 8.1 (2004) 92. I thank Professor Hardin for corresponding with me about this article.

70. Hardin, *Morality within the Limits of Reason*, 169.

71. Ibid., 170.

72. Hayek, *Fatal Conceit*, 95.

73. Perhaps they interpret these sources mistakenly, but I will not address this issue.

74. Hayek, *Mirage of Social Justice*, 25.

75. Hardin, *Morality within the Limits of Reason*, 191.

76. Ibid., 192.

Five   No Reason to Torture:
Dirty Hands and Spiritual Damage

1. Machiavelli, *The Discourses*, I, 26, 177.

2. Michael Stocker, *Plural and Conflicting Values* (New York: Oxford University Press, 1992), 9.

3. Walzer, "Political Action: The Problem of Dirty Hands," 66.

4. Ibid., 62.

5. Ibid., 67.

6. Ibid. J.L. Austin is the source of Walzer's distinction between excuse and justification.

7. Walzer, "The Problem of Dirty Hands," 68.

8. Ibid., 71.

9. Ibid., 72.

10. Ibid., 73.

11. Elshtain, "Reflections on the Problem of 'Dirty Hands,'" 83.

12. Ibid., 88.

13. Ibid., 87–88.

14. Ibid., 88.

15. Ibid.

16. Machiavelli, *The Prince*, chapter 25.
17. Weber, "Politics as a Vocation," 125–126.
18. Ibid., 127.
19. Niebuhr, *Moral Man and Immoral Society*, 257.
20. Thomas Nagel, "War and Massacre" in *Mortal Questions*, ed. Thomas Nagel (Cambridge, NY: Cambridge University Press, 1991), 74.
21. Edmund Santurri carefully explores the idea of "moral blind alley," discussing whether it reflects an ontological clash of values or merely our epistemological ignorance; see Edmund N. Santurri, *Perplexity in the Moral Life: Philosophical and Theological Considerations. Studies in Culture* (Charlottesville, VA: University of Virginia Press), 1988. I am grateful to professor Santurri for helpful e-mail correspondence on this topic.
22. Bernard Williams, "Conflicts of Values," *Moral Luck: Philosophical Papers, 1973–1980* (Cambridge, NY: Cambridge University Press, 1981), 72.
23. Bernard Williams, "Moral Luck," *Moral Luck: Philosophical Papers, 1973–1980* (Cambridge, NY: Cambridge University Press), 20.
24. Williams, "Conflicts of Values," 71.
25. Goldsmith, *The Terror Presidency*, 175.
26. Ibid.
27. Kant is the target for many contemporary dirty hands thinkers.
28. Niccoló Machiavelli, "The History of Florence," in *Machiavelli: The Chief Works and Others*, Vol. 3. Translated by Allan Gilbert (Durham, NC: Duke University Press, 1989), book three, chapter 8, 1150.
29. Kai Nielsen, "There Is No Dilemma of Dirty Hands," in *Cruelty and Deception: The Controversy over Dirty Hands in Politics*, ed. David Shugarman and Paul Rynard (Ontario, Canada: Broadview Press, 1999), 140; italics in the original.
30. Stephen de Wijze, "Tragic Remorse: The Anguish of Dirty Hands," *Ethical Theory and Moral Practice*, 7.5 (November 2004), 460.
31. Deontic logic is the logic of obligation. See Williams, "Conflicts of Values." For another treatment of deontic logic, see Walter Sinnott-Armstrong, *Moral Dilemmas* (Boston, MA: Blackwell, 1988). I have also learned from Edmund Santurri's work and appreciate his helpful correspondence: see Edmund N. Santurri, *Perplexity in the Moral Life*.
32. Williams, "Moral Luck," 28.
33. Wijze, "Tragic Remorse," 464.
34. Weber, "Politics as a Vocation," 127.
35. Josef Pieper, *The Four Cardinal Virtues: Prudence, Justice, Fortitude, Temperance* (Notre Dame, IN: University of Notre Dame Press, 1966), 33.
36. For one discussion of *virtú*, see Machiavelli, *The Prince*, chapter 25.
37. Aristotle, "Nicomachean Ethics," section 1107, in *Introduction to Aristotle*, 2nd edn,. ed. Richard McKeon (Chicago, IL: University of Chicago Press, 1973).
38. Williams, "Conflicts of Values," 81.
39. Pieper, *The Four Cardinal Virtues*, 10. Pieper repeatedly links prudence with other virtues.
40. Ibid., 14. For an excellent discussion of prudence, see Yves R. Simon, *The Tradition of Natural Law: A Philosopher's Reflections*, ed. Vukan Kuis with an introduction by Russell Hittinger (New York: Fordham University Press), 93, 154–155. I pass over complex questions about the unity of the virtues and the relationship between theoretical and practical reasons. Both Simon and Pieper address them carefully.
41. Goldsmith, *The Terror Presidency*, 189.
42. Ibid., 192.
43. Maritain, "The End of Machiavellianism," 148.
44. Jacques Maritain, *Existence and the Existent*. English version by Lewis Galantiere and Gerald B. Phelan (New York: Pantheon Books, 1948), 93.

45. Max Scheler, "Repentance and Rebirth," in *Person and Self-Value: Three Essays*. With an Introduction, and Edited and Partially Translated by M.S. Frings (Dordrecht, The Netherlands: Martinus Nijhoff, 1987), 112.

46. Sokolowski, *Moral Acts*, 66.

47. Maritain, "The End of Machiavellianism," 149.

48. Jacques Maritain, "Freedom in the Modern World," in *Integral Humanism, Freedom in the Modern World, and a Letter on Independence*. Translated and edited by Otto Bird. Translated by Joseph Evans and Richard O'Sullivan (Notre Dame, IN: University of Notre Dame Press, 1996), 91.

49. Scheler, "Repentance and Rebirth," 99.

50. Maritain, "Freedom in the Modern World," 91.

51. Jacques Maritain, *On the Philosophy of History*. Edited by Joseph Evans (New York: Charles Scribner, 1957), 59.

52. Mayer, *The Dark Side*, 79.

53. For one account of what happened, see Savage, *Takeover*, 134–139. Mayer provides good background on the decisions about the Geneva Conventions: see Mayer, *The Dark Side*, chapters 5 and 6.

54. Colin L. Powell, "Draft Decision Memorandum for the President on the Applicability of the Geneva Conventions to the Conflict with Afghanistan," in *The Torture Papers: The Road to Abu Ghraib*, ed. Karen J. Greenberg and Joshua L. Dratel. With an introduction by Anthony Lewis (Cambridge, NY: Cambridge University Press, 2005), 123.

55. William H. Taft, IV, "Comments on Your Paper on the Geneva Convention," February 2, 2002, in *The Torture Papers: The Road to Abu Ghraib*, ed. Karen J. Greenberg and Joshua L. Dratel. With an introduction by Anthony Lewis (Cambridge, NY: Cambridge University Press, 2005), 129.

56. Alberto R. Gonzales, "Decision RE Application of the Geneva Conventions on Prisoners of War to the Conflict with al-Qaeda and the Taliban," January 25, 2002, in *The Torture Papers: The Road to Abu Ghraib*, ed. Karen J. Greenberg and Joshua L. Dratel. With an introduction by Anthony Lewis (Cambridge, NY: Cambridge University Press, 2005), 134. Mayer maintains that David Addington, Vice President Cheney's lawyer, was the real author of this memo: see Mayer, *The Dark Side*, 124.

57. Bush, "Humane Treatment," 134.

58. Ibid.

59. Eric Posner, "Applying the Golden Rule to al-Qaeda?" *Wall Street Journal*, July 15, 2006, available at http://www.ericposner.com/goldenrule.html.

60. Gonzales, "Decision RE Application of the Geneva Conventions," 121.

61. Posner, "Applying the Golden Rule to al-Qaeda?"

62. Margulies, *Guantánamo and the Abuse of Presidential Power*, 54.

63. "Geneva Conventions Relative to the Treatment of Prisoners of War," available at http://www.unhchr.ch/html/menu3/b/91.htm.

64. Margulies, *Guantánamo and the Abuse of Presidential Power*, 55. For some of this debate, see Goldsmith, *The Terror Presidency*, chapter 4, and Derek P. Jinks, "*Hamdan* and the Law of War: The Applicability of the Geneva Conventions to the 'Global War on Terrorism,'" available at http://www.law.uga.edu/intl/jinks.pdf. I have followed Jinks in my interpretation of reciprocity and Common Article Three.

65. For a discussion of this history, see Judge James Roberson, "United States District Court for the District of Columbia, Salim Ahmed Hamdan, Plaintiff vs. Donald H. Rumsfeld," November 8, 2004, http://fl1.findlaw.com/news.findlaw.com/hdocs/docs/tribunals/hamdanrums110804opn.pdf.

66. I find the Bush administration's interpretation of Common Article Three completely unpersuasive and uninformed by the history of its drafting in the 1940s. For good histories, see Francois Bugnion, "The Geneva Conventions of 12 August 1949: From the 1949

Diplomatic Conference to the Dawn of the New Millennium," *International Affairs (Royal Institute of International Affairs 1944)*, 76.1 (January 2000), 41–50; Lindsay Moir, *The Law of Internal Armed Conflict* (Cambridge: Cambridge University Press, 2007), chapters 1 and 2, and Jean S. Pictet, "The New Geneva Protections for War Victims," *American Journal of International Law*, 45.3 (July 1951), 462–475.

67. This quote is from section 33, line 19 of the transcript of oral arguments in the *Hamdan case*, available at http://www.supremecourtus.gov/oral_arguments/argument_transcripts/05-184.pdf.

68. Jinks, "*Hamdan* and the Law of War," 10.

69. My concern is to establish only a case for Common Article Three as a moral minimum. Other elements of international law may be similar, but I cannot make this case in this book.

70. Eric Posner never mentions spirituality, embracing instead a cost–benefit form of consequentialism. He repeatedly attacks attempts to ground international law in extralegal moral norms. Jack Goldsmith follows him in this approach. For an example, see Eric Posner and Jack Goldsmith, *The Limits of International Law* (Oxford: Oxford University Press, 2006). Posner and Goldsmith embrace many of the defective consequentialist arguments I criticize in chapter four.

71. For a collection of Rumsfeld's derisive statements about the Geneva Conventions, see Human Rights Watch, "Getting Away with Torture: Command Responsibility for the U.S. Abuse of Detainees," April 24, 2005, available at http://www.hrw.org/reports/2005/us0405/.

72. See Savage, *Takeover*, chapter 8. Mayer describes how Alberto Mora (the Navy's general counsel) fought nobly but unsuccessfully to stop torture at Guantánamo: see Mayer, *The Dark Side*, chapter 9.

73. Savage, *Takeover*, 188–192.

74. See Mayer's book, *The Dark Side,* for a full account of these deceptions, particularly chapter 12.

75. Goldsmith, *The Terror Presidency*, 120.

76. *Hamdan* dealt with many complex issues, and although scholars embraced its conclusions, some argued that the decision was poorly reasoned. For an example, see Cass R. Sunstein, "Clear Statement Principles and National Security: Hamdan and Beyond," in *Supreme Court Review* 1, ed. Dennis J. Hutchinson, David A. Strauss, and Geoffrey R. Stone (Chicago, IL: University of Chicago Press, 2007).

77. Goldsmith, *The Terror Presidency*, 139. Goldsmith heavily criticizes the Bush administration, but remains a supporter of strong executive power.

78. Maritain, "The End of Machiavellianism," 149.

79. Elshtain, "Reflections on the Problem of 'Dirty Hands,'" 87.

80. Ibid., 88.

81. Bernard Williams, "Utilitarianism and Moral Self-Indulgence," *Moral Luck: Philosophical Paper, 1973–1980* (Cambridge, NY: Cambridge University Press, 1981), 41. In this section, I draw heavily on Williams's excellent essay.

82. Jacques Maritain, "Integral Humanism," in Maritain, *Integral Humanism*, 309.

83. Mark J. Osiel, "The Mental State of Torturers: Argentina's Dirty War," in *Torture: A Collection*, ed. Sanford Levinson (Oxford: Oxford University Press, 2006), 129.

84. Williams, "Utilitarianism and Moral Self-Indulgence," 45.

85. Posner and Vermeule, "Should Coercive Torture Be Legal?" 3, available at http://www.michiganlawreview.org/archive/104/4/Posner_Vermeule.pdf.

86. Alan M. Dershowitz, "Tortured Reasoning," in *Torture: A Collection*, ed. Sanford Levinson (Oxford: Oxford University Press, 2006), 257.

87. For an excellent (but depressing) study of the efficacy of laws against torture, see Oona A. Hathaway, "The Promise and Limits of the International Law of Torture," in *Torture: A Collection*, ed. Sanford Levinson (Oxford: Oxford University Press, 2006), chapter 11.

88. John Paul II, "Veritatis Splendor," section 63.

89. Ibid.

90. Osiel, "The Mental State of Torturers," 132.

91. Mark J. Osiel, *Mass Atrocity, Ordinary Evil, and Hannah Arendt: Criminal Consciousness in Argentina's Dirty War* (New Haven, CT: Yale University Press, 2001). Addressing subjective culpability requires that we have a clear conception of conscience and its deformations. This is a topic many theologians have struggled to understand. For an excellent account of conscience, see Eric D'Arcy, *Conscience and Its Right to Freedom* (New York: Sheed and Ward, 1961).

92. Dershowitz, "Tortured Reasoning," 276.

93. I first learned about this case when lecturing at the Philipps-Universität in Marburg, Germany in 2004. I thank faculty members in ethics who offered critical comments on my lecture, particularly Wolfgang Nethofel and Peter Dabrock.

94. For details of this case, see BBC News, "German Officer Guilty of Threats," December 20, 2004, available at http://news.bbc.co.uk/2/hi/europe/4111483.stm. *Washington Post*, "Police Torture Threat Sparks Painful Debate in Germany," March 8, 2003, http://personal.ecu.edu/conradtd/pols2010/spring2010/2010sp0383.htm and Florien Jessberger, "Bad Torture—Good Torture? What International Criminal Lawyers may Learn from the Recent Trial of Police Officers in Germany," *Journal of International Criminal Justice*, 3 (2005), 1059–1073, available at http://jicj.oxfordjournals.org/cgi/reprint/3/5/1059. I have learned much from Jessberger's excellent essay.

95. Perhaps the judge was too lenient in this case, a point some German commentators made. I do not, however, feel competent to comment on this issue.

96. Jessberger, "Bad Torture—Good Torture?" 1065.

97. Ibid.

98. Kent Greenwalt, "The Perplexing Borders of Justification and Excuse," *Columbia Law Review*, 84.4 (1984), 1900. Greenwalt expresses skepticism about enshrining the excuse/justification distinction into law. On torture, I obviously reject such skepticism. For a careful discussion of excuses, see Moore, *Placing Blame,* 481–595.

99. For an excellent discussion of justification and excuse, see Yuval Ginbar, *Why Not Torture Terrorists?: Moral, Practical and Legal Aspects of the "Ticking Bomb" Justification for Torture*, Oxford Monographs in International Law. (Oxford: Oxford University Press, 2008), 304–339.

100. Responding to allegations of torture in its security forces, in the 1980s and the 1990s, Israel experimented with different legal regimes. Unfortunately, it failed to keep torture's objective wrongness clear, thus legitimizing the torture of many Palestinians. For an excellent discussion of the Israel experience, see Ginbar, *Why Not Torture Terrorists?* 171–223. For a different account of this experience, see Michael L. Gross, "Regulating Torture in a Democracy: Death and Indignity in Israel," *Policy*, 36.3 (2004), 367–388.

101. For some examples, see Bowden, "The Dark Art of Interrogation."

102. Jessberger, "Bad Torture—Good Torture?" 1073.

103. Weber, "Politics as a Vocation," 127; italics in the original.

104. Machiavelli, *The Prince*, book XXV.

105. Maritain, *On the Philosophy of History*, 50.

106. John Paul II, *"Veritatis Splendor"*, 92.

Conclusion

1. International Theological Commission, *Memory and Reconciliation: The Church and the Faults of the Past*, section 5.1, December 1999, available at http://www.vatican.va/roman_curia/

congregations/cfaith/cti_documents/rc_con_cfaith_doc_20000307_memory-reconc-itc_en.html.

2. Machiavelli, *The Prince*, chapter 18, 149.

3. Leo Strauss uses this term to describe Machiavelli: see Leo Strauss, *Thoughts on Machiavelli* (Chicago, IL: University of Chicago Press, 1995).

4. For details on the Arar case, see Mayer, *The Dark Side*, 129–133. For lawyers' account of their experience representing detainees, see Margulies, *Guantánamo and the Abuse of Presidential Power*, and Clive S. Smith, *The Eight O'Clock Ferry to the Windward Side: Fighting the Lawless World of Guantánamo Bay* (New York: Nation Books, 2008).

5. Mark Osiel, *Mass Atrocity, Collective Memory and the Law* (New Brunswick, NJ: Transaction Publishers, 1999).

6. *Military Commissions Act of 2006*, section 7, public Law 109–366, October 17, 2006, available at http://frwebgate.access.gpo.gov/cgi-bin/getdoc.cgi?dbname=109_cong_public_laws&docid=f:publ366.109.pdf.

7. U.S. Supreme Court, *Biomedicine et al. v. Bush, President of the United States, et al.*, June 12, 2008, available at http://www.supremecourtus.gov/opinions/07pdf/06-1195.pdf.

8. *Military Commissions Act of 2006*, section 948r.

9. The Military Commissions Act is problematic for many other reasons that I will not analyze here. For a good survey of them in light of the Geneva Conventions, see Jack M. Beard, "The Geneva Boomerang: The Military Commissions Act of 2006 and U.S. Counterterror Operations," *American Journal of International Law*, 101.1 (January 2007), 56–73.

10. For a good discussion of the attempt to indict Pinochet, see Dinges, *The Condor Years*, chapter 14.

11. Christopher Hitchens proposed trying Kissinger for war crimes, but the courts paid no attention to him: see Christopher Hitchens, *The Trial of Henry Kissinger* (Scranton, PA: Verso, 2001).

12. See "Human Rights First and ACLU Express Disappointment at Dismissal of Rumsfeld Torture Case," March 27, 2007, available at http://www.humanrightsfirst.org/media/etn/2007/alert/321/index.htm.

13. Marty Lederman, a former official in the Office of Legal Counsel, maintained a useful blog on torture and other matters. He expressed skepticism about the prospect of war crimes trials, see Marty Lederman, "A Dissenting View on Prosecuting the Waterboarders," February 8, 2008, available at http://balkin.blogspot.com/2008/02/dissenting-view-on-prosecuting.html.

14. I thank Alfred McCoy for discussions about the JAGs. For an insightful account of war crime trials, see Samantha Power, *"A Problem from Hell": America and the Age of Genocide* (New York: Basic Books, 2002), chapters 13–14.

15. Thomas Ricks argues that General Sanchez made major mistakes in important areas, see Thomas E. Ricks, *Fiasco: The American Military Adventure in Iraq* (New York: Penguin, 2007).

16. Conroy, *Unspeakable Acts, Ordinary People*, 242.

17. Sands, *Torture Team*, chapter 26.

18. Conroy, *Unspeakable Acts, Ordinary People*, 244. Weinstein discusses how Ewen Cameron's victims encountered difficulties in seeking justice from the CIA and Canadian government: see Weinstein, *Psychiatry and the CIA*.

19. BBC News, "Tipton Three Complain of Beatings," March 14, 2004, available at http://news.bbc.co.uk/1/hi/uk/3509750.stm. Rose, *Guantánamo* and *San Francisco Chronicle*, "All Eyes on Guantánamo Movie, Court Rulings Intensify Focus on Military Prisons," July 2, 2006, available at http://www.sfgate.com/cgi-bin/article.cgi?f=/c/a/2006/07/02/INGJNJMQF51.DTL.

20. *Washington Post*, "Shiite Militias Control Prisons, Official Says," June 16, 2006, available at http://www.washingtonpost.com/wp-dyn/content/article/2006/06/15/AR2006061502180_pf.html. *Washington Post*, "New Detainees Strain Iraq's Jails: Sharp Rise Follows Start of Security Plan; Suspects Housed with Convicts," May 15, 2007, available at http://www.washingtonpost.com/wp-dyn/content/article/2007/05/14/AR2007051402265.html.

21. *Human Rights Watch*, "Locked up Alone: Detention Conditions and Mental Health at Guantánamo," part II, camp 7, June 2008, available at http://hrw.org/reports/2008/us0608/us0608web.pdf.

22. For a discussion of 62 detainees and their condition, see Human Rights Center, University of California, Berkley, "Guantánamo and Its Aftermath": U.S. Detention and Interrogation Practices and their Impact on Former Detainees, November 2008, available at http://hrc.berkeley.edu/pdfs/Gtmo-Aftermath.pdf.

23. *World Public Opinion*, "American and International Opinion on the Rights of Terrorism Suspects," July 17, 2006, available at http://www.worldpublicopinion.org/pipa/pdf/jul06/TerrSuIn sspect_Jul06_rpt.pdf.

24. *The Pew Global Attitudes Project*, "American Character Gets Mixed Reviews: U.S. Image Slightly up, but Still Negative," June 23, 2005, available at http://pewglobal.org/reports/pdf/247.pdf.

25. *The Pew Global Attitudes Project*, "No Global Warming Alarm in the U.S., China: America's Image Slips, but Allies Share U.S. Concerns," June 13, 2006, available at http://pewglobal.org/reports/display.php?ReportID=252.

26. Rejali, *Torture and Democracy*, 519.

27. In what follows, I draw heavily from Scheler's masterful essay, "Repentance and Rebirth." I use it only selectively because it is a rich text and deserves more attention from contemporary scholars.

28. Améry, *At the Mind's Limit*, 40.

29. Scheler, "Repentance and Rebirth," 95; italics in the original.

30. International Theological Commission, *Memory and Reconciliation*, Section 5.1.

31. Scheler, "Repentance and Rebirth," 100–101; italics in the original.

32. Scheler, "Repentance and Rebirth," 101.

33. Ibid., 96.

34. Ibid., 114.

35. For a good discussion of this problem, see Osiel, *Mass Atrocity, Collective Memory*, chapter 6.

36. *Canadian Broadcast Company*, "Harper's Apology Means the World: Arar," January 26, 2007, available at http://www.cbc.ca/canada/story/2007/01/26/harper-apology.html.

37. For an interesting consideration of public apologies, see Luigi Accatoli and Jordan Aumann, *When a Pope Asks Forgiveness: The Mea Culpas of John Paul II* (Boston, MA: Pauline Books, 1998). See also Elazar Barkan and Alexander Karn, eds., *Taking Wrongs Seriously: Apologies and Reconciliation* (Stanford, CA: Stanford University Press, 2006).

38. Elazar Barkan and Alexander Karn, "Group Apology as an Ethical Imperative," in Barkan and Karn, *Taking Wrongs Seriously*, chapter 1.

39. *Canadian Broadcast Company*, "U.S. Legislators Apologize to Maher Arar," October 19, 2007, available at http://www.cbc.ca/world/story/2007/10/18/arar.html.

40. For a disturbing analysis of Bush administration apologies, see Elazar Barkan, "The Worst Is Yet to Come: Abu Ghraib and the Politics of Not Apologizing," in *Taking Wrongs Seriously*, ed. Barkan and Karn, chapter 14.

41. Barkan and Karn, "Group Apology as an Ethical Imperative," in *Taking Wrongs Seriously*, ed. Barkan and Karn, 14.

42. Several journalists and public figures have called for truth commissions. For an excellent proposal for one dealing with U.S. torture, see International Center for Transitional Justice,

Policy Brief: U.S. Inquiry into Human Rights Abuses in the "War on Terror," Lisa Magarrell, International Center for Transitional Justice, November 2008.

43. Robert L. Rotberg "Apology, Truth Commissions, and Intrastate Conflict," in *Taking Wrongs Seriously: Apologies and Reconciliation*, ed. Elazar Barkan and Alexander Karn (Stanford, CA: Stanford University Press, 2006), 36. My discussion in this paragraph owes much to Rotberg's article. He carefully discusses the complexities of how to convene and empower truth commissions.

44. Jacques Maritain, "The Possibilities for Co-Operation in a Divided World: Inaugural Address to the Second International Conference of UNESCO," *The Range of Reason* (New York: Charles Scribner's, 1952), 177.

WORKS CITED

ABC News, "Coming in From the Cold: CIA Spy Calls Waterboarding Necessary but Torture. Former Agent Says the Enhanced Technique Was Used on al-Qaeda Chief Abu Zubaydah," available at http://abcnews.go.com/Blotter/story?id=3978231&page=1.

Accatolli, Luigi and Aumann, Jordan. *When a Pope Asks Forgiveness: The Mea Culpas of John Paul II*. Boston, MA: Pauline Books, 1998.

Alter, Jonathan. "Time to Think about Torture," *Newsweek*, November 5, 2001, available at http://www.newsweek.com/id/76304/.

American Bar Association. "Task Force on Presidential Signing Statements and the Separation of Powers Doctrine," August 2006, available at http://www.abanet.org/op/signingstatements/aba_final_signing_statements_recommendation-report_7-24-06.pdf.

American Civil Liberties Union. "FBI Inquiry Details Abuses Reported by Agents at Guantánamo," available at http://www.aclu.org/safefree/torture/27816prs20070103.html.

American Civil Liberties Web site, available at http://www.aclu.org/projects/foiasearch/pdf/DODDOACID013960.pdf.

Améry, Jean. *At the Mind's Limit: Contemplations by a Survivor of Auschwitz and Its Realities*. Translated by Sidney Rosenfeld and Stella P. Rosenfeld. Bloomington, IN: Indiana University Press, 1980.

Amnesty International. *United States of America: A Case to Answer. From Abu Ghraib to Secret CIA Custody: The Case of Khaled al-Maqtari*, March 14, 2008, available at http://www.amnesty.org/en/library/asset/AMR51/013/2008/en/1788d961-f1d3-11dc-adcd-cdafd0ab0dfe/amr510132008eng.pdf/.

An Evangelical Declaration against Torture: Protecting Human Rights in the Age of Terror, section 7:9, available at http://www.evangelicalsforhumanrights.org/Declaration.pdf.

Andrews, George. *MKULTRA: The CIA's Top Secret Program in Human Experimentation and Behavior Modification*. Winston-Salem, NC: Healthnet Press, 2001.

Annas, George J. and Grodin, Michael A., eds. *The Nazi Doctors and the Nuremburg Code: Human Rights in Human Experimentation*. Oxford, England: Oxford University Press, 1995.

Anscombe, Elizabeth. *Intention*, 2nd edn. Ithaca, NY: Cornell University Press, 1957.

———. "Modern Moral Philosophy," *The Collected Philosophical Papers of G.E.M. Anscombe*. Minneapolis, MN: University of Minnesota Press, 1981.

Aquinas, Thomas. *On Being and Essence*. Translated by Joseph Bobick. Notre Dame, IN: University of Notre Dame Press, 1965.

———. *Questions on the Soul*. Translated by James H. Robb. Milwaukee, WI: Marquette University Press, 1984.

Aquinas, Thomas. *Summa Contra Gentiles*. Translated with an introduction and notes by James F. Anderson. Notre Dame, IN: University of Notre Dame Press, 2001.

———. *The Summa Theologica of St. Thomas Aquinas*, 2nd rev. edn, 1920. Literally translated by Fathers of the English Dominican Province, online edn. Grand Rapids, MI. Copyright 2008 Kevin Knight. 2008.

Aristotle, "Nicomachean Ethics," in Richard McKeon, ed., *Introduction to Aristotle*, 2nd edn. Chicago: University of Chicago Press, 1973.

Army Field Manual, FM 34–52, "Intelligence Interrogation," available at http://www.fas.org/irp/doddir/army/fm34-52.pdf.

Bagaric, Mirko and Clarke, Julie. *Torture: When the Unthinkable Is Morally Permissible*. Albany, NY: State University of New York Press, 2007.

Barkan, Elazar and Karn, Alexander, eds. *Taking Wrongs Seriously: Apologies and Reconciliation*. Stanford, CA: Stanford University Press, 2006.

Basoglu, Metin, ed. *Torture and Its Consequences: Current Treatment Approaches*. Cambridge: Cambridge University Press, 1992.

Basoglu, M. Livanou, M. and Crnobaric, C. "Torture versus Other Cruel, Inhuman and Degrading Treatment: Is the Distinction Real or Apparent?" *Archives of General Psychiatry*, 64 (2007), 277–285.

BBC News. "German Officer Guilty of Threats," December 20, 2004, available at http://news.bbc.co.uk/2/hi/europe/4111483.stm.

———. "Tipton Three Complain of Beatings," March 14, 2004, available at http://news.bbc.co.uk/1/hi/uk/3509750.stm.

Beard, Jack M. "The Geneva Boomerang: The Military Commissions Act of 2006 and U.S. Counterterror Operations," *American Journal of International Law*, 101.1 (January 2007), 56–73.

Beaver, Diane. "Memorandum for Commander, Joint Task Force 170, October 11, 2002," in Karen J. Greenberg and Joshua L. Dratel, eds., *The Road to Abu Ghraib*. With an Introduction by Anthony Lewis. Cambridge, NY: Cambridge University Press, 2005, 229–235.

Bennett, M.R. and Hacker, P.M.S. *Philosophical Foundations of Neuroscience*. Boston, MA: Wiley-Blackwell, 2003.

Benzoni, Francisco. *Ecological Ethics and the Human Soul: Aquinas, Whitehead, and the Metaphysics of Value*. Notre Dame, IN: University of Notre Dame Press, 2007.

Biderman, Albert D. "Communist Attempts to Elicit False Confessions from Air Force Prisoners," *Bulletin of the New York Academy of Medicine*, 33.9 (September 1957), 616–625, available at http://www.pubmedcentral.nih.gov/picrender.fcgi?artid=1806204&blobtype=pdf.

Biderman, Albert and Zimmer, Herbert, eds. *The Manipulation of Human Behavior*. New York: John Wiley, 1961.

Blanchette, Oliva. *The Perfection of the Universe According to Aquinas: A Teleological Cosmology*. Pennsylvania: Pennsylvania State University Press, 1992.

Borum, Randy. "Approaching Truth: Behavioral Science Lessons on Educing Information from Human Sources," in *Educing Information: Interrogation: Science and Art Foundations for the Future*, Intelligence Science Board, December 2006, section I, available at http://www.fas.org/irp/dni/educing.pdf.

Bowden, Mark. "The Dark Art of Interrogation," *Atlantic Monthly*, 293.3 (October 2003), 51–76.

Brandt, Richard. "Utilitarianism and the Rules of War," in T.M. Scanlon, Marshall Cohen, and Thomas Nagel, eds., *War and Moral Responsibility: A Philosophy and Public Affairs. Reader* Princeton, NJ: Princeton University Press, 1974.

Brecher, Bob. *Torture and the Ticking Bomb*. Malden, MA: Blackwell, 2007.

Brown, Richard E. "Alfred McCoy, Hebb, the CIA and Torture," *Journal of the History of the Behavioral Sciences*, 43.2 (April 2007), 205–213.

Bugnion, Francois. "The Geneva Conventions of 12 August 1949: From the 1949 Diplomatic Conference to the Dawn of the New Millennium," *International Affairs (Royal Institute of International Affairs 1944)*, 76.1 (January 2000), 41–50.

Bush, George W. "Executive Order: Interpretation of the Geneva Conventions Common Article 3 as Applied to a Program of Detention and Interrogation Operated by the Central Intelligence Agency," available at http://www.whitehouse.gov/news/releases/2007/07/20070720-4.html.

———. "Humane Treatment of al-Qaeda and Taliban Detainees," February 7, 2002, in Karen J. Greenberg and Joshua L. Dratel, eds., *The Torture Papers: The Road to Abu Ghraib*. With an introduction by Anthony Lewis. Cambridge, NY: Cambridge University Press, 2005, 134–135.

———. "Statement by the President," June 26, 2003, available at http://www.whitehouse.gov/news/releases/2003/06/20030626-3.html.

Cahill, Lisa S. "Accent on the Masculine," in Michael E. Allsopp and John J. O'Keefe, eds., *Veritatis Splendor: American Perspectives*. Kansas City, MO: Sheed and Ward, 1995.

Canadian Broadcast Company. "Harper's Apology Means the World: Arar," January 26, 2007, available at http://www.cbc.ca/canada/story/2007/01/26/harper-apology.html.

———. "U.S. Legislators Apologize to Maher Arar," October 19, 2007, available at http://www.cbc.ca/world/story/2007/10/18/arar.html.

Cavanaugh, William T. *Torture and Eucharist: Theology, Politics, and the Body of Christ*. Malden, MA: Blackwell, 1998.

Center for Human Rights and Global Justice, NYU Law School. "On the Record: U.S. Disclosures on Rendition, Secret Detention, and Coercive Interrogation," 2008, available at http://www.chrgj.org/projects/docs/ontherecord.pdf.

———. *Surviving the Darkness: Testimony from the U.S. "Black Sites."* New York: NYU School of Law, 2007, available at http://www.chrgj.org/projects/docs/survivingthedarkness.pdf.

Chalmers, David A. "Consciousness and Its Place in Nature," 2001, available at http://consc.net/papers/nature.pdf.

Chinnery, Philip. *Korean Atrocity! Forgotten War Crimes, 1950–1953*. Annapolis, MD: U.S. Naval Institute Press, 2000.

Chisholm, Roderick M. *Perceiving: A Philosophical Study*. Ithaca, NY: Cornell University Press, 1957.

Clarke, W. Norris, S.J. "Action as the Self-Revelation of Being: A Central Theme in the Thought of Thomas Aquinas," in W. Norris Clarke, S.J., ed., *Explorations in Metaphysics: Being, God, Person*. Notre Dame, IN: University of Notre Dame Press, 1994, 45–64.

———. "Living on the Edge: The Human Person as 'Frontier Being' and Microcosm," *International Philosophical Quarterly*, 36.2 issue no. 142 (June 1996), 183–199.

———. *Person and Being*. Milwaukee, WI: Marquette University Press, 1993.

———. *The Philosophical Approach to God: A New Thomistic Perspective*. New York: Fordham University Press, 2007.

CNN. "CIA Director: Waterboarding Necessary but Potentially Illegal," February 7, 2008, available at http://www.cnn.com/2008/POLITICS/02/07/mukasey.waterboarding/index.html?eref=rss topstories.

Cole, David. *Enemy Aliens: Double Standards and Constitutional Freedoms in the War on Terrorism*. New York: New Press, 2003.

Conroy, John. *Unspeakable Acts, Ordinary People: The Dynamics of Torture*. Berkley, CA: University of California Press, 2002.

Council of Europe, Parliamentary Assembly. "Secret Detentions and Illegal Transfers of Detainees Involving Council of Europe Member States: Second Report," Committee on Legal Affairs and Human Rights, Rapporteur: Mr. Dick Marty, Switzerland, Alliance of Liberals and Democrats for Europe, June 11, 2007, section 247, available at http://assembly. coe.int/Documents/WorkingDocs/Doc07/edoc11302.pdf.

"Counter Resistance Strategy Meeting Minutes," October 2, 2002, available at http://levin. senate.gov/newsroom/supporting/2008/Documents.SASC.061708.pdf.

Crelinsten, Ronald D. "In Their Own Words: The World of the Torturer," in Ronald D. Crelinsten and Alex P. Schmid, ed., *The Politics of Pain: Torturers and Their Masters*. Boulder, CO: Westview Press, 1995, chapter 4.

Crosby, John F. *Personalist Papers*. Washington, DC: Catholic University Press of America, 2004.

Curcio, Sharon. "Generational Differences in Waging Jihad," *Military Review* (July–August 2005), 84–88.

Curran, Charles E. and McCormick, Richard A. *Moral Norms and Catholic Tradition: Readings in Moral Theology No. I*. New York: Paulist Press, 1979.

Danner, Mark. *Torture and Truth: America, Abu Ghraib, and the War on Terror*. New York: New York Review of Books, 2004.

D'Arcy, Eric. *Conscience and Its Right to Freedom*. New York: Sheed and Ward, 1961.

———. *Human Acts: An Essay in Their Moral Evaluation*. Oxford, England: Clarendon Press, 1965.

Davis, Michael. "The Moral Justifiability of Torture and Other Cruel, Inhuman and Degrading Treatment," *International Journal of Applied Philosophy*, 19.2 (2005), 161–178.

Deely, John N. *Intentionality and Semiotics: A Story of Mutual Fecundation*. Scranton, PA: University of Scranton Press, 2007.

———. *What Distinguishes Human Understanding?* South Bend, IN: St. Augustine's Press, 2002.

Dershowitz, Alan M. "Tortured Reasoning," in Sanford Levinson, ed., *Torture: A Collection*. Oxford: Oxford University Press, 2006, chapter 14.

———. *Why Terrorism Works*. New Haven, CT: Yale University Press, 2002.

Destro, Robert A. "Foreword," *Educing Information: Interrogation: Science and Art Foundations for the Future*, Intelligence Science Board, December 2006, available at http://www.fas.org/ irp/dni/educing.pdf.

"Detainee Treatment Act of 2005," December 13, 2005, available at http://www.pegc.us/ detainee_act_2005.html.

Dinges, John. *The Condor Years: How Pinochet and His Allies brought Terrorism to Three Continents*. New York: New Press, 2005.

Donagan, Alan. *The Theory of Morality*. Chicago, IL: The University of Chicago Press, 1977.

Donceel, Joseph F. *Natural Theology*. New York: Sheed and Ward, 1962.

Dratel, Joshua. "The Curious Debate," in Karen J. Greenberg, ed., *The Torture Debate in America*. Cambridge: Cambridge University Press, 2006.

Eban, Katherine. "Rorschach and Awe," *Vanity Fair*, July 17, 2007, available at http://www. vanityfair.com/politics/features/2007/07/torture200707?printable=true&curre ntPage=all.

Educing Information: Interrogation: Science and Art Foundations for the Future, Intelligence Science Board, December, 2006, available at http://www.fas.org/irp/dni/educing.pdf.

Ellu, Jacques. *The Technological Society*. New York: Vintage Press, 1967.

Elshtain, Jean B. "Reflections on the Problem of 'Dirty Hands,'" in Sanford Levinson, ed., *Torture: A Collection*. Oxford: Oxford University Press, 2006, chapter 4.

European Court of Human Rights. *Ireland v. United Kingdom*, January 18, 1978, available at http://www.echr.coe.int/echr/.

Fabro, Cornelio. *La nozione metafisica di partecipazione secondo S. Tomasso d'Aquino*. Torino: Società editrice internazionale, 1950.

Finance, Joseph de, S.J. *Citoyen de Deux Mondes: La place de l'homme dans la création*. Rome: Università Gregorian Editrice, 1980.

———. *Essai sur l'agir humain*. Rome: Presses de l'Université grégorienne, 1962.

———. *Être et agir dans la philosophie de S. Thomas*. Rome: Università Gregoriana, 1960.

Foster, John. *The Immaterial Mind: A Defence of the Cartesian Dualist Conception of the Mind*. London: Routledge, 1991.

Gellman, Barton. *Angler: The Cheney Vice Presidency*. New York: Penguin Press, 2008.

"Geneva Conventions Relative to the Treatment of Prisoners of War," available at http://www.unhchr.ch/html/menu3/b/91.htm.

Gilson, Etienne. *Being and Some Philosophers*. Toronto, Canada: Pontifical Institute of Medieval Studies, 1952.

Ginbar, Yuval. *Why Not Torture Terrorists?: Moral, Practical and Legal Aspects of the "Ticking Bomb" Justification for Torture*, Oxford Monographs in International Law. Oxford: Oxford University Press, 2008.

Goldsmith, Jack. *The Terror Presidency: Law and Judgment inside the Bush Administration*. New York: W.W. Norton, 2007.

Gonzales, Alberto R. "Decision RE Application of the Geneva Conventions on Prisoners of War to the Conflict with al-Qaeda and the Taliban," January 25, 2002, in Karen J. Greenberg and Joshua L. Dratel, eds., *The Torture Papers: The Road to Abu Ghraib*. With an introduction by Anthony Lewis. Cambridge: Cambridge University Press, 2005, 118–121.

Gourevitch, Philip and Morris, Errol. "Exposure: The Woman Behind the Camera at Abu Ghraib," *New Yorker*, March 24, 2008, available at http://www.newyorker.com/reporting/2008/03/24/080324fa_fact_gourevitch.

———. *Standard Operating Procedure*. New York: Penguin, 2008.

Grassian, Stuart, M.D. "Neuropsychiatric Effects of Solitary Confinement," in Almerindo E. Ojeda, ed., *The Trauma of Psychological Torture*. Westport, CT: Praeger, 2008, chapter 6.

———. "Psychiatric Effects of Solitary Confinement," available at http://www.prisoncommission.org/statements/grassian_stuart_long.pdf.

Gray, John. *Hayek on Liberty*, 3rd edn. London: Routledge, 1998.

Greenberg, Karen J., ed. *The Torture Debate in America*. Cambridge, NY: Cambridge University Press, 2006.

Greenwalt, Kent. "The Perplexing Borders of Justification and Excuse," *Columbia Law Review* 84.4 (1984), 1897–1927.

Gross, Michael L. "Regulating Torture in a Democracy: Death and Indignity in Israel," *Policy*, 36.3 (2004), 367–388.

Gurwitsch, Aron. *Phenomenology and the Theory of Science*. Edited by Lester Embree. Evanston, IL: Northwestern University Press, 1974.

Gustafson, James M. *Ethics from a Theocentric Perspective: Volume Two, Ethics and Theology*. Chicago, IL: The University of Chicago Press, 1984.

Gutierrez, Gitanjali S., Esq. "The Case of Mohammed al-Qahtani," in Almerindo E. Ojeda, ed., *The Trauma of Psychological Torture*. Westport, CT: Praeger, 2008, chapter 11.

Habermas, Jürgen. *The Theory of Communicative Action, Volume 1: Reason and the Rationalization of Society*. Boston, MA: Beacon Press, 1985.

Harbury, Jennifer K. *Truth, Torture and the American Way: The History and Consequences of U.S. Involvement in Torture*. Boston, MA: Beacon Press, 2005.

Hardin, Russell. "Civil Liberties in the Era of Mass Terrorism," *Journal of Ethics*, 8.1 (2004), 77–95.

———. *Indeterminacy and Society*. Princeton, NJ: Princeton University Press, 2003.

———. *Morality within the Limits of Reason*. Chicago, IL: University of Chicago Press, 1988.

Hathaway, Oona A. "The Promise and Limits of the International Law of Torture," in Sanford Levinson, ed., *Torture: A Collection*. Oxford: Oxford University Press, 2006, chapter 11.

Hayek, Friedrich A. *The Constitution of Liberty*. Chicago, IL: The University of Chicago Press, 1960.

———. *The Fatal Conceit: The Errors of Socialism*. Edited by W.W. Barthley III. Chicago, IL: University of Chicago Press, 1988.

———. *The Mirage of Social Justice*. Chicago, IL: University of Chicago Press, 1976.

———. *The Road to Serfdom*. With a new introduction by Milton Friedman. Chicago, IL: University of Chicago Press, 1994.

Heidegger, Martin, "The Question Concerning Technology," in William Lovett, ed., *The Question Concerning Technology and Other Essays*. New York: Harper Torchbooks, 1977, 3–35.

Hinkle, Leonard Jr. and Wolff, Harold. *Communist Control Techniques: An Analysis of the Methods Used by Communist State Police in the Arrest, Interrogation, and Indoctrination of Persons Regarded as "Enemies of the State,"* April 1956, available at http://www.americantorture.com/documents/cold_war/01.pdf.

Hitchens, Christopher. *The Trial of Henry Kissinger*. Scranton, PA: Verso, 2001.

Hochschild, Adam. "What's in a Word? Torture," *New York Times*, May 23, 2004.

Horne, Alistair. *A Savage War of Peace: Algeria 1954–1962*. With a new preface by the author. New York: New York Review of Books, 2006.

"Human Rights First and ACLU Express Disappointment at Dismissal of Rumsfeld Torture Case," March 27, 2007, available at http://www.humanrightsfirst.org/media/etn/2007/alert/321/index.htm.

Human Rights Watch. "Enduring Freedom: Abuses by U.S. Forces in Afghanistan," March 2004, available at http://hrw.org/reports/2004/afghanistan0304/.

———. "Getting Away with Torture: Command Responsibility for the U.S. Abuse of Detainees," April 24, 2005, available at http://www.hrw.org/reports/2005/us0405/.

———. "Locked up Alone: Detention Conditions and Mental Health at Guantánamo," June 2008, available at http://hrw.org/reports/2008/us0608/us0608web.pdf.

———. "The Road to Abu Ghraib," June 2004, available at http://www.hrw.org/reports/2004/usa0604/3.htm#_Toc74483696.

Human Rights Center, University of California, Berkley. *Guantánamo and Its Aftermath: U.S. Detention and Interrogation Practices and Their Impact on Former Detainees,* November 2008, available at http://hrc.berkeley.edu/pdfs/Gtmo-Aftermath.pdf.

Hunsinger, George, ed. *Torture Is a Moral Issue: Christians, Jews, Muslims, and People of Conscience Speak Out*. Grand Rapids, MI: William B. Eerdmans, 2008.

Hunt, Linda. *Secret Agenda: The United States Government, Nazi Scientists and Project Paperclip, 1945 to 1990*. New York: St. Martin's Press, 1991.

Husserl, Edmund. *Logical Investigations*. Translated by J.N. Findlay with a new preface by Michael Dummett and edited with a new introduction by Dermot Moran. London: Routledge, 2001.

International Center for Transitional Justice. *Policy Brief: U.S. Inquiry into Human Rights Abuses in the "War on Terror,"* Lisa Magarrell, International Center for Transitional Justice, November 2008.

"The ICRC Report: Report of the International Committee of the Red Cross (ICRC) on the Treatment by the Coalition Forces of Prisoners of War and Other Protected Persons by the Geneva Conventions in Iraq during Arrest, Internment, and Interrogation," February 2004, in Karen J. Greenberg and Joshua L. Dratel, eds., *The Torture Papers: The Road to Abu Ghraib*. With an introduction by Anthony Lewis. Cambridge: Cambridge University Press, 2005, 384–404.

International Theological Commission. *Memory and Reconciliation: The Church and the Faults of the Past*, December 1999, available at http://www.vatican.va/roman_curia/congregations/ cfaith/cti_documents/rc_con_cfaith_doc_20000307_memory-reconc-itc_en.html.

Interrogation Log, Detainee 063, November 23, 2002 to January 11, 2003, available at http:// www.americantorture.com/documents/featured/featured_02.pdf.

Jacobs, Uwe. "Documenting the Neurobiology of Psychological Torture: Conceptual and Neuropsychological Observations," in Almerindo E. Ojeda, ed., *The Trauma of Psychological Torture*. Westport, CT: Praeger, 2008, chapter 9.

Jessberger, Florien. "Bad Torture—Good Torture? What International Criminal Lawyers May Learn from the Recent Trial of Police Officers in Germany," *Journal of International Criminal Justice*, 3 (2005), 1059–1073, available at http://jicj.oxfordjournals.org/cgi/ reprint/3/5/1059.

Jinks, Derek P. "*Hamdan* and the Law of War: The Applicability of the Geneva Conventions to the 'Global War on Terrorism,'" available at http://www.law.uga.edu/intl/jinks.pdf.

John Paul II. "Salvifici Doloris," section 5, available at http://www.vatican.va/holy_father/ john_paul_ii/apost_letters/documents/hf_jp-ii_apl_11021984_salvifici-doloris_en.html.

———. "Veritatis Splendor," available at http://www.vatican.va/holy_father/john_paul_ii/ encyclicals/documents/hf_jp-ii_enc_06081993_veritatis-splendor_en.html.

Kass, Leon R. "The New Biology: What Price Relieving Man's Estate?" *Toward a More Natural Science: Biology and Human Affairs*. New York: Free Press, 1985, chapter 1.

Kelman, Herbert C. "The Social Context of Torture: Policy Process and Authority Structure," in Ronald D. Crelinsten and Alex P. Schmid, eds., *The Politics of Pain: Torturers and Their Masters*. Boulder, CO: Westview Press, 1995, chapter 3.

Kenny, Anthony. "Intention and Purpose," *Journal of Philosophy*, 63 (1966), 642–651.

Kim, Jaegwon. *Physicalism or Something Near Enough*. Princeton, NJ: Princeton University Press, 2007.

Kirk, Kenneth E. *Conscience and Its Problems: An Introduction to Casuistry*. Westminster: Westminster John Knox Press, 1999.

Kleinman, Steven M. M.S. "KUBARK Counterintelligence Interrogation Review: Observations of an Interrogator: Lessons Learned and Avenues for Further Research," *Educing Information: Interrogation: Science and Art Foundations for the Future*, Intelligence Science Board, December 2006, chapter 5, available at http://www.fas.org/irp/dni/educing.pdf.

Klima, Gyula. "Aquinas on the Immateriality of the Human Soul," available at http://www. phil-inst.hu/~gyula/FILES/immat.doc.

———. "Nulla virtus cognoscitiva circa proprium obiectum decipitur," available at http:// www.fordham.edu/gsas/phil/klima/APA.htm.

———. "Tradition and Innovation in Medieval Theories of Mental Representation," *Proceedings of the Society for Medieval Logic and Metaphysics*, vol. 4, 2004, available at http://www.fordham. edu/gsas/phil/klima/SMLM/PSMLM4/PSMLM4.pdf.

Krauthammer, Charles. "The Truth about Torture," *Weekly Standard*, 11.12, December 5, 2005, available at http://www.weeklystandard.com/Content/Public/Articles/000/000/006/ 400rhqav.asp.

Kristof, Nicholas. "The Truth Commission," *New York Times*, July 6, 2008, available at http:// www.nytimes.com/2008/07/06/opinion/06kristof.html?_r=1&oref=slogin.

KUBARK Counterintelligence Interrogation, July 1963, available at http://www.americantorture. com/documents/cold_war/03.pdf.

Langguth, A.J. *Hidden Terrors*. New York: Pantheon Books, 1978.

Lederman, Marty. "A Dissenting View on Prosecuting the Waterboarders," February 8, 2008, available at http://balkin.blogspot.com/2008/02/dissenting-view-on-prosecuting.html.

Lee, Patrick. "Interrogational Torture," *American Journal of Jurisprudence*, 51 (2006), 131–147.

Lee, Patrick and George, Robert P. *Body-Self Dualism in Contemporary Ethics and Politics*. Cambridge, NY: Cambridge University Press, 2007.

Lemov, Rebecca. *World as Laboratory: Experiments with Mice, Mazes, and Men*. New York: Hill & Wang, 2005.

Levin, Daniel. "Legal Standards Applicable under 18 U.S.C. 2340–2340A," December 30, 2004, available at http://www.humanrightsfirst.org/us_law/etn/gonzales/memos_dir/levin-memo-123004.pdf.

Levinson, Sanford. "Contemplating Torture: An Introduction," in Sanford Levinson, ed., *Torture: A Collection*. Oxford: Oxford University Press, 2006.

Luban, David. "Liberalism, Torture and the Ticking Bomb," in Karen J. Greenberg, ed., *The Torture Debate in America*. Cambridge, NY: Cambridge University Press, 2006, 35–84.

———. "The Torture Lawyers of Washington," *Legal Ethics and Human Dignity*. Cambridge, NY: Cambridge University Press, 2007, chapter 5.

Lyons, David. *Forms and Limits of Utilitarianism*. Oxford: Clarendon Press, 1965.

Machiavelli, Niccoló. *The Discourses*. Edited with an introduction by Bernard Crick. Translated by Leslie J. Walker, S.J. with revisions by Brian Richardson. New York: Penguin Books, 1970.

———. "The History of Florence," *Machiavelli: The Chief Works and Others*, vol. 3. Translated by Allan Gilbert. Durham, NC: Duke University Press, 1989.

———. *The Prince*. Translated and edited by Mark Musa. New York: St. Martin's Press, 1964.

Marcel, Gabriel. *Being and Having: An Existentialist Diary*. Translated by Katherine Farrer, with an introduction by James Collins. New York: Harper Torchbooks, 1965.

———. "Incarnate Being," *Creative Fidelity*. Translated by Robert Rosthal. New York: Farrar, Straus, 1964.

———. "Phenomenological Notes," *Creative Fidelity*. Translated by Robert Rosthal. New York: Farrar, Straus, 1964.

Maréchal, Joseph. *A Maréchal Reader*. Edited by Joseph Donceel. St. Louis, MO: Herder & Herder, 1970.

Margulies, Joseph. *Guantánamo and the Abuse of Presidential Power*. New York: Simon & Schuster, 2007.

Maritain, Jacques. *Distinguish to Unite or the Degrees of Knowledge*. Translated by Gerald B. Phelan. New York: Charles Scribner's, 1959.

———. "The End of Machiavellianism," *The Range of Reason*. New York: Charles Scribner's, 1952, 134–164.

———. *Existence and the Existent*. English version by Lewis Galantiere and Gerald B. Phelan. New York: Pantheon Books, 1948.

———. "Freedom in the Modern World," *Integral Humanism, Freedom in the Modern World, and a Letter on Independence*. Translated and edited by Otto Bird. Translated by Joseph Evans and Richard O'Sullivan. Notre Dame, IN: University of Notre Dame Press, 1996.

———. "The Immortality of the Soul," *The Range of Reason*. New York: Charles Schribner's, 1952.

———. *On the Philosophy of History*. Edited by Joseph Evans. New York: Charles Scribner's, 1957.

———. "The Possibilities for Co-Operation in a Divided World: Inaugural Address to the Second International Conference of UNESCO," *The Range of Reason*. New York: Charles Schribner's, 1952, chapter 13.

Marks, John. *The Search for the "Manchurian Candidate": The CIA and Mind Control*. New York: Times Books, 1979, chapter 9.

Mayer, Jane. "The Black Sites: A New Look at inside the CIA's Secrete Interrogation Program," *New Yorker,* August 13, 2007, available at http://www.newyorker.com/reporting/2007/08/13/070813fa_fact_mayer?printable=true.

———. *The Dark Side: The Inside Story of How the War on Terror Turned into a War on American Ideals.* New York: Doubleday, 2008.

———. "The Experiment," *New Yorker,* July 11, 2005, available at http://www.newyorker.com/archive/2005/07/11/050711fa_fact4.

———. "The Memo: How an Internal Effort to Ban the Abuse and Torture of Detainees Was Thwarted," *New Yorker,* February 27, 2006, available at http://www.newyorker.com/archive/2006/02/27/060227fa_fact.

McCormick, Richard A. "Document Begs Many Legitimate Moral Questions," *National Catholic Reporter,* October 15, 1993, 17–18.

McCoy, Alfred W. "Legacy of a Dark Decade: CIA Mind Control, Classified Behavioral Research, and the Origins of Modern Medical Ethics," in Almerindo E. Ojeda, ed., *The Trauma of Psychological Torture.* Westport, CT: Praeger, 2008, chapter 3.

———. *A Question of Torture: CIA Interrogation from the Cold War to the War on Terror.* New York: Henry Holt, 2007.

———. "Science in Dachau's shadow: Hebb, Beecher, and the Development of CIA Psychological Torture and Modern Medical Ethics," *Journal of the History of the Behavioral Sciences,* 43.4 (October 2007), 401–417.

McDonald, Heather. "How to Interrogate Terrorists," in Karen J. Greenberg, ed., *The Torture Debate in America.* Cambridge, NY: Cambridge University Press, 2006.

McKelvey, Tara. *Monstering: Inside America's Policy of Secret Interrogations and Torture in the Terror War.* New York: Carroll & Graff, 2007.

Meilaender, Gilbert. *Bioethics: A Primer for Christians.* Grand Rapids, MI: William B. Eerdmans, 1996.

Miles, Steven. *Oath Betrayed: Torture, Medical Complicity and the War on Terror.* New York: Random House, 2006.

Military Commissions Act of 2006, October 17, 2006, available at http://frwebgate.access.gpo.gov/cgibin/getdoc.cgi?dbname=109_cong_public_laws&docid=f:publ366.109.pdf.

Miller, Gail H. "Defining Torture," Floersheimer Center for Constitutional Democracy, Occasional Paper #3, available at http://www.cardozo.yu.edu/cms/uploadedFiles/FLOERSHEIMER/Defining%20Torture.pdf.

Miller, Seumus. "Is Torture Ever Morally Justified?" *International Journal of Applied Philosophy,* 19.2 (2005), 179–192.

———. "Torture," *The Stanford Encyclopedia of Philosophy,* 2006, available at http://plato.stanford.edu/entries/torture/.

Moir, Lindsay. *The Law of Internal Armed Conflict* (Cambridge: Cambridge University Press, 2007).

Moore, Michael S. *Placing Blame: A General Theory of the Criminal Law.* Oxford: Clarendon Press, 1997.

Moreland, J.P., *Universals.* Montreal: McGill-Queen's University Press, 2001.

Moreno, Jonathan D. *Mind Wars: Brain Research and National Defense.* New York: Dana Press, 2006.

Morgenthau, Hans J. and Thompson, Kenneth W. *Politics among Nations: The Struggle for Power and Peace,* 6th edn. Edition. New York: Alfred A. Knopf, 1985.

Mounier, Emmanuel. *Personalism.* Translated by Philip Mairet. Notre Dame, IN: University of Notre Dame Press, 1970.

Nagel, Thomas. *The View from Nowhere.* New York: Oxford University Press, 1989.

Nagel, Thomas. "War and Massacre," in Thomas Nagel, ed., *Mortal Questions*. Cambridge, NY: Cambridge University Press, 1991.

Nemesius of Emesa, "On the Nature of Man," *Cyril of Jerusalem and Nemesius of Emesa*. Translated by William Telfer. London: SCM Press, 1955.

New York Times. "China Inspired Interrogations at Guantánamo," July 2, 2008, available at http://www.nytimes.com/2008/07/02/us/02detain.html?_r=1&hp=&pagewanted=all&oref=slogin.

———. "Padilla Is Guilty on All Charges in Terror Trial," August 16, 2007, available at http://www.nytimes.com/2007/08/17/us/17padilla.html?_r=1&oref=slogin.

———. "Psychologists Vote to End Interrogation Consultations," September 17, 2008, available at http://www.nytimes.com/2008/09/18/us/18psych.html?fta=y.

———. "The Reach of War: Sexual Humiliation; Forced Nudity of Iraqi Prisoners Is Seen as Pervasive Pattern, not Isolated Incidents," June 8, 2004, available at http://query.nytimes.com/gst/fullpage.html?res=9E01EFD71E31F93BA35755C0A9629C8B63.

———. "Video Is a Window into Terror Suspect's Isolation," December 4, 2006, available at http://www.nytimes.com/2006/12/04/us/04detain.html.

Niebuhr, Reinhold. *Moral Man and Immoral Society: A Study in Ethics and Politics*. New York: Charles Scribner's, 1960.

Nielsen, Kai. "There Is No Dilemma of Dirty Hands," in David Shugarman and Paul Rynard, eds., *Cruelty and Deception: The Controversy over Dirty Hands in Politics*. Ontario, Canada: Broadview Press, 1999.

The 9/11 Commission Report: Final Report of the National Commission on Terrorist Attacks upon the United States. New York: W.W. Norton, 2004.

O'Callaghan, John P. *Thomist Realism and the Linguistic Turn: Toward a More Perfect Form of Existence*. Notre Dame, IN: University of Notre Dame Press, 2003.

Ogrisseg, Jerald F. "Psychological Effects of Resistance Training," July 24, 2002, available at http://levin.senate.gov/newsroom/supporting/2008/Documents.SASC.061708.pdf.

Ojeda, Almerindo E. *The Trauma of Psychological Torture*. Westport, CT: Praeger, 2008.

Osiel, Mark J. *Mass Atrocity, Collective Memory and the Law*. New Brunswick, NJ: Transaction Publishers, 1997.

———. *Mass Atrocity, Ordinary Evil, and Hannah Arendt: Criminal Consciousness in Argentina's Dirty War*. New Haven, CT: Yale University Press, 2001.

———. "The Mental State of Torturers: Argentina's Dirty War," in Sanford Levinson, ed., *Torture: A Collection*. Oxford: Oxford University Press, 2006, chapter 7.

Otterman, Michael. *American Torture: From the Cold War to Abu Ghraib and Beyond*. Ann Arbor, MI: University of Michigan Press, 2007.

Pareto, Vilfredo. *The Mind and Society*, vol. 4. Edited by Arthur Livingston. Translated by Andrew Bongiorno and Arthur Livingston, with the advice and active cooperation of James Harvey Rogers. New York: Harcourt, Brace, 1935.

Parry, John T. "The Shape of Modern Torture: Extraordinary Rendition and Ghost Detainees," *Melbourne Journal of International Law*, 6 (2005), 516–533.

Pasnau, Robert. *Theories of Cognition in the Middle Ages*. Cambridge: Cambridge University Press, 1997.

———. *Thomas Aquinas on Human Nature: A Philosophical Study of "Summa Theologica" Ia 75–89*. Cambridge, UK and NY: Cambridge University Press, 2002.

Pavlischek, Keith. "'Human Rights and Justice in an Age of Terror' An Evangelical Critique of 'An Evangelical Declaration against Torture,'" *Books and Culture*, September/October 2007, available at http://www.christianitytoday.com/books/web/2007/sept24a.html.

Peters, Edward. *Torture*. New York: B. Blackwell, 1985.

Pew Global Attitudes Project. "American Character Gets Mixed Reviews: U.S. Image Slightly Up, but Still Negative," June 23, 2005, available at http://pewglobal.org/reports/pdf/247.pdf.

————. "No Global Warming Alarm in the U.S., China: America's Image Slips, but Allies Share U.S. Concerns," June 13, 2006, available at http://pewglobal.org/reports/display.php?ReportID=252.

Phifer, Jerald. "Memorandum for Commander, Joint Task Force 170," October 11, 2002, in Karen J. Greenberg and Joshua L. Dratel, eds., *The Torture Papers: The Road to Abu Ghraib.* With an introduction by Anthony Lewis. Cambridge: Cambridge University Press, 2005, 227–228.

Physicians for Human Rights. "Break Them Down: Systematic Use of Psychological Torture by U.S. Forces," 2005, available at http://physiciansforhumanrights.org/library/documents/reports/break-them-down-the.pdf.

Pico della Mirandola, Giovanni. *Oration on the Dignity of Man.* Translated by Robert Caponigni. Chicago, IL: Henry Regnery, 1956.

Pictet, Jean S. "The New Geneva Protections for War Victims," *American Journal of International Law*, 45.3 (July 1951), 462–475.

Pieper, Josef. *The Four Cardinal Virtues: Prudence, Justice, Fortitude, Temperance.* Notre Dame, IN: University of Notre Dame Press, 1966.

————. *Living the Truth: The Truth of All Things and Reality and the Good.* San Francisco, CA: St. Ignatius Press, 1989.

Pinckaers, Servais, O.P. "A Historical Perspective on Intrinsically Evil Acts," in John Berkman and Craig S. Titus, eds., *The Pinckaers Reader: Renewing Thomistic Moral Theology.* Translated by Sr. Mary Thomas Noble, O.P., Craig S. Titus, Michael Sherwin, O.P., and Hugh Connolly. Washington, DC: Catholic University Press of America, 2005, 194–198.

————. "Revisionist Understandings of Actions in the Wake of Vatican II," in John Berkman and Craig S. Titus, eds., *The Pinckaers Reader: Renewing Thomistic Moral Theology.* Translated by Sr. Mary Thomas Noble, O.P., Craig S. Titus, Michael Sherwin, O.P., and Hugh Connolly. Washington, DC: Catholic University Press of America, 2005, chapter 12.

Pinker, Steven. *The Blank Slate: The Modern Denial of Human Nature.* New York: Penguin Books, 2002.

Plato. *Timaeus.* Translated with an introduction by Donald J. Zeyl. Indianapolis: Hackett, 2000.

Plotinus. *The Enneads.* Translated by Stephen McKenna. Abridged with an introduction and notes by John Dillon. London: Penguin Books, 1991.

Pokempner, Dinah. "Command Responsibility for Torture," in Kenneth Roth and Minky Worden, eds., *Torture: Does it Make Us Safer? Is it Ever OK? A Human Rights Perspective.* Amy D. Bernstein, contributing editor. Published in conjunction with Human Rights Watch. New York: New Press, 2005, chapter 14.

Porter, Jean. *Nature as Reason: A Thomistic Theory of the Natural Law.* Grand Rapids, MI: William B. Eerdmans, 2005.

Posner, Eric. "Applying the Golden Rule to al-Qaeda? *Wall Street Journal*, July 15, 2006, available at http://www.ericposner.com/goldenrule.html.

Posner, Eric and Goldsmith, Jack. *The Limits of International Law* (Oxford: Oxford University Press, 2006).

Posner, Eric A. and Vermeule, Adrian. "Should Coercive Torture Be Legal?" *Chicago: Public Law and Legal Theory Working Paper No. 84*, February 2006, available at http://papers.ssrn.com/sol3/papers.cfm?abstract_id=690902#PaperDownload.

Posner, Richard. "Torture, Terrorism, and Interrogation," in Sanford Levinson, ed., *Torture: A Collection.* Oxford: Oxford University Press, 2006, 291–299.

Powell, Colin L. "Draft Decision Memorandum for the President on the Applicability of the Geneva Conventions to the Conflict with Afghanistan," in Karen J. Greenberg and Joshua

L. Dratel, eds., *The Torture Papers: The Road to Abu Ghraib*. With an introduction by Anthony Lewis. Cambridge: Cambridge University Press, 2005, 122–125.

Power, Samantha. *"A Problem from Hell": America and the Age of Genocide*. New York: Basic Books, 2002.

President's Council on Bioethics. *Beyond Therapy: Biotechnology and the Pursuit of Happiness*, October 2003, available at http://www.bioethics.gov/reports/beyondtherapy/beyond_therapy_final_webcorrected.pdf.

Reinach, Adolph. *The Apriori Foundations of the Civil Law*. Translated by John F. Crosby. "Aletheia" III (1983), 1–142.

Rejali, Darius. *Torture and Democracy*. Princeton, NJ: Princeton University Press, 2007.

Rhonheimer, Martin. "Intentional Actions and the Meaning of the Object: A Reply to Richard McCormick," *The Thomist*, 59.2 (April 1995), 279–311.

———. *Natural Law and Practical Reason: A Thomist View of Moral Autonomy*. Translated by Gerald Malsbary. New York: Fordham University Press, 2000.

Ricks, Thomas E. *Fiasco: The American Military Adventure in Iraq*. New York: Penguin, 2007.

Risen, James. *State of War: The Secret History of the CIA and the Bush Administration*. New York: Free Press, 2006.

Roberson, James. "United States District Court for the District of Columbia, Salim Ahmed Hamdan, Plaintiff vs. Donald H. Rumsfeld," November 8, 2004, http://fl1.findlaw.com/news.findlaw.com/hdocs/docs/tribunals/hamdanrums110804opn.pdf.

Rocca, Gregory. *Speaking the Incomprehensible God: Thomas Aquinas on the Interplay of Positive and Negative Theology*. Washington, DC: Catholic University of America Press, 2004.

Rockwood, Lawrence P. *Walking Away from Nuremberg: Just War and the Doctrine of Command Responsibility*. Amherst, MA: University of Massachusetts Press, 2007.

Rose, David. *Guantánamo: The War on Human Rights*. New York: New Press, 2006.

Ross, Colin A, M.D. *The CIA Doctors: Human Rights Violations by American Psychiatrists*. Richardson, TX: Manitou Communications, 2006.

Rumsfeld, Donald. "Action Memo," November 27, 2002, in Karen J. Greenberg and Joshua L. Dratel, eds., *The Road to Abu Ghraib*. With an Introduction by Anthony Lewis. Cambridge, NY: Cambridge University Press, 2005, 237.

———. "Memorandum for the Commander, Southern Command," April 16, 2003, in Karen J. Greenberg and Joshua L. Dratel, eds., *The Torture Papers: The Road to Abu Ghraib*. With an introduction by Anthony Lewis. Cambridge: Cambridge University Press, 2005, 360–361.

Rotberg, Robert L. "Apology, Truth Commissions, and Intrastate Conflict," in Elazar Barkan, and Alexander Karn, eds., *Taking Wrongs Seriously: Apologies and Reconciliation*. Stanford, CA: Stanford University Press, 2006, chapter 2.

San Francisco Chronicle. "All Eyes on Guantánamo Movie, Court Rulings Intensify Focus on Military Prisons," July 2, 2006, available at http://www.sfgate.com/cgi-bin/article.cgi?f=/c/a/2006/07/02/INGJNJMQF51.DTL.

Sands, Philippe. *Torture Team: Rumsfeld's Memo and the Betrayal of American Values*. New York: Palgrave Macmillan, 2008.

Santurri, Edmund N. *Perplexity in the Moral Life: Philosophical and Theological Considerations. Studies in Religion and Culture*. Charlottesville, VA: University of Virginia Press, 1988.

Sargant, William. *Battle for the Mind: A Physiology of Conversion and Brain-Washing*. Garden City, NY: Doubleday, 1957.

Savage, Charlie. *Takeover: The Return of the Imperial Presidency and the Subversion of American Democracy*. New York: Little, Brown, 2007.

Scarry, Elaine. *The Body in Pain: The Making and Unmaking of the World*. New York: Oxford University Press, 1985.

Scheler, Max. *Formalism in Ethics and Non-Formal Ethics of Values: A New Attempt toward the Foundation of an Ethical Personalism*. Translated by Manfred S. Frings and Roger L. Funk. Evanston, IL: Northwestern University Press, 1973.

———. "Repentance and Rebirth," in M.S. Frings, ed., *Person and Self-Value: Three Essays*. With an introduction, edited, and partially translated by M.S. Frings. Dordrecht, The Netherlands: Martinus Nijhoff, 1987.

"The Schlesinger Report: Final Report of the Independent Panel to Review DOD Detention Operations," August 2004, in Karen J. Greenberg and Joshua L. Dratel, eds., *The Torture Papers: The Road to Abu Ghraib*. With an introduction by Anthony Lewis. Cambridge: Cambridge University Press, 2005, 908–975.

Schmiesing, Kevin. "A History of Personalism," available at the Acton Institute Web site at http://www.acton.org/research/pubs/papers/history_personalism.html.

Schmitz, Kenneth L. "The First Principle of Personal Becoming," *The Texture of Being: Essays in First Philosophy*. Washington, DC: Catholic University Press of America, 2007.

———. "The Geography of the Human Person," *The Texture of Being: Essays in First Philosophy*. Washington, DC: Catholic University Press of America, 2007.

———. "Purity of Soul and Immorality," *The Texture of Being: Essays in First Philosophy*. Washington, DC: Catholic University Press of America, 2007.

Searle, John R. *The Rediscovery of the Mind*. Cambridge, MA: MIT Press, 1992.

Shue, Henry. "Torture," in Sanford Levinson, ed., *Torture: A Collection*. Oxford: Oxford University Press, 2006, 47–61.

———. "Torture in Dreamland: Disposing of the Ticking Bomb," *Case Western Reserve Journal of International Law*, 37.2/3 (2006), 231–239.

Simon, Yves R. *An Introduction to the Metaphysics of Knowledge*. Edited and translated by Vukan Kuic and Richard J. Thompson. New York: Fordham University Press, 1990.

———. *Practical Knowledge*. Edited by Robert J. Mulvaney. New York: Fordham University Press, 1991.

———. *The Tradition of Natural Law: A Philosopher's Reflections*. Edited by Vukan Kuic with an introduction by Russell Hittinger. New York: Fordham University Press, 1992.

Singer, Peter and Dawn, Karen. "Echoes of Abu Ghraib in Chicken Slaughterhouse," *Los Angeles Times*, July 25, 2004, 4, available at http://articles.latimes.com/2004/jul/25/opinion/oe-singer25.

Sinnot-Armstrong, Walter. *Moral Dilemmas*. Boston: Blackwell, 1988.

Smart, J.C. and Williams, Bernard. *Utilitarianism: For and Against*. Cambridge, UK: Cambridge University Press, 1973.

Smith, Clive S. *The Eight O'Clock Ferry to the Windward Side: Fighting the Lawless World of Guantánamo Bay*. New York: Nation Books, 2008.

Smith, Janet E. *Humanae Vitae*. Washington, DC: Catholic University of America Press, 1991.

Sokolowski, Robert. *Moral Action: A Phenomenological Analysis*. Bloomington: Indiana University Press, 1984.

Soldz, Stephen and Olson, Brad. "Psychologists, Detainee Interrogations, and Torture: Varying Perspectives on Nonparticipation," in Almerindo E. Ojeda, ed., *The Trauma of Psychological Torture*. Westport, CT: Praeger, 2008, chapter 4.

Southern District of Florida Miami Division. *United States of America vs. Jose Padilla, Defendant. Motion to Dismiss for Outrageous Government Conduct*, October 4, 2006, available at http://www.discourse.net/archives/docs/Padilla_Outrageous_Government_Conduct.pdf.

Steenberghen, Fernand Van. *Ontology*. Translated by the Reverend Martin J. Flynn. New York: J.F. Wagner, 1952.

Stein, Edith. *On the Problem of Empathy*. Washington DC: ICS, 1989.

Stocker, Michael. *Plural and Conflicting Values*. New York: Oxford University Press, 1992.

Strauss, Leo. *Thoughts on Machiavelli*. Chicago, IL: University of Chicago Press, 1995.

Strauss, Marcy S., "Torture," Loyola-LA Public Law Research Paper No. 2003-7, January 2003, available at SSRN: http://ssrn.com/abstract=370680 or DOI: 10.2139/ssrn.370680.

Stump, Eleonore. *Aquinas. Arguments of the Philosophers*. London: Routledge, 2003.

Sullivan, Andrew. "The Abolition of Torture," in Sanford Levinson, ed., *Torture: A Collection*. Oxford: Oxford University Press, 2006.

Suskind, Ron. *The One-Percent Doctrine: Deep Inside America's Pursuit of Its Enemies since 9/11*. New York: Simon & Schuster, 2007.

Sunstein, Cass R. "Clear Statement Principles and National Security: Hamdan and Beyond," in Dennis J. Hutchinson, David A. Strauss, and Geoffrey R. Stone, eds., *Supreme Court Review* 1. Chicago, IL: University of Chicago Press, 2007.

Sussman, David. "Defining Torture," *Case Western Reserve Journal of International Law*, 37.2/3 (2006), 225–230.

———. "What's Wrong with Torture?" *Philosophy and Public Affairs*, 33 (2005), 1–33.

Swinburne, Richard. *The Evolution of the Soul*. Oxford: Oxford University Press, 1997.

Taft, William H., IV, "Comments on Your Paper on the Geneva Convention," February 2, 2002, in Karen J. Greenberg and Joshua L. Dratel, eds., *The Torture Papers: The Road to Abu Ghraib*. With an introduction by Anthony Lewis. Cambridge: Cambridge University Press, 2005, 129–133.

"The Taguba Report: Article 15–6 Investigation of the 800th Military Police Brigade," in Karen J. Greenberg and Joshua L. Dratel, eds., *The Torture Papers: The Road to Abu Ghraib*. With an introduction by Anthony Lewis. Cambridge: Cambridge University Press, 2005, 405–556.

Taliaferro, Charles. *Consciousness and the Mind of God*. Cambridge, NY and UK: Cambridge University Press, 1994.

Thomas, Gordon. *Journey into Madness: The True Story of Secret CIA Mind Control and Medical Abuse*. New York: Bantam Books, 1989.

Timerman, Jacobo. *Prisoner without a Name, Cell without a Number*. Translated from the Spanish by Toby Talbot. New York: Alfred Knopf, 1981.

United Nations Convention against Torture and Other Cruel, Inhuman or Degrading Treatment or Punishment, June 26, 1987, available at http://www.unhchr.ch/html/menu3/b/h_cat39.htm.

U.S. Department of Justice, Office of the Inspector General. *A Review of the FBI's Involvement in and Observations of Detainee Interrogations in Guantánamo Bay, Afghanistan, and Iraq*, May 2008, available at http://www.usdoj.gov/oig/special/s0805/final.pdf.

U.S. Senate, "The Origin of Aggressive Interrogation Techniques: Part I of the Committee's Inquiry into the Treatment of Detainees in U.S. Custody," available at http://levin.senate.gov/newsroom/supporting/2008/Documents.SASC.061708.pdf.

———. "Senate Armed Services Inquiry into the Treatment of Detainees in U.S. Custody," December 2008, available at http://levin.senate.gov/newsroom/release.cfm?id=305735.

U.S. Supreme Court. *Biomedicine et al. v. Bush, President of the United States, et al.* June 12, 2008, available at http://www.supremecourtus.gov/opinions/07pdf/06-1195.pdf.

———. *Hamdan v. Rumsfeld, Secretary of Defense, et al.*, available at http://www.supremecourtus.gov/opinions/05pdf/05-184.pdf.

Velde, Rudi te. *Participation and Substantiality in Thomas Aquinas*. Leiden, The Netherlands: E.J. Brill, 1995.

Verbeke, Gerard. "Man as a 'Frontier' according to Aquinas," in Gerard Verbeke and D. Verhults, eds., *Aquinas and the Problems of His Time*. Leuven, Belgium: Leuven University Press, 1976, 195–233.

Waldron, Jeremy. "Torture and Positive Law: Jurisprudence for the White House," *Columbia Law Review*, 105 (October 2005), 1681–1750.

Wallace, William A. *The Modeling of Nature: Philosophy of Science and Philosophy of Nature in Synthesis*. Washington, DC: Catholic University of America Press, 1997.

Walzer, Michael. "Political Action: The Problem of Dirty Hands," in Sanford Levinson, ed., *Torture: A Collection*. Oxford: Oxford University Press, 2006, 61–77.

Washington Post. "New Detainees Strain Iraq's Jails: Sharp Rise Follows Start of Security Plan; Suspects Housed with Convicts," May 15, 2007, available at http://www.washingtonpost.com/wp-dyn/content/article/2007/05/14/AR2007051402265.html.

———. Shiite Militias Control Prisons, Official Says," June 16, 2006, available at http://www.washingtonpost.com/wp-dyn/content/article/2006/06/15/AR2006061502180_pf.html.

———. "Police Torture Threat Sparks Painful Debate in Germany," March 8, 2003, available at http://personal.ecu.edu/conradtd/pols2010/spring2010/2010sp0383.htm.

———. "U.S. Decries Abuse but Defends Interrogations 'Stress and Duress' Tactics Used on Terrorism: Suspects Held in Secret Overseas Facilities," December 26, 2002, available at http://www.washingtonpost.com/ac2/wp-dyn/A37943-2002Dec25.

Weber, Max. "Politics as a Vocation," *From Max Weber: Essays in Sociology.* Translated, edited, and with an introduction by C. Wright Mills and Hans H. Gerth. Oxford: Oxford University Press, 1958.

Weinstein, Harvey M. *Psychiatry and the CIA: Victims of Mind Control*. Washington, DC: American Psychiatric Press, 1990.

Wijze, Stephen de. "Tragic Remorse: The Anguish of Dirty Hands," *Ethical Theory and Moral Practice*, 7.5 (November 2004), 453–471.

Williams, Bernard. "Conflicts of Values," *Moral Luck: Philosophical Papers, 1973–1980*. Cambridge, NY: Cambridge University Press, 1981, chapter 5.

———. "Moral Luck," *Moral Luck: Philosophical Papers, 1973–1980*. Cambridge, NY: Cambridge University Press, 1981, chapter 2.

———. "Utilitarianism and Moral Self-Indulgence," *Moral Luck: Philosophical Papers, 1973–1980*. Cambridge, NY: Cambridge University Press, 1981, chapter 3.

Wippel, John F. *The Metaphysical Thought of Thomas Aquinas*. Washington, DC: Catholic University Press of America, 2000.

Wiredu, Kwasi. *Cultural Universals and Particulars: An African Perspective*. Bloomington, IN: Indiana University Press, 1996.

Wojtyla, Karol. "The Constitution of Culture through Human Praxis," *Person and Community: Selected Essays*. Translated by Theresa Sandok. New York: Peter Lang, 1993.

———. *Love and Responsibility*. Translated by H.T. Willetts. New York: Farrar, Straus, & Giroux, 1960.

———. "Thomistic Personalism," in *Person and Community: Selected Essays*. Translated by Theresa Sandok. New York: Peter Lang, 1993.

Wolff, Harold and Hinkle, Lawrence, Jr. "Communist Control Techniques: An Analysis of the Methods Used by Communist State Police in the Arrest, Interrogation, and Indoctrination of Persons Regarded as 'Enemies of the State,'" April 2, 1956, available at http://americantorture.com/documents/cold_war/01.pdf.

"Working Group Report on Detainee Interrogations," in Karen J. Greenberg and Joshua L. Dratel, eds., *The Torture Papers: The Road to Abu Ghraib*. With an introduction by Anthony Lewis. Cambridge: Cambridge University Press, 2005, 241–359.

World Public Opinion. "American and International Opinion on the Rights of Terrorism Suspects," July 17, 2006, available at http://www.worldpublicopinion.org/pipa/pdf/jul06/TerrSuIn sspect_Jul06_rpt.pdf.

Worthington, Andy. *The Guantánamo Files: The Stories of the 744 Detainees in America's Illegal Prison*. London: Pluto Press, 2007.

Yoo, John. *War by Other Means: An Insider's Account of the War on Terror*. New York: Atlantic Monthly Press, 2006.

Yoo, John and Bybee, Jay. "Standards of Conduct for Interrogation under U.S.C. 2340–2340A," August 1, 2002, in Karen J. Greenberg and Joshua L. Dratel, eds., *The Torture Papers: The Road to Abu Ghraib*. With an introduction by Anthony Lewis. Cambridge: Cambridge University Press, 2005.

Zelikow, Philip. "Legal Policy for a Twilight War," April 26, 2007, available at http://hnn.us/articles/39494.html.

Zimbardo, Philip. *The Lucifer Effect: Understanding Why Good People Turn Evil*. New York: Random House, 2007.

INDEX